Expert C++/CLI: .NET for Visual C++ Programmers

Marcus Heege

Apress®

Expert C++/CLI: .NET for Visual C++ Programmers

Copyright © 2007 by Marcus Heege

ISBN-13: 978-1-4302-1168-6

ISBN-10: 1-4302-1168-7

Lead Editor: James Huddleston

Technical Reviewer: Stanley Lippman

Editorial Board: Steve Anglin, Ewan Buckingham, Gary Cornell, Jason Gilmore, Jonathan Gennick, Jonathan Hassell, James Huddleston, Chris Mills, Matthew Moodie, Jeff Pepper, Paul Sarknas, Dominic Shakeshaft, Jim Sumser, Matt Wade

Project Manager: Elizabeth Seymour

Copy Edit Manager: Nicole Flores

Copy Editor: Damon Larson

Assistant Production Director: Kari Brooks-Copony

Production Editor: Lori Bring

Compositor: Gina Rexrode

Proofreader: Patrick Vincent

Indexer: Brenda Miller

Artist: April Milne

Cover Designer: Kurt Krames

Manufacturing Director: Tom Debolski

For information on translations, please contact Apress directly at 2560 Ninth Street, Suite 219, Berkeley, CA 94710. Phone 510-549-5930, fax 510-549-5939, e-mail info@apress.com, or visit http://www.apress.com.

The source code for this book is available to readers at http://www.apress.com in the Source Code/ Download section.

Contents at a Glance

Contents

About the Author

MARCUS HEEGE has over 20 years of experience developing software for Microsoft languages and platforms. He is a course author and instructor for DevelopMentor, where he developed the Essential C++/CLI: Building and Migrating Applications and Components with C++/CLI seminar. He also serves as a troubleshooter and mentor for many professional software developers.

Marcus blogs about C++ and .NET topics at www.heege.net/blog, and he has written dozens of articles for a wide variety of magazines. Marcus is an MVP for Visual C++ and has been a Microsoft Certified Solution Developer and Microsoft Certified Trainer since 1997.

About the Technical Reviewer

STANLEY LIPPMAN served as architect with the Visual C++ team during the four-year development of C++/CLI. He is currently a senior software engineer with Emergent Game Technologies, a provider of middleware software for massive multiplayer online games. Stan also writes "Netting C++," a bimonthly column for *MSDN* magazine.

Acknowledgments

Writing this book was only possible because I got a lot of help from people that deserve to be named here. From the team at Apress I would like to thank Elizabeth Seymour, Lori Bring, Jim Huddleston, and Damon Larson.

I would also like to thank Stan Lippman, the technical reviewer of my book. His feedback constantly pushed me to make the book better. Without his feedback, the book would have been less correct and much less readable. I also got valuable reviews from Richard Dutton.

Several members of the Visual C++ team have been great sources for in-depth information about implementation details of C++/CLI and the CLR. These guys are Martyn Lovell, Brandon Bray, Arjun Bijanki, Jeff Peil, Herb Sutter, Ayman Shoukry, and Bill Dunlap. Many topics that I cover in this book are insights that I got from them.

Over the last few years, I have learned a lot about various areas of software development in discussions with my DevelopMentor colleagues, including Dominick Baier, Richard Blewett, Mark Vince Smit, and Mark Smith, as well as from other smart software developers, including Mirko Matytschak, Klaus Jaroslawsky, and Ian Griffiths.

Furthermore, I would like to thank the students of my C++/CLI classes. By asking me many interesting questions, they have allowed me to review my knowledge in many different practical contexts.

The biggest thank you goes to my wife, Marion, and my two kids, Lisa Maria and Jule. Since the time they started being the center of my world, they have continuously supported me with all the love and power they have. For the many months that I was writing this book, they had to accept that I had to spend most of my time researching and writing instead of being a good husband and a good daddy.

Marcus Heege
Kaisersesch, Germany
February 2007

CHAPTER 1

■ ■ ■

Why C++/CLI?

The road to C++/CLI began some 30 years ago with a very small C program:

```
// HelloWorld.cpp
// compile with "CL HelloWorld.cpp"

#include <stdio.h>

int main()
{
  printf("hello, world");
}
```

To be precise, this code is not just a C program, but also a C++ program, since C++ derived from C. Because C++ has a high degree of source code compatibility with C, you can mix many C constructs with C++ constructs, as the following code shows:

```
// HelloWorld2.cpp
// compile with "CL /EHs HelloWorld2.cpp"

#include <stdio.h>
#include <iostream>

int main()
{
  printf("hello");
  std::cout << ", world";
}
```

Extending C++ with .NET Features

In a very similar way, C++/CLI is layered on top of C++. C++/CLI provides a high degree of source code compatibility with C++. As a consequence, the following code is valid if you build the program with a C++/CLI compiler:

```
// HelloWorld3.cpp
```

```
#include <stdio.h>
#include <iostream>

int main()
{
  // use a C function to print "hello"
  printf("hello");

  // use a C++ object  to print a comma followed by a space
  std::cout << ", ";

  // use a .NET class to print "world"
  System::Console::WriteLine("world");
}
```

The interesting aspect of this code is that it uses C, C++, and .NET constructs to implement main. First, it calls the native function printf to write the string "hello", then it uses the C++ object std::cout to write ", ", and finally it uses the .NET class System::Console to write the last part of that well-known message.

What Is .NET?

Before looking at the steps necessary to build the preceding application, I should cover what the term *.NET* means and what it offers to a software developer. .NET is an infrastructure that provides two major benefits: productivity and security. Using .NET, a developer can write code for many modern problem domains faster, and during coding, the developer faces fewer pitfalls that could end up in security vulnerabilities. Furthermore, .NET code can be implemented so that it can be executed with restricted access to APIs. All these benefits are achieved by two components: a runtime and a class library.

The .NET runtime and core parts of the base class library are specified as an open standard. This standard is called the *Common Language Infrastructure (CLI)*, and it is published as the ECMA-335 standard and as the ISO standard 23271. There are several implementations of this standard. The *Common Language Runtime (CLR)* is the most important implementation because it is the most powerful one, and it targets Microsoft Windows operating systems, the most common platform for .NET development.

In the context of .NET, you very often hear the term *managed*. .NET code is often called managed code, .NET types are managed types, objects in .NET are managed objects, and for the heap on which managed objects are instantiated, the term *managed heap* is used. In all these cases, the term *managed* means "controlled by the .NET runtime." The .NET runtime influences most aspects of managed execution. Managed code is JIT-compiled to machine-specific (native) code. For managed types, you can easily retrieve runtime type information, and managed objects are garbage-collected. (Memory management is discussed in Chapter 2, and other runtime services are covered in Chapter 4.)

To differentiate between .NET concepts and non-.NET concepts, the term *unmanaged* is used quite often.

What Is C++/CLI?

C++/CLI is a set of extensions made to the C++ language to benefit from the services that an implementation of the CLI offers. These extensions are published as the ECMA-372 standard. With the help of these extensions, a programmer can use .NET constructs in existing C++ code, as shown previously. Visual C++ 2005 implements the C++/CLI standard to support executing code on the CLR.

Building C++/CLI Applications

To make the switch from C to C++, a new file extension was used. As you can see in the preceding HelloWorld3.cpp example, the file extension for C++/CLI applications remains unchanged. However, there is still a need to distinguish between C++ compilation and C++/CLI compilation—the result of native C++ compilation is native code, whereas the result of C++/CLI compilation is managed code. If you try to compile the code on the command line, as shown in the following, you'll get compiler errors.

```
CL.EXE HelloWorld3.cpp
```

These errors will complain that System is neither a class nor a namespace name, and that the identifier WriteLine is not found. Both the namespace System and the method WriteLine are the managed aspects of your code. The Visual C++ compiler can act as a normal C++ compiler or as a C++/CLI compiler. By default, it remains a native compiler. To use it as a C++/CLI compiler, you use the compiler switch /clr, as in the following command line:

```
CL.EXE /clr HelloWorld3.cpp
```

This simple HelloWorld3 application shows one of the advantages that C++/CLI has over all other commonly used .NET languages: it provides source code compatibility with a good old native language.

C++/CLI is a superset of the C++ language. A valid C++ program is also a valid C++/CLI program. As a consequence, your existing code base is not lost. Instead of reimplementing existing applications with a completely new language and programming infrastructure, you can seamlessly extend existing code with .NET features.

The HelloWorld3.exe file created by the C++/CLI compiler and linker is a so-called .NET assembly. For this chapter, it is sufficient to consider assemblies as the deployable units of the .NET world. Chapter 4 will provide a more detailed definition of this term. The HelloWorld3.exe assembly differs from assemblies created by other .NET languages because it contains native code as well as managed code. An assembly like HelloWorld3.exe is also called a *mixed-code assembly*.

A migration strategy based on C++/CLI can preserve huge investments in existing C++ source code. This is extremely important because there is a vast amount of C++ code that is already written, tested, accepted, and in service. Furthermore, this strategy allows a partial migration with small iterations. Instead of switching everything to .NET in one chunk, you can flexibly use different .NET features when they seem appropriate.

Object File Compatibility

Partial migration obviously depends heavily on source code compatibility. Once existing C++ source code is compiled to managed code, you can straightforwardly and seamlessly integrate other .NET components and benefit from the many features the .NET Framework offers. However, there is a second pillar that you must understand to use C++/CLI efficiently. I like to refer to this feature as *object file compatibility*.

Like source code compatibility, the object file compatibility feature of C++/CLI has an interesting analogy to the shift from C to C++. As shown in Figure 1-1, the linker accepts object files compiled from C and C++ sources to produce a single output.

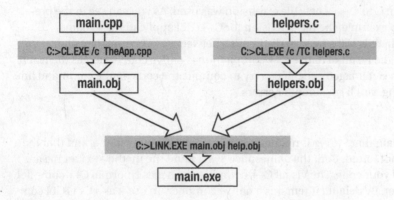

Figure 1-1. *Linking C and C++ based object files into an application*

The compiler switch /c produces just an object file instead of an executable output. In this sample, one file is compiled with the C++ compiler and a second file is compiled with the C compiler. (The /TC switch is used for that.) Both resulting object files are linked to produce the application.

When a source file is compiled with /clr, the compiler produces a managed object file. Equivalent to the scenario with C and C++ based object files, the linker can get managed and unmanaged object files as an input. When the linker detects that at least one input is a managed input, it generates a managed output. Figure 1-2 shows how you can link a managed and an unmanaged object file into a single output file.

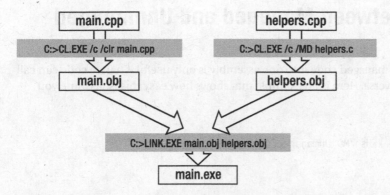

Figure 1-2. *Linking managed and unmanaged object files into an application*

As Figure 1-3 demonstrates, you can also create a managed static library that itself can be an input to the linker. In this figure, TheLib.obj is a managed object file. Therefore, TheLib.lib is a managed static library. TheApp.obj is also a managed object file. The linker gets two managed inputs, so the resulting TheApp.exe is a .NET assembly. Feel free to ignore the keyword __clrcall in TheApp.cpp. It will be discussed extensively in Chapter 9.

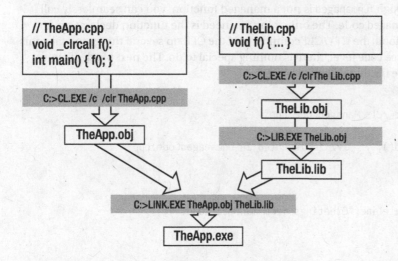

Figure 1-3. *Linking with managed library inputs*

Object file compatibility is an important feature because it allows you minimize the overhead of managed execution. If you use C++/CLI to integrate .NET code into existing C++ code, you will likely decide to compile most or even all of your existing code without /clr, and to compile only new files to managed code. In Chapter 7, I will explain what you should consider before you modify your project settings to turn on the /clr compiler switch, and I will give step-by-step instructions for modifying your project configurations.

Interaction Between Managed and Unmanaged Code

Linking native code and managed code into one assembly is only useful if native code can call managed code and vice versa. Here is an example that shows how easy this is. Assume you have a file like this one:

```
// UnmanagedCode.cpp
// compile with "CL /c /EHs /MD UnmanagedCode.cpp"

#include <iostream>
using namespace std;

void fUnmanaged()
{
  cout << "Hello again from unmanaged code.\n" << endl;
}
```

If you compile this file with the command mentioned in the comment, you will get an unmanaged object file named UnmanagedCode.obj. Obviously, fUnmanaged will be compiled to unmanaged code. Although fUnmanaged is not a managed function, you can seamlessly call it in a file compiled to managed code. The only thing you need is the function declaration for fUnmanaged. Under the hood, the C++/CLI compiler and the CLR do several things to make this possible, but at the source code level, there is nothing special to do. The next block of code shows a managed source file that calls fUnmanaged:

```
// ManagedCode.cpp
// compile with "cl /c /clr ManagedCode.cpp"

extern void fUnmanaged();      // implemented in UnmanagedCode.cpp

void fManaged()
{
  System::Console::WriteLine("Greetings from managed code!");
  fUnmanaged();
}
```

The next example shows a native caller for the managed function fManaged. Again, only the normal function declaration is necessary, and under the hood the compiler and the runtime make sure the code works as intended.

```
// HelloWorld4.cpp
// compile with "cl /MD HelloWorld4.cpp /link ManagedCode.obj UnmanagedCode.obj"

#include <stdio.h>

extern void fManaged();      // implemented in ManagedCode.cpp

int main()
{
  printf("Hi from native code.\n");
  fManaged();
}
```

If you use the command shown in the comment of this code, the C++/CLI compiler will generate a native object file, HelloWorld4.obj, and link it together with ManagedCode.obj and UnmanagedCode.obj into the application HelloWorld4.exe. Since HelloWorld4.obj is a native object file, HelloWorld4.exe has a native entry point. The printf call in main is a native call from a native function. This call is done without a switch between managed and unmanaged code. After calling printf, the managed function fManaged is called. When an unmanaged function like main calls a managed function like fManaged, an unmanaged-to-managed transition takes place. When fManaged executes, it uses the managed Console class to do its output, and then it calls the native function fNative. In this case, a managed-to-unmanaged transition occurs.

The HelloWorld4 application was written to explain both kinds of transitions. It is extremely helpful to have both these options and to control in a very fine-grained way when a transition from managed code to unmanaged code, or from unmanaged code to managed code, takes place. In real-world applications, it is important to avoid these transitions, because method calls with these transitions are slower. Reducing these transitions is key to avoiding performance penalties in C++/CLI. To detect performance problems, it can be very important to identify transitions between managed and unmanaged code. Reducing performance penalties is often done by introducing new functions that replace a high number of managed/unmanaged transitions with just one. Chapter 9 gives you detailed information about internals of managed/unmanaged transitions.

The code samples used so far have used the simplest possible method signature. However, the interoperability features of C++/CLI allow you to use any native type in code that is compiled to managed code. This implies that methods called via managed/unmanaged transitions can use any kind of native type. Chapter 8 will discuss all details of type transitions.

DLLs with Managed Entry Points

You can also factor managed code out into a separate DLL so that your existing projects remain completely unmanaged. Figure 1-4 shows a simple example of such a scenario.

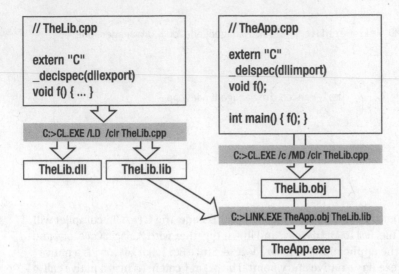

Figure 1-4. *Separating managed code in DLLs*

In this simple scenario, `TheApp.cpp` shall represent your existing project. To extend it with managed features, a new DLL is created from the source file `TheLib.cpp`. Notice that `TheLib.cpp` is compiled with `/clr`. Therefore, the exported function `f()` is a managed function. When `main` calls the managed function `f`, the CLR is delay-loaded.

Using mixed-code DLLs like `TheLib.dll` from the preceding sample, you can minimize the impact that managed execution has on your project. However, there are some pitfalls that you should know before you start writing mixed-code DLLs. Chapter 12 gives you all the necessary information to avoid these pitfalls.

Compilation Models

So far, I have discussed the following two major features, sometimes summarized as C++/CLI interoperability:

- Existing C++ source code can be compiled to managed code (source code compatibility).

- Native code and managed code can be linked into a mixed-code assembly (object file compatibility).

Compared to the interoperability features that other .NET languages provide, C++/CLI interoperability is much more powerful. It is a significant simplification for interoperating with native code, and it enables developers to save huge investments of existing C++ code.

On the other hand, these powerful features have side effects. Often, these side effects can be ignored, but it is also possible that these side effects are incompatible with other constraints and requirements of a project. To handle situations that are incompatible with the side effects caused by C++/CLI interoperability, Visual C++ allows you to turn either the object file compatibility or both C++/CLI interoperability features off. This can be done by choosing different compilation models supported by Visual C++. If the command-line option `/clr` is not used, the compiler chooses the native compilation model. To compile to managed code, the compiler argument /clr, or one of its alternatives—/clr:pure or /clr:safe—can be chosen.

As shown in the preceding samples, the /clr compiler option enables you to use both interoperability features mentioned previously. The compiler option /clr:pure still allows you to compile existing C++ code to managed code (source code compatibility), but you cannot produce mixed-code assemblies, which would require object file compatibility. The linker does not allow you to link object files produced with /clr:pure with native object files. An assembly linked from object files compiled with /clr:pure will have only managed code; hence the name.

Assemblies containing only managed code can be used to bypass two special restrictions of mixed-code assemblies. However, these restrictions apply only to very special scenarios, and understanding them requires knowledge of .NET features discussed later in this book. Therefore, I defer this discussion to Chapter 7.

Another restriction that applies to mixed-code assemblies as well as to assemblies built with /clr:pure is much more relevant: neither kind of assembly contains verifiable code, which is a requirement for .NET's new security model, called Code Access Security (CAS). CAS can be used to execute assemblies with restricted abilities to use features of the runtime and base class libraries. For example, pluggable applications are often implemented so that plug-ins do not have any permission on the file system or the network. This is sometimes called *sandboxed execution*.

Certain features of the runtime could be misused to easily bypass a sandbox of restricted permissions. As an example, all features that allow you to modify random virtual memory could be used to overwrite existing code with code that is outside of the runtime's control. To ensure that none of these dangerous features are used by a sandboxed assembly, its code is verified before it is actually executed. Only if code has passed the verification can it be executed in a sandbox. The powerful interoperability features that are supported with the compilation models /clr and /clr:pure use nonverifiable features intensively. To produce verifiable code, it is required to use the compilation model /clr:safe. Source code that is compiled with /clr:safe can only contain .NET constructs. This implies that native C++ types cannot be used.

Wrapping Native Libraries

C++/CLI is not only the tool of choice for extending existing C++ applications with .NET features, but it is also the primary tool for creating mixed-code libraries. These libraries can be simple one-to-one wrappers for native APIs; however, in many scenarios it is useful to do more than that. Making existing C++ libraries available to .NET developers so that they can make the best use of them requires giving an existing API a .NET-like face.

In .NET, there is a new type system with new features, and there are also new philosophies related to class libraries, error reporting, data communication, and security that all have to be considered to make a wrapper a successful .NET library. Several chapters of this book are dedicated to different tasks of wrapping native libraries. Chapters 5 and 6 explain how to define the various kinds of managed types and type members, and show the .NET way to map different kinds of relationships to a system of managed types. In Chapter 10, important design and implementation aspects of wrapper libraries are discussed. Finally, Chapter 11 explains how to use the reliability features provided by .NET to ensure that the wrapped resources are cleaned up even in critical scenarios like stack overflows. High reliability is of special importance if a wrapper library is used in long-running servers.

Summary

This chapter has introduced some of the salient features of C++/CLI. Using C++/CLI, you can combine the good old world of native C++ and the fancy new world of .NET. As you've seen, you can integrate managed code into existing C++ code and also link native and managed inputs into a single output file. Furthermore, you can seamlessly call between managed and unmanaged code. These features are extremely useful, both for extending existing applications and libraries with .NET features and for writing new .NET applications and libraries that require a lot of interoperability between managed and unmanaged code.

CHAPTER 2

■ ■ ■

Managed Types, Instances, and Memory

.NET's CLI introduces a new type system called the Common Type System (CTS). A major design goal of the CTS is language interoperability. This means that the CTS is used by all .NET languages—hence the name *Common* Type System. Language interoperability is helpful for users of class libraries as well as for developers writing class libraries for others. Due to the CTS's language interoperability, many .NET class libraries can be used by all .NET languages. Even if you switch from one .NET language to another, your knowledge about the .NET class libraries and their types is likely not lost. This is especially helpful because the Microsoft .NET Framework SDK ships with a huge, powerful base class library. Throughout this book, I will call this base class library the Framework Class Library (FCL).

Class library developers benefit from the CTS because all potential client languages use the CTS, too. Without such a language-interoperable type system, it would be necessary to use only a very limited set of interoperable types in signatures of methods visible to library users. As an example, C++ developers writing COM components callable by Visual Basic cannot use character pointers or the type std::string for string arguments. Parameters of type BSTR, a special COM-specific language-interoperable string type, are required instead. For a developer of a .NET class library, the situation is different. Not all .NET languages support all possible types that can be defined with the CTS, but the number of types known by all .NET languages is significantly greater.

Figure 2-1 shows a schema of the CTS that is not complete, but sufficient for the current discussion.

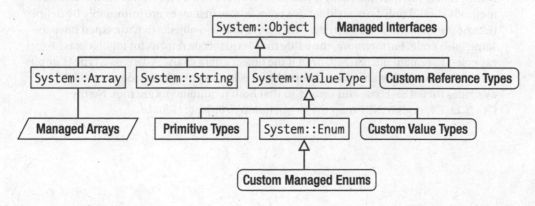

Figure 2-1. *The CTS*

As Figure 2-1 shows, System::Object is a central type of the CTS. Apart from managed interfaces and a few other types ignored here, all CTS types are directly or indirectly inherited from System::Object. Therefore, the CTS is sometimes called a single-rooted type system. Similar to the C++ type system, the CTS supports a set of primitive types. Even primitives indirectly inherit System::Object. A string is not just an array of characters, but an individual type. The CTS also allows the definition of certain special kinds of types. These include arrays, interfaces, custom value types, and custom managed enums.

System::Object

Since System::Object acts as the lowest common denominator of almost all .NET types, there are certain similarities to void*, which is the lowest common denominator of all C++ pointer types. However, System::Object is much more powerful than void*. System::Object provides a set of methods that is available for all expressions resulting in .NET types. These methods are as follows:

ToString: This is a virtual function that returns a string that represents the object. The default implementation provided by System::Object simply returns the name of the object's type. Many types in the FCL provide an overload for this function. For example, System::Enum, the base class of all managed enums, overloads ToString so that the string literal of the current value is returned. The ToString overload of System::String simply returns the string value.

GetType: This function is the entry point to the very powerful runtime type information features of .NET. Using this method, you can obtain a .NET object that allows the investigation of almost any static aspect of a managed type. Starting from the type's identity, name, and characteristics, all its type members can be inspected down to the level of method implementations. Furthermore, types can be instantiated and invoked dynamically based on runtime type information objects.

GetHashCode: As the name says, GetHashCode is supposed to return a hash code of the object. Like ToString, it is a virtual function. The FCL has a couple of collection classes that internally use this function.

Equals: Various collection classes in the FCL use Object::Equals for search operations. Notice that if you override Equals, you must override GetHashCode, too. However, both methods should only be overridden for types whose instances are immutable by definition. Some collection classes in the FCL expect that two objects that are equal have the same hash code. Furthermore, the value that GetHashCode returns for an object is expected to remain unchanged, even if the object's data changes. Unless a type is implemented so that its instances are immutable, it is impossible to provide nontrivial overrides for GetHashCode and Equals so that both requirements are met. Neither C++/CLI, C#, nor VB .NET map the == operation to Object::Equals.

Primitive Types

If code is compiled with /clr, the System::Object methods can be called on any expression that evaluates to a managed type. An expression of type std::string is obviously not a managed type; therefore it is illegal to call one of the methods mentioned previously on an expression that evaluates to std::string. However, in managed compilation, literals for Boolean and numeric values are of managed types. The following code uses this feature:

```
// managedExpressions.cpp
// build with "cl /clr managedExpressions.cpp"

using namespace System;

int main()
{
  System::Console::WriteLine((3+39).ToString());
  System::Console::WriteLine((42).GetType());
}
```

Even though it seems so, the int literals 3 and 39 are not simply literals of the native type int. Because the file is compiled to managed code, these literals are of managed primitive types. The expression (3+39) is also of a managed primitive type; therefore ToString can be called on it. For the managed int primitive, ToString is overloaded to return the string literal of the current value. In this case, it is 42, which will be written to the console. Since (42) is a managed expression, too, you can also call GetType on it. As described previously, GetType returns a .NET type information object. When such a type information object is passed to Console::WriteLine, a different overload of this method is called. This method internally calls ToString on the object passed. The .NET type information object's ToString method simply returns the type name. The output that this sample application writes to the console is probably surprising:

```
42
System.Int32
```

The managed int literal is in fact different from a native one. It is an instance of a type with the name System.Int32. This type inherits methods like ToString and GetType from System::Object. In this type name, the dot character (.) is used as a separator for namespace names and type names. The FCL uses this type-naming schema because most .NET languages, including C# and VB .NET, use it, too. Even though a C++/CLI developer has to write System::Int32 with two colons (::) instead, it is important to know about the other naming schema used by the FCL, especially if you search the MSDN documentation or the Web for information about a type.

Table 2-1 shows commonly used primitives provided by the runtime.

Table 2-1. *CTS Primitives and C++/CLI Type Names*

C++/CLI Type Name	Class Name	Literals
bool	System::Boolean	true, false
unsigned char	System::Byte	
signed char	System::SByte	'a'
short	System::Int16	
unsigned short	System::UInt16	
int	System::Int32	1L
unsigned int	System::UInt32	1U
long long	System::Int64	1LL
unsigned long long	System::UInt64	1ULL
float	System::Single	1.0f, -1e-4f
double	System::Double	1.0, -1e-4
wchar_t	System::Char	L'a'
void	System::Void	

Since all the primitives shown here, and their native equivalents, have the same binary layout, a primitive type in managed code can still be used as a native primitive, if this is required by the context. The following sample code shows this. Even though a variable of type System::Double is passed to std::cout, the code compiles and works as expected.

```
// primitives.cpp
// build with "CL /clr primitives.cpp"

#include <iostream>
using namespace std;

int main()
{
  System::Double PI = 3.14159265358979;
  cout << PI;
}
```

Custom CTS Type Definitions

To distinguish the definition of CTS types from native type definitions, a set of new keywords has been introduced. These new keywords include white spaces, which avoids conflicts with identifiers (names for variables, types, and type members) in existing C++ code. As an example, the keyword ref class is used to define a custom CTS class. The following code shows a simple managed type definition:

```
ref class ManagedReferenceType
{
  int aPrivateField;
public:
  void APublicFunction();
};
```

The CTS supports the definition of various other kinds of types and type members. These will be discussed in Chapter 5.

Managed Memory

Like native code, managed code supports two major options for memory allocations: a stack and a heap. The managed stack has a lot of similarities to the native stack. Both stacks contain stack frames (also called activation records) to store data that is bound to a method call, like parameters, local variables, and temporary memory. In fact, the CLR implements the managed stack mainly in terms of the native stack. Due to the similarities between the native and managed stacks, it is often sufficient to see both concepts as one. However, sometimes an explanation of certain internals, like the garbage collection and .NET's security model, requires differentiating them.

Managed Heap

Similar to the C++ free store (new/delete) and the heap (malloc/free), the lifetime of a memory allocation on the managed heap is not bound to a method call or a scope within a method call. The lifetime of a memory allocation on the managed heap is controlled by a garbage collector (GC). Therefore, this managed heap is also referred to as the "garbage-collected" heap, or simply the "GC" heap.

To differentiate allocations on the native heap from allocations on the managed heap, the operator gcnew is used. The following program creates a new instance of System::String with the value aaaaaaaaaa on the GC heap, and writes its value to the console:

```
// gcnew.cpp
// compile with "cl /clr gcnew.cpp"

int main()
{
  System::Console::WriteLine(gcnew System::String(L'a', 10));
}
```

Only instances of managed types can be allocated on the GC heap. Trying to instantiate a native type like `std::string` via gcnew will cause a compiler error. However, since primitives are managed types in the managed compilation model, they can be instantiated on the managed heap, too. The following expression is legal if you compile with `/clr`:

```
gcnew int(0);
```

Since the managed compilation model can treat primitives as native primitives if the actual context requires this, the following expression is also legal if you compile to managed code:

```
int* pi = new int(0);
```

When a local variable is supposed to refer to an object on the GC heap, a simple native pointer is not sufficient. The following line of code is illegal:

```
int* pi = gcnew int(0);
```

A native pointer could easily be copied into an unmanaged memory location. The copied pointer would be outside of the runtime's control. This would conflict with the requirements of .NET's GC—to decide whether an object's memory can be reclaimed or not, the GC must be aware of all variables referring to the GC heap.

The CLR implements the GC heap with a compacting algorithm. Instead of managing fragments of deallocated memory, objects can be relocated during a garbage collection so that one object follows the next and there is one free memory block at the end of the heap. To ensure that the moved objects are still accessible, the runtime must update all variables referring to relocated objects. This is another reason why the GC must be aware of all references.

Although this implementation strategy sounds like a huge amount of work during a garbage collection, a defragmenting GC can be very helpful for implementing performant and scalable applications. Allocating memory on the GC heap is an extremely scalable operation compared to unmanaged allocation, particularly in scenarios in which many threads allocate memory synchronously. The GC heap maintains a pointer to the start of the free memory area. To allocate memory on the GC heap, it is often enough to block other allocating threads only for a very short time. In a simplified view, it is sufficient to block other threads only to save the free memory pointer into a temporary variable and to increment the free memory pointer. The temporarily saved pointer can then act as the pointer to the allocated memory.

Tracking Handles

Since a native pointer is not sufficient to refer to a location on the GC heap, another kind of variable is introduced by C++/CLI. It is called a *tracking handle*, because the GC keeps track of variables of this kind. Instead of an asterisk, a caret (`^`) is used to define a tracking handle:

```
int^ i = gcnew int(0);
```

In the same way, a handle to the String object can be stored in a local variable:

```
System::String^ str = gcnew System::String(L'a', 10);
```

A tracking handle either refers to an object on the GC heap, or is a variable referring to nothing. To avoid confusions with the value 0, the keyword `nullptr` has been introduced for this null value.

```
System::String^ str = nullptr;
```

The keyword `nullptr` can also be used to check if a tracking handle refers to an object or not:

```
bool bRefersToAnObject = (str != nullptr);
```

As an alternative, you can use this construct:

```
bool bRefersToAnObject = !str;
```

There are significant differences between native pointers and tracking handles. A tracking handle can only be used as a simple handle to an object—for example, to call a method of an object. Its binary value must not be used by your code. You cannot perform pointer arithmetic on a tracking handle. Allowing pointer arithmetic would imply that a programmer can control internals of the GC—for example, the order in which objects are allocated on the GC heap. Even if a thread creates two objects in two continuous operations, a different thread can create an object that is allocated between the two objects. A garbage collection can also be implemented so that the order of the objects can change during a garbage collection, or the memory for new objects can be allocated so that newer objects are allocated at lower addresses. All this is outside of the programmer's control.

Although the concept of tracking handles differs from the concept of native pointers, there are a lot of similarities. As with native pointers, the size of a tracking handle is platform dependent. On a 32-bit CLR, a tracking handle's size is 32 bits; on a 64-bit CLR, it is 64 bits. In fact, both native pointers and tracking handles store addresses in the virtual memory of the process. In the current implementation of the CLR (version 2.0), a tracking handle points to the middle of an object's header. Figure 2-2 shows that an object header is 8 bytes long: 4 bytes for a type identifier, 4 bytes for flags, and some other object-specific data that the CLR uses to provide different services. The actual member variables of the object follow the object header.

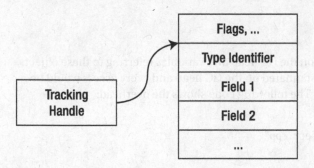

Figure 2-2. *A tracking handle referring to a managed object*

The type identifier shown in Figure 2-2 can be compared to the vtable pointer of a C++ object. However, it is used not only for method dispatching and dynamic casting, but also for certain other services of the runtime environment. For this chapter, it is sufficient to know that an object has an 8-byte object header followed by its fields, as shown in Figure 2-2.

Since a tracking handle has certain similarities to a native pointer, C++/CLI uses the arrow operator, ->, to access an object via a tracking reference:

```
System::String^ strUpper = str->ToUpper();
```

Values and Objects

There are different object-oriented systems with different definitions of an object. Early object-oriented systems like Smalltalk consider everything to be an object. In such a world, all local variables refer to objects on the heap, like tracking handles in C++/CLI. In contrast to Smalltalk, .NET does not have a purely object-oriented type system. The CLI differentiates between objects and values.

Objects can be defined as instances created on .NET's managed heap. As discussed previously, objects always have an 8-byte object header, and they are always accessed in a referenced way. On the one hand, the object header is required by many runtime services. Garbage collection is the most obvious one. Virtual method dispatching is another straightforward service based on the object header. But there are other services, too, which will be discussed in later chapters. On the other hand, an explicit allocation operation per object, plus the 8-byte object header, plus at least 4 bytes for a tracking handle to the object, plus the costs of accessing the object's state indirectly is an overhead that you will not want for every instance. Consider an instance that is supposed to simply act as an iterator variable of a loop:

```
// intAsAValue.cpp
// compile with "cl /clr intAsAValue.cpp"

int main()
{
  for (int i = 0; i < 10; ++i)
    System::Console::WriteLine(i);
}
```

If the CTS supported only objects on the GC heap and variables referring to these objects, the index variable would have to be instantiated on the GC heap and every access would be done with an extra level of indirection. The following code shows the overhead:

```
// intAsAnObject.cpp
// compile with "cl /clr intAsAnObject.cpp"

int main()
{
  for (int^ i = gcnew int(0); *i < 10; ++(*i))
    System::Console::WriteLine(*i);
}
```

This code compiles and executes as expected, but the runtime provides many more services for the variable i than actually needed. For example, there is no need to decouple i's memory allocation from main's execution time. Using the integer as an object here is a significant overhead, for the following reasons:

- The object instantiation is an explicit operation.

- 12 bytes are allocated on the managed heap (the 8-byte object header plus 4 bytes for the integer value).

- The object's memory is not deallocated when main exits, but when the GC decides to clean it up.

- A tracking handle is used as a local variable.

- All access to the integer object is done via the tracking handle.

Values, on the other hand, do not have this overhead. Compared to the previous example, a loop that uses values as in the sample code before the last one has several benefits as follows:

- The memory for the value is implicitly allocated on the managed stack as part of main's stack frame when main starts.

- Only 4 bytes of memory are allocated on the managed stack. There is no additional memory needed—neither for an 8-byte object header nor for a variable referring to the instance.

- The memory for the value is automatically deallocated when main returns. There is no extra garbage collection overhead.

- All operations on i can directly operate on i's memory. There is no need to calculate i's address before i can be accessed.

In contrast to objects, values are not independently garbage-collected. Similar to the rules for C++ variables, values are a part of the context in which they are defined. The preceding example uses a value as a local variable. In this case, a value is part of the stack frame of the function that defines the local variable. A value can also be defined as a member variable of a managed type. If it is a non-static member variable, every instance of the type contains such a value. If the value is a static member variable, it is part of the type itself. Table 2-2 summarizes the three cases.

Table 2-2. *Locations and Lifetimes of Values*

Value Defined As	Contained By
Local variable	The stack frame of the function defining the variable
Non-static member variable	An instance of the type that defines the variable
Static member variable	The type that defines the variable

The memory for a value is allocated and deallocated with its container. Values used as local variables are allocated when the function starts and deallocated when the function returns. When a value is defined as a non-static member variable of a type, it is part of an instance of the containing type, and is therefore automatically allocated and deallocated with the instance. If this instance is an object, the memory for the value is indirectly controlled by the GC. Values used as static variables of a type live as long as the type lives. As I will explain later, a type is loaded when it is used the first time and unloaded when the so-called application domain is unloaded. For most applications, this happens at application shutdown.

Value Types and Reference Types

Not all types can be instantiated as values. The CLI separates types into value types and reference types. As Figure 2-1 shows, the base class System::ValueType is used to differentiate value types from reference types. Everything that is derived from this class is a value type; all other types are reference types. Value types like System::Int32 can be instantiated either as an object (on the GC heap) or as a value. In contrast to value types, reference types can only be instantiated as an object. Instead of the actual instance, the declaring context can contain only tracking handles (and other referencing types not discussed yet). Figure 2-3 shows a managed stack and a managed heap of a simple application that instantiates a System::String, which is a reference type. Two tracking handles reference this new instance. Furthermore, the type int is instantiated twice, once as an object on the managed heap and once as a value on the stack.

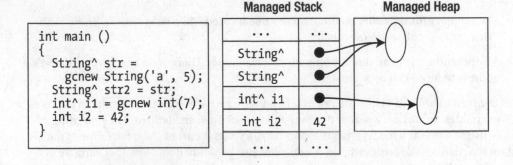

Figure 2-3. *Objects and values*

Boxing

As just discussed, a value type can be instantiated in two different ways: as a value or as an object. The variant instantiated on the managed heap is often called a *boxed object*. The object acts only as a box for the real value. Like many other .NET languages, C++/CLI supports an implicit conversion from a value V to a tracking handle of type V^.

```
int i = 5;
int^ i2 = i;
```

Since System::Object is the lowest common denominator of all possible instances, a conversion to System::Object^ exists, too.

```
int i = 5;
System::Object^ o = i;
```

Conversions like the two mentioned here look quite strange at first sight. What should the result of this cast be? Should the value 5 be treated as the pointer to the object? This would obviously end up in an invalid pointer, because no managed object will ever end up at the address 0x00000005. Should the address of the value be returned? In this case, 5 would be regarded as a part of the object header. The 4 bytes prior to that would be the first part of the object header, and the 4 bytes after that would be considered the actual value. Both solutions would soon end up in chaos. Instead of these nonsense approaches, a new instance of a boxed object is created on the managed heap by the cast operation. Since the new object is a boxed object, this is described as *boxing*.

The compiler automatically emits code that performs a boxing operation whenever a conversion from a value to a reference type occurs. You should be aware that every implicit or explicit cast from a value to a reference type causes a boxing operation. In the following code, two boxing operations occur:

```
// boxing1.cpp
// compileWith cl /clr boxing1.cpp

using namespace System;

int main()
{
  int i = 5;

  Console::WriteLine(Object::ReferenceEquals(i, i));
}
```

ReferenceEquals is a static helper method of System::Object that expects two arguments of type System::Object^, and returns true if both tracking handles refer to the same object. Although the same value is passed for these two arguments, two boxed objects are created here. Since these are two different objects, ReferenceEquals will return false.

Boxing often occurs silently under the hood. In the following code, 1,000,000 boxed objects of the value type System::DateTime from the FCL are created:

```
// boxing2.cpp
// compileWith cl /clr boxing2.cpp

using namespace System;

void f(DateTime^ dt)
{
  Console::WriteLine(dt->ToLongDateString());
}
```

```
int main()
{
  DateTime dt = DateTime::Now;
  for (int i = 0; i < 1000000; ++i)
    f(dt);
}
```

Every iteration of the for loop calls f passing the dt value. Since f expects an argument of type DateTime^—a tracking handle to DateTime—the dt value is boxed. This can be a significant overhead for the memory allocations as well as for the GC. To avoid this overhead, the object can be boxed before the loop starts:

```
DateTime^ dt = DateTime::Now;
for (int i = 0; i < 1000000; ++i)
  f(dt);
```

However, this approach can have side effects. If the f is implemented so that it calls a function on its argument that modifies the state of the boxed value, the same object will be modified by all iterations. If a value is passed instead of a boxed object, every iteration will create a new boxed object. This new boxed object will be modified and the value passed to the function will remain unchanged. To avoid these problems, System::DateTime does not have functions that modify the state of an object. Functions like DateTime::AddDays return a new value with the modified state instead of returning an existing one. Many other value types from the FCL, and other libraries, however, do have functions that can be used to modify the value. It is important to understand that a boxed object and the value used to create it are independent instances.

Unboxing

To retrieve the value from the boxed object, an operation called *unboxing* is performed. The most obvious example of an unboxing operation is dereferencing a tracking handle to a boxed object:

```
void f(V^ boxedV)
{
  V v = *boxedV;  // unboxing and assignment of unboxed value
  ...
}
```

If the tracking handle is not of type V^, a cast, instead of a dereferencing operation, is necessary. In this case, unboxing takes place, too:

```
void f(Object^ o)
{
  int i = (int)o; // unboxing and assignment of unboxed value
  ...
}
```

It is important to differentiate between a normal cast and an assignment of an unboxed value. Unboxing is a typed operation—to unbox an object, it is necessary to know the type of the boxed object. If the boxed object does not exactly match the type into which it should be unboxed, a System::InvalidCastException is thrown. The following code shows an example:

```
System::Object^ o = 5;
short s = (short)o;
```

The literal 5 is of type int. To assign it to an Object^, it is implicitly boxed. In the next line, the cast to a short is compiled into an unboxing operation. Even though there is a standard conversion from int to short, it is not legal to unbox a boxed int to a short value. Therefore, an InvalidCastException is thrown.

To avoid this InvalidCastException, you have to know the type of the boxed object. The following code executes successfully:

```
System::Object^ o = 5;
short s = (int)o;
```

In this sample, the boxed int is unboxed to an int value, and then the standard conversion is performed.

System::String

The CTS type System::String is implemented in a special way. For most CTS types, it is correct to say that all its instances are of the same size. System::String is an exception to this rule. Different instances of System::String can be of different sizes. However, .NET objects are fixed in their size. Once an object has been instantiated, its size does not change. This statement is true for strings, as well as for any other .NET objects, and it has significant impacts on the implementation of System::String. Since the size of a string once created cannot be changed afterwards, string objects cannot be extended or shrunk. To make string manipulations behave consistently, it has been defined that strings are immutable and that any function modifying a string's content returns a new string object with the modified content. The following code shows some examples:

```
String^ str1 = String::Empty;
str1 += "a";
str1 = str1 + "a";
str1 = String::Concat(str1, "a");
String^ str2 = str1->ToUpper();
```

In this code, all the operations that extend the string with an "a" are compiled into the same managed code, which uses String::Concat to concatenate the strings. Instead of modifying an existing string's content, Concat creates a new string object with the concatenated content and returns this new string object.

The fact that strings are immutable is quite helpful in multithreaded scenarios. There is no need to ensure that modifications to a string are synchronized with other threads. When two threads are simultaneously modifying the same string object, the string itself remains unchanged. Instead, every thread is creating its own string object containing the modified state.

On the other hand, creating new objects for each modification has its price. Using String::Concat directly or indirectly to concatenate many strings to a new string can easily end up in poor performance. For every concatenation, a new object has to be allocated on the managed heap. Even though memory allocation on the managed heap is a very fast operation, this can be an overhead. Due to the many objects created, the GC has to do much more than necessary. Furthermore, for every concatenation, the result of the previous concatenation, as well as the string to add, must be copied to the new string's memory. If there are many strings to concatenate, you should use the helper type StringBuilder from the namespace System::Text.

```
using System::Text::StringBuilder;
StringBuilder^ sb = gcnew StringBuilder(1024);
sb->Append("Rows: \n");
for (int i = 0; i < 100; ++i)
    sb->AppendFormat("Row {0}\n", i);
System::String^ strResult = sb->ToString();
```

Another special aspect of managed strings is the fact that they can be pooled. The CLR provides a pool for managed strings. The string pool can be helpful to save memory if the same string literal is used several times in your code, and to provide a certain optimization of comparisons against string literals. If you create your assembly with C++/CLI, all managed string literals used inside your assembly end up in the string pool. Some other .NET languages, including the C# version that comes with Visual Studio 2005, do not pool their string literals. (See the MSDN documentation for System::Runtime::CompilerServics::CompilationRelaxiationAttribute for more details.)

Managed Arrays

Even though there are various collection classes in the FCL, arrays are often the simplest and most effective option for storing data. Arrays are a special kind of type in the CTS.

One of the most special aspects of a managed array type is the fact that it is not created by a compiler at build time, but by the just-in-time (JIT) compiler at runtime. When the compiler generates some code that uses a managed array, it emits only a description of this array instead of a full type definition. Such a description is often found as part of the assembly's internal data structures. These can be, for example, data structures describing a method's signature or a local variable. When the JIT compiler has to create an array type, it extends a new type from System::Array. This class provides several helper functions—for example, to copy one array to another one, to search sequentially for an element, to sort an array, and to perform a binary search over a sorted array.

An array description inside an assembly contains only two pieces of information. These are the element type and the number of dimensions, called the *rank*. The C++/CLI syntax for managed arrays reflects this fact, too. The type name for a two-dimensional array of integers is as follows:

```
array<int, 2>
```

Since the default rank of this construct is 1, it is possible to define a one-dimensional array of short elements, like this:

```
array<short>
```

In native C++, array is not a keyword. It is possible that the keyword array conflicts with an identifier. Assume you have defined a variable named array. Such a naming conflict can be resolved by using the pseudo-namespace cli. In the sample that follows, a variable named array is declared as a tracking handle to a managed array of integers:

```
cli::array<int, 1>^ array;
```

It is illegal to define a managed array as a local variable. You can only define tracking handles to arrays as local variables. Like normal reference types, arrays are always instantiated on the managed heap. To instantiate a managed array, you can use a literal-like syntax or a constructor-like syntax. The following code shows a literal-like syntax:

```
array<int, 2>^ intsquare = {
    {1, 2, 3},
    {4, 5, 6},
    {7, 8, 9}
};
```

This code instantiates a 3 × 3 int array on the managed heap and implicitly initializes all its values. The alternative would be to instantiate the array with the constructor-like syntax first and initialize it separately, as follows:

```
array<int, 2>^ intsquare2 = gcnew array<int, 2>(3, 3);
intsquare2[0, 0] = 1; intsquare2[0, 1] = 2; intsquare2[0, 2] = 3;
intsquare2[1, 0] = 4; intsquare2[1, 1] = 5; intsquare2[1, 2] = 6;
intsquare2[2, 0] = 7; intsquare2[2, 1] = 8; intsquare2[2, 2] = 9;
```

Although both approaches look quite different, the C++/CLI compiler generates the same code. The first approach is used quite often to pass an array as a method argument without defining an extra variable. This code calls a function named average, which expects a double array:

```
double result = average(gcnew array<double> { 1, 3.5, -5, 168.5 });
```

In contrast to a native array, the number of elements is not part of the array's type. While the type char[3] is different from the type char[4], a one-dimensional managed byte array with three elements is of the same type as a one-dimensional managed array with four elements. Like managed strings, different array instances can have different sizes; but like any .NET object, an array, once created, cannot change its size. This sounds strange, given that there is a method System::Array::Resize. Instead of resizing an existing array, this method creates a new array and initializes it according to the source array's elements.

Managed Array Initialization

When a managed array is created, the data for all elements is implicitly set to zero values, and the default constructor—if available—is called. This behavior differs from the initialization of native arrays. To initialize a native array, the default constructor would be called for every single argument. If no constructor is present, the native array's data is not initialized.

Initializing a managed array with zero values first and then calling a potential default constructor sounds like an overhead. However, in most cases, there is no default constructor that could be called. None of the public value types from the FCL has a default constructor. To support fast array initialization, most .NET languages, including C++/CLI and C#, do *not* allow defining value types with default constructors.

However, there are a few .NET languages that support creating value types with default constructors. C++ Managed Extensions (the predecessor of C++/CLI) is one of them. If you instantiate an array of value types that have a default constructor, C++/CLI first instantiates the array normally, which implies zero-initialization, and then calls Array::Initialize on it. This method calls the default constructor for all elements. Most other .NET languages, including C#, do not initialize arrays of value types with custom default constructors correctly! To ensure a correct initialization in these languages, you have to call Array::Initialize manually, after instantiating such an array. If you migrate old C++ Managed Extensions code from .NET 1.1 to .NET 2.0, I strongly recommend making sure that no value types have default constructors.

Iterating Through an Array

A C++/CLI programmer can use different alternatives to iterate through a managed array. To obtain an element from an array, the typical array-like syntax can be used. This allows you to iterate through an array with a normal for loop. To determine the number of elements (in all dimensions) of an array, the implicit base class System::Array offers a public member called Length.

```
array<int>^ arr = { 1, 2, 3, 4, 5 };
for (int i = 0; i < arr->Length; ++i)
  System::Console::WriteLine(arr[i]);
```

C++/CLI also provides a for each loop to iterate through an array. This construct is often more convenient:

```
array<int>^ arr = GetManagedArrayFromSomeWhere();
for each (int value in arr)
  System::Console::WriteLine(value);
```

Finally, it is possible to access elements of a value array in a pointer-based way. As Figure 2-4 shows, the elements of a one-dimensional managed array are laid out and ordered sequentially. Multidimensional arrays, and some seldom-used arrays with arbitrary bounds, have a different layout, but their elements are laid out and ordered sequentially, too.

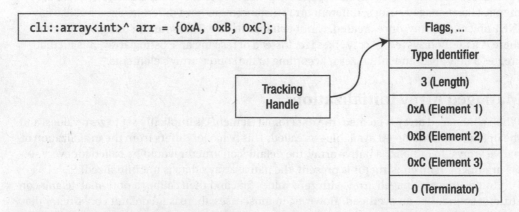

Figure 2-4. *Memory layout of a one-dimensional managed array of value types*

However, using native pointers would not be sufficient here. Since managed arrays are instantiated on the managed heap, where they can be relocated to defragment the managed heap, a special kind of pointer is necessary. Like a tracking handle, pointers of this type need to be updated when the managed array is moved. However, the tracking handle would not be sufficient either. As you can see in Figure 2-4, a tracking handle always refers to a managed object's header. The pointer type needed here should refer to an object's data area. For this new pointer concept, a template-like syntax is used. The keyword `interior_ptr` intends to make clear that this managed pointer concept refers to an object's data, not to an object's header. To differentiate a tracking handle from an interior pointer, a tracking handle is sometimes called whole-object pointer. Figure 2-5 shows the difference between a tracking handle and an interior pointer.

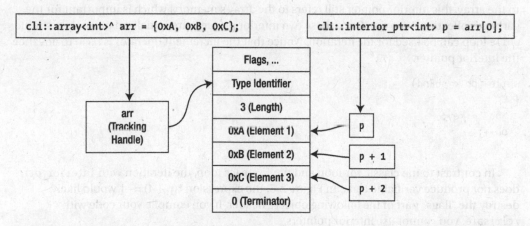

Figure 2-5. *Tracking handles and interior pointers*

In cases in which the keyword `interior_ptr` would conflict with an identifier, the pseudo-namespace `cli` can be used again. The following code shows how to use interior pointers to iterate through a one-dimensional array of integers:

```
void WeakEncrypt(array<unsigned char>^ bytes, unsigned char key)
{
  cli::interior_ptr<unsigned char> pb = &(bytes[0]);
  interior_ptr<unsigned char> pbEnd = pb + bytes->Length;
  while (pb < pbEnd)
  {
    *pb ^= key;
    pb++;
  }
}
```

The function `WeakEncrpyt` expects a managed byte array that will be encrypted and a byte that is used as the encryption key. `WeakEncrpyt` is probably the weakest possible encryption algorithm. When you need to encrypt data in your projects, use types from the `System::Security::Cryptography` namespace instead. Nevertheless, this function is sufficient to show how interior pointers can be used.

In WeakEncrypt, two variables of type interior_ptr<unsigned char> are defined. The first one (pb) is initialized with the address of the first element of the array, as follows:

```
cli::interior_ptr<unsigned char> pb = &(bytes[0]);
```

Since the array is a managed one, pb points to memory on the GC heap. The GC is aware of all interior pointers. When the array is relocated during a garbage collection, the interior pointer will automatically be updated.

The second interior pointer is initialized relative to the first one:

```
interior_ptr<unsigned char> pbEnd = pb + bytes->Length;
```

pbEnd points behind the last element of the array. Since the terminating bytes still belong to the array, this interior pointer still refers to the array's memory, which is important for the garbage collection behavior. Once these two interior pointers are initialized properly, a simple while loop can be used for the iteration. Notice that the increment operator is used to advance the interior pointer.

```
while (pb < pbEnd)
{
  *pb ^= key;
  pb++;
}
```

In contrast to the classic for loop and the for each loop, the iteration with interior_ptr does not produce verifiable code. In Figure 2-5, the expression *(p + 4) = −1 would likely destroy the "flags" part of the following object's header. If you compile your code with /clr:safe, you cannot use interior pointers.

Managed Arrays of Tracking Handles

In all the managed arrays discussed so far, each element of the array is an instance of a value type. There is no option to create managed arrays of managed objects; the type name array<System::String> is illegal. However, you can create managed arrays of tracking handles—for example, array<System::String^>. To create a managed array of tracking handles the same syntax as for creating value arrays is used:

```
array<String^>^ arr1 = { "1", "2", "3" };
array<String^>^ arr2 = gcnew array<String^>(3);
```

There are special rules for managed arrays of tracking handles. Similar to value arrays, a tracking handle array is initialized by setting all tracking handle elements to nullptr. The objects that the array elements refer to are created and destroyed independent of the array. Creating an array of ten string handles does not create ten strings.

An array of ten System::String handles has the same size as an array of ten System::Object handles. Due to the similar object layout that arrays of different tracking handles have, there is a special conversion option. Since there is an implicit conversion from String^ to Object^, all elements of an array<String^> can be treated as Object^. Therefore, there is also an implicit conversion from an array of string handles to an array of object handles.

Since there is an implicit conversion from any tracking handle to System::Object^, there is also an implicit conversion from an array<T^>^ to array<Object^>^, where T may be any managed type. There is even a conversion from an array<T^, n> to <Object^, n>. This behavior is called *covariance*.

Covariance does not apply to arrays of values. Although there is also an implicit conversion from a managed value to Object^, there is no implicit conversion from a value array to an array<Object^>^. The implicit conversion from a managed value to Object^ performs a boxing operation. Extending such a cast for the array would require creating a new array in which every element is a boxed object. To cover arrays of value types as well as arrays of tracking handles, the type System::Array can be used.

There is also no implicit conversion from an array<Object^>^ to an array<String^>^. On the one hand, this is quite obvious, because there is no implicit upcast from Object^ to String^; on the other hand, upcasting all elements of an array is often needed in the real-life code. The for each loop can often provide a solution to this problem, because it implies a special type-safe cast for each iteration. (It is called "safe cast," and will be explained in the next chapter.) The following code is legal, but the implicit casts may throw a System::InvalidCastException when the current element of the arrObj array cannot be cast to String^:

```
array<Object^>^ arrObj = GetObjectArrayFromSomewhere();
for each (String^ str in arrObj)
  Console::WriteLine(str);
```

Summary

With its new type system and the GC, .NET introduces new concepts for managing and using memory that has certain differences to the native model. Native C++ allows you to define any level of indirection by supporting direct variables, as well as any level of pointer-to-pointer types. The CTS differentiates only between values and objects, where values are instances that are directly accessible in their defined context and objects are instances that are always accessed indirectly. To achieve further levels of indirection, you have to define new classes with fields referencing other objects.

CHAPTER 3

■■■

Writing Simple .NET Applications

This chapter covers basics that you need to know to understand explanations in later chapters. I will familiarize you with a few fundamental types from the FCL that are used in different contexts throughout this book. Through the discussion of small applications that act as clients of the FCL, this chapter also explains how C++/CLI language concepts for common tasks like using libraries, using namespaces, exception handling, and casting can be used in the managed world, and how these concepts differ from their native counterparts.

Referencing Assemblies

Like native libraries and COM servers, assemblies are used to share code. Allowing your C++/CLI code to use another assembly requires certain steps that differ from the way native libraries and COM servers are made available to your projects. To understand these differences and the reasons behind them, it makes sense to take a step back and look at the way the compiler is enabled to call foreign code in the old ways of code sharing.

Using a native library requires including the library's header files. The declarations in the header file describe what types and functions are available to the library user. For COM servers, a similar kind of server description usually resides in type libraries. Visual C++ offers a Microsoft-specific extension to the C++ language that is often used to make this information available to the C++ compiler:

```
#import "AComTypeLibrary.tlb"
```

While information in a header file is used only at compile time, information in a COM type library is also used for different runtime features. Based on information in type libraries, COM can dynamically create proxies for remote procedure calls and dynamically invoke functions for scripting scenarios. Due to the required runtime availability, the type library is often embedded in the COM server. #import can also extract a type library from an existing COM server, as follows:

```
#import "AComServerWithAnEmbeddedTypeLibrary.dll"
```

For .NET assemblies, a description of the assembly itself, as well as its contents, is a mandatory part of the assembly; not an optional part, as in COM. In .NET, this description is called *metadata*. Metadata in .NET is mandatory because it is required by runtime services like garbage collection. Most (but not all) metadata is bound to the .NET types defined by an assembly. Therefore, the term *type information* is often used instead of metadata. In this book, I will use the more comprehensive term *metadata*, unless I really mean metadata describing types only. In that case, I will use the more precise term *type information*.

Analogous to the #import extension, C++/CLI comes with the #using directive to reference .NET assemblies. The following code references the assembly System.dll via a #using directive:

```
// referencingAssemblies1.cpp
// compile with "cl /clr:safe referencingAssemblies1.cpp"

#using <System.dll>

using namespace System;

int main()
{
  // System::Uri is defined in the assembly System.dll
  Uri^ uri = gcnew Uri("http://www.heege.net");
  Console::WriteLine(uri->Host);  // output: "www.heege.net"
}
```

This sample uses the type System::Uri, which is defined in the assembly System.dll. Without the #using directive, the compiler would complain that an undefined type System::Uri is used. To use the type System::Console, no #using directive is necessary. System::Console is defined in a very special assembly called mscorlib.dll. It defines many core types like System::Object, and even the types for the managed primitives. Therefore, mscorlib is automatically referenced by the C++/CLI compiler.

There is no mandatory relationship between an assembly name and the name of the namespace in which the assembly's types are defined. As an example, System.dll and mscorlib.dll define types in the namespace System.

If you're using make files or the new MSBUILD tool, or if you're building simple test solutions from a command shell, you can also set assembly references via the /FU command-line switch, as follows:

```
// referencingAssemblies2.cpp
// compile with "cl /clr:safe /FUSystem.dll referencingAssemblies2.cpp"

// no need for #using <System.dll>
using namespace System;

int main()
{
  Uri^ uri = gcnew System::Uri("http://www.heege.net");
  Console::WriteLine(uri->Host);  // output: "www.heege.net"
}
```

Assembly References in Visual Studio

To configure the /FU compiler switch in a Visual Studio 2005 project, you can add an assembly reference to the project. This can be done with the dialog shown in Figure 3-1.

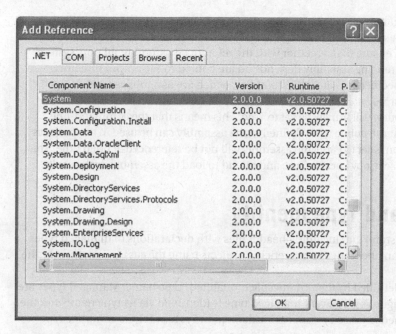

Figure 3-1. *Adding assembly references in Visual Studio projects*

You can choose various options for defining an assembly reference. The .NET tab shows a selection of often-referenced assemblies. You can configure this list via subkeys of the registry key HKEY_LOCAL_MACHINE\SOFTWARE\Microsoft\.NETFramework\v2.0.50727\ AssemblyFoldersEx. The COM tab is used for COM interoperability. Via the Browse tab, you can select any assembly in the file system.

The Projects tab is used very often. It is more convenient to pick a project from a list of the projects in the solution than to browse to an assembly output, but there are also important side effects. A project reference automatically implies a project dependency. The referencing project implicitly depends on the referenced project. Therefore, the referenced project is built before the referencing one.

Assembly references in Visual Studio can also have properties that influence post-build steps. Figure 3-2 shows the default properties for a project reference.

⊟ Build Properties	
Copy Local	**True**
Copy Local Dependencies	**True**
Copy Local Satellite Assemblies	**True**
Use Dependencies In Build	**True**
Use In Build	**True**

Figure 3-2. *Properties of an assembly reference in Visual Studio*

The most important property is Copy Local. When this property is set to True, the referenced assembly is copied to the output directory of the referencing project. This output directory depends on the configuration currently selected for the solution.

When the Copy Local property is set to True, the Copy Local Dependencies and Copy Local Satellite Assemblies properties are inspected as well. The Copy Local Dependencies property can be used to ensure that, together with the referenced assembly, all non-system assemblies that the referencing assembly depends on are copied to the output directory, too. The same can be specified for satellite assemblies, which are assemblies containing language-specific resources.

The Use in Build option will usually be set to True. This means that the command-line option /FU is used so that the public types defined in the assembly can be used in the project's source code. If this option is set to False, the assembly will not be referenced at build time. This only makes sense if you set Copy Local to True and intend to load the assembly dynamically.

Assemblies and Type Identity

It is important to understand that including header files with declarations of managed types in other projects is not an alternative to referencing projects using the #using construct or the /FU compiler switch.

In C++, types are identified by their (namespace-qualified) type name. Managed types are identified in a less ambiguous way. Every managed type is identified via its type name *and* the assembly that has defined it. Since System::Uri is defined in System.dll, its complete type name is as follows:

```
System.Uri, System, Version=2.0.0.0, Culture=neutral,
PublicKeyToken=b77a5c561934e089
```

This type name is called the assembly-qualified type name. It includes the namespace-qualified type name System.Uri (with a dot [.] as the namespace separator), and the complete name of the assembly in which it is defined. As you can see, a complete assembly name has several parts. These will be discussed in Chapter 4. So far, it is sufficient to realize that a complete CTS type name contains the assembly name.

The type identity of managed types is much stronger than the type identity of native types. Even if two types in different assemblies have the same namespace-qualified name, the runtime sees them as two different types.

This precise type identity concept is required to ensure .NET's security features, but it can also cause trouble. As a C++/CLI programmer, you must be aware of the different identity concepts for managed types. If you include a header file with managed type declarations in your project, the compiler expects these types to be defined in your project, not in the library you would like to reference. Including header files with declarations of managed types only makes sense if a managed type is used by source files from the same project that implements the managed type. The only way to tell your compiler about the managed types in other libraries is to set assembly references, as discussed before.

The different type identity concepts of the CTS and the C++ type system will also be important for later discussions in this book, so keep this information in mind—CTS types are identified via type name and assembly name, whereas C++ types are only identified via their type name.

Avoiding Naming Conflicts

Chapter 1 summarized the evolution from C to C++/CLI. In all the different phases of this evolution, new names have been introduced for types, functions, templates, variables, and so on. C++ has introduced the concept of namespaces to avoid naming conflicts. The CTS supports namespaces for the same reason. C++/CLI allows you to manage CTS namespaces with language syntax you already know from C++.

As a C++/CLI programmer, chances are good that you have to solve naming conflicts between names of these different phases. Many C++ programs written for the Windows platforms use a variety of libraries including the C runtime, the STL, the Win32 API, ATL, and MFC. All these libraries include new names. Since the FCL also introduces a huge amount of new names, naming conflicts can easily happen. The following code shows a simple example:

```
// nameingTrouble.cpp
// compile with "cl /c /clr namingTrouble.cpp"

using namespace System;
#include <windows.h>
```

This simple source file does not implement any function. Will it compile?

Well, would I ask you this question if the answer was what you expect? Try to compile this file with the command line mentioned in the comment and you will get a couple of strange errors telling you something about an IServiceProvider type that you have never written in the few lines of your code.

Since you compile with /clr, the assembly mscorlib is automatically referenced. The mscorlib assembly defines many types in the namespace System. The using declaration allows you to use all of these types without the namespace qualifier. The interface System::IServiceProvider is one of these types. If you include windows.h (the standard header file for the Win32 API), many new types and functions are declared. One of these types is the COM interface IServiceProvider. Since this type is not declared in the namespace System, this type declaration itself does not cause a naming conflict. However, after this COM interface is declared, several other declarations depend on the type name IServiceProvider. For example, there are methods using the type IServiceProvider in their signature. Since the type name IServiceProvider is ambiguous in this case, the compiler complains.

Even though these compiler errors look very irritating, it is easy to solve the problem. Just write the using declaration after including windows.h, as follows:

```
// noNameingTrouble.cpp
// compile with "cl /c /clr noNamingTrouble.cpp"

#include <windows.h>
using namespace System;
```

Since the namespace is opened later in this sample, none of the declarations in windows.h causes naming conflicts. To minimize the potential for naming conflicts, it can be useful to reduce the number of names that are visible without namespace qualifiers. This can be done in two ways. First, you can use using declarations instead of using directives. While a using directive introduces all names of a namespace, a using declaration only introduces a special name. Second, you can introduce new names only in a special scope. The following code introduces new names defensively by combining both suggestions:

```cpp
// introducingNamesCarefully.cpp
// compile with "cl /clr:safe introducingNamesCarefully.cpp"

#using <System.dll>

int main()
{
  // scoped using declaration introducing only System::Uri
  using System::Uri;

  // scoped using declaration introducing only System::Console
  using System::Console;

  Uri^ uri = gcnew Uri("http://www.heege.net");
  Console::WriteLine(uri->Host);     // writes www.heege.net
}
```

Command-Line Arguments

The next sample application simply dumps the command-line arguments passed:

```cpp
// dumpArgs.cpp
// build with "CL /clr dumpArgs.cpp"

using namespace System;

int main(array<String^>^ args)
{
  for (int i = 0; i < args->Length; ++i)
  {
    Console::WriteLine("Argument {0}: {1}", i, args[i]);
  }
}
```

Since the source file is compiled with /clr, the entry point main is a managed function. A managed main can receive command-line arguments via a managed string array parameter. The application shown here iterates through the array of arguments and dumps them to the console. The overload of Console::WriteLine used here expects a format string and a variable number of arguments. The format string "Argument {0}: {1}" contains two different placeholders. Each of these placeholders specifies an index identifying the argument written in a pair of curly braces. The index 0 refers to the argument following the format string, the index 1 refers to the next one, and so on. The formatted output string contains the formatted arguments instead of the placeholders.

Formatting an argument can be done by calling `ToString` on the argument. However, the placeholder can also contain further formatting information. As an example, the placeholder `{0:X}` specifies that the first argument following the format string should be formatted as a hexadecimal number with capital letters as hex digits. (For further information on this topic, search the MSDN documentation for "composite formatting.")

Stream-Based IO

The majority of applications and components need to read bytes from or write bytes to data sources. To simplify this task, the FCL provides rich support for stream-based IO. The central type for the FCL's IO features is the abstract class `System::IO::Stream`. Various classes representing different media are derived from `Stream`. Figure 3-3 shows a couple of them.

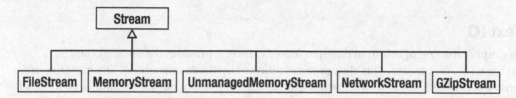

Figure 3-3. *Streams in the FCL*

The `Stream`-derived classes include `System::IO::FileStream` for file IO operations, `System::IO::MemoryStream` for stream-based access of a managed byte array, `System::IO::UnmanagedMemoryStream` for access to a continuous range of unmanaged memory with a managed API, and `System::Net::NetworkStream` for network-based IO operations. Other stream implementations provide additional features (e.g., the `GZipStream` from the namespace `System::IO::Compression` can be used for the compressed storage of data in any underlying stream).

All concrete stream implementations provide constructors that allow you to specify the underlying media. As an example, the following code instantiates `FileStream` with a constructor that expects the name of the text file:

```
FileStream^ fs = gcnew FileStream("SampleFile.txt", FileMode::Open);
```

The second constructor argument passed here specifies that a file with that name is expected to exist. If this is not the case, an exception is thrown. The `FileMode` enumeration provides various alternative flags. As an example, `FileMode::OpenOrCreate` ensures that a new instance is created if the file does not exist, instead of throwing an exception.

To determine the number of bytes in the stream, the member `Stream::Length` can be used:

```
int bytesInFile = fs->Length;
```

Depending on the concrete stream type, the capabilities of a stream can be different. As an example, `NetworkStream` does not support retrieving the length of the stream or repositioning the stream's internal cursor (Seek). Attempts to use these members will cause a `System::NotSupportedException`.

Streams support IO operations using either `System::Byte` (or the native equivalent type name, unsigned char) or a managed array of `System::Byte`. As an example, the whole contents of `FileStream` can be written into a byte array:

```
array<Byte>^ bytes = gcnew array<Byte>(bytesInFile);
```

```
// write whole file contents into bytes, starting from position 0
fs->Read(bytes, 0, bytesInFile);
```

To get a string from the byte array, it is necessary to know how the file's text is encoded into bytes. The FCL provides different encoder implementations. If simple ASCII encoding can be assumed, the following code provides an easy decoding:

```
String^ textInFile = Encoding::ASCII->GetString(bytes);
```

Text IO

To simplify reading of text from different sources, the FCL provides the abstract class `System::IO::TextReader`. This class provides different methods to read text. The most important ones are `ReadLine` to read a single line and `ReadToEnd` to read all the remaining contents of the stream. There are two concrete `TextReader` implementations: `System::IO::StringReader`, which can be used to read multiline .NET strings line by line, and `System::IO::StreamReader`, which uses a stream as its source.

As Figure 3-4 shows, there is also the abstract class `TextWriter` and concrete types for writing text into a stream or into a `StringBuilder` object.

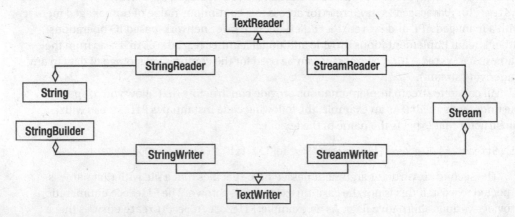

Figure 3-4. *TextReader and TextWriter classes in the FCL*

The concrete classes `StreamReader` and `StreamWriter` are especially helpful. `StreamReader` automatically decodes bytes read from a stream, and `StreamWriter` implicitly encodes the text that should be written to a stream. Both use UTF-8 encoding by default, but you can use any available text encoder instead.

The following application treats the command-line arguments as names of text files and dumps the files' content to the console. To achieve this, it uses `TextReader` and `TextWriter`.

```
// dumpFiles.cpp
// build with "CL /clr:safe dumpFiles.cpp"

using namespace System;
using namespace System::IO;

void DumpTextReader(TextReader^ tr, TextWriter^ tw);

int main(array<String^>^ args)
{
  for each (String^ arg in args)
  {
    StreamReader^ sr = gcnew StreamReader(arg);
    TextWriter^ tw = Console::Out;
    tw->WriteLine("File {0}", arg);
    DumpTextReader (sr, tw);

    sr->Close();
  }
}

void DumpTextReader (TextReader^ tr, TextWriter^ tw)
{
  String^ line;
  int iLine = 0;
  while ((line = tr->ReadLine()) != nullptr)
    tw->WriteLine("Line {0}: {1}", iLine++, line);
}
```

Reading and Writing Binary Data

If a stream is supposed to contain binary data instead of text, two other helpers can be used. To serialize primitive types to a `Stream` instance, `System::IO::BinaryWriter` provides several typed overloads of the function `Write`. The following code shows how this class can be used:

```
void WriteData(Stream^ strm, int i, double d)
{
  BinaryWriter^ writer = gcnew BinaryWriter(strm);
  writer->Write(i);
  writer->Write(d);
  writer->Close();
}
```

For reading primitive data types from a stream, the type System::IO::BinaryReader, with several type-specific reader functions, can be used:

```
void DumpData(Stream^ strm)
{
  BinaryReader^ reader = gcnew BinaryReader(strm);
  Console::WriteLine(reader->ReadInt32());
  Console::WriteLine(reader->ReadDouble());
  reader->Close();
}
```

Managed Exception Handling

For historical reasons, many native libraries use a mixture of error reporting strategies. The Win32 API reports errors either via HRESULT values returned by functions or via error codes returned by the GetLastError API. Many C++ class libraries use C++ exception handling instead.

.NET also has a widely accepted exception handling infrastructure. The CLR, the FCL, and third-party libraries use managed exceptions to report all kinds of errors.

The try...catch construct of C++/CLI can be used to handle C++ exceptions as well as managed exceptions. Managed exceptions are tracking handles. Any tracking handle referring to an object can be thrown as a managed exception. The catch block shown here catches any managed exception:

```
catch (Object^ o)
{ /* ... */ }
```

However, to support language interoperability, the CLR, the FCL, and most other class libraries throw only exceptions of type System::Exception^ or tracking handles to classes derived from System::Exception. Languages like C# 2.0 and VB .NET 2.0 have only limited support for exceptions that do not derive from System::Exception, and earlier versions of these languages do not support other exception types at all.

The text file dumper application shown before will run successfully only if all command-line arguments are paths to files that are not locked by other processes and are accessible for the current user. In theory, it is even possible that the application is able to write to the console. As an example, assume you have piped the console output to a file and your hard disk is running out of space, or you have reached your quota on the hard disk.

In all these error cases, the FCL types used by the application will throw managed exceptions. The preceding code does not handle managed exceptions so far. The default behavior for unhandled exceptions is to write an error message describing the exception to the console's error stream and to create an entry in the operating system's event log. (If you are interested in overriding this behavior, consult the documentation for AppDomain::UnhandledException.)

StreamReader's constructor can throw exceptions of type System::IO::FileNotFoundException^, System::IO::PathNotFoundException^, and System::IOException^. An IOException^ can also be thrown from the stream writer Console::Out. Figure 3-5 shows the inheritance tree for these exception classes.

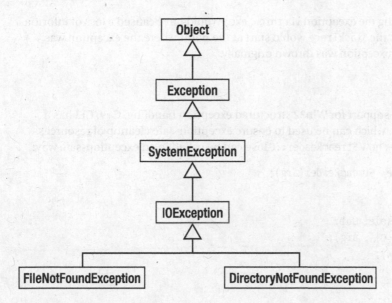

Figure 3-5. *Managed exceptions*

The base class System::Exception can give you useful information: In addition to a simple text message describing the exception, you can obtain an inner exception and the call stack from the method where the exception is thrown to the method where the exception is handled. The following code shows how you can use this information:

```
void ReportException(Exception^ exc)
{
  for (Exception^ exc2 = exc;
       exc2 != nullptr;
       exc2 = exc2->InnerException)
    Console::WriteLine(exc2->Message);
  Console::WriteLine("Stacktrace: {0}", exc->StackTrace);
}
```

The class System::SystemException, which extends System::Exception, does not provide additional functionality. It is simply used to differentiate exception classes defined in the base class library from other exception classes.

Like native C++, C++/CLI allows you to rethrow exceptions by using the throw statement without an operand:

```
try
{
  /* guarded block */
}
catch (Exception^ exc)
{
  ... partially handle the exception here ...

  throw;
}
```

Notice that rethrowing the exception via throw exc; would have caused a loss of information because in this case, the StackTrace would start at the point where the exception was rethrown, not where the exception was thrown originally.

try...finally

Similar to the Visual C++ support for Win32 structured exception handling, C++/CLI has a try...finally construct, which can be used to ensure exception-safe cleanup of resources. The following code shows how StreamReader::Close can be called in an exception-safe way:

```
StreamReader^ sr = gcnew StreamReader(arg);
try
{
  TextWriter^ tw = Console::Out;
  tw->WriteLine("File {0}", arg);
  DumpTextReader(sr, tw);
}
finally
{
  sr->Close();
}
```

This code follows a common pattern for resource management. Resources are typically wrapped in objects. As an example, the StreamReader object in the sample code wraps a FileStream object, which wraps the file handle it receives by calling an API of the operating system. The allocation of the FileStream object is done in the StreamReader constructor. If this resource allocation fails, the constructor throws one of the exceptions mentioned previously. If no exception is thrown, then the resource was allocated successfully. In this case, cleanup of the resource should be ensured even if an exception is thrown later. To achieve exception-safe cleanup, the resource is used inside a try block that immediately follows the resource allocation, and the resource cleanup is implemented in a finally block.

In addition to this try...finally pattern, C++/CLI provides an alternative for ensuring cleanup of resources that is derived from common C++ patterns for resource management. This alternative will be discussed in Chapter 6. In some cases, even the try...finally pattern mentioned here can cause resource leaks. Chapter 11 explains why this is possible.

Web Requests

A lot of features of the FCL are layered on top of the stream IO APIs. These features include a web request API for polymorphic URL-based access to resources. By default, this API supports the protocols HTTP, HTTPS, and FTP. To access resources on the file system in a polymorphic way, file://-based URLs can be requested, too. Furthermore, custom implementations for further protocols can be plugged into this architecture. The following sample code shows how to request resources via this API:

```
// UrlDumper.cpp
// build with "cl /clr:safe UrlDumper.cpp"
```

```
#using "System.dll"

using namespace System;
using namespace System::IO;
using namespace System::Net;

void DumpTextReader(TextReader^ tr, TextWriter^ tw);

int main(array<String^>^ args)
{
  for each (String^ url in args)
  {
    WebRequest^ req = WebRequest::Create(url);
    WebResponse^ rsp = req->GetResponse();
    DumpTextReader(gcnew StreamReader(rsp->GetResponseStream()),
                   Console::Out);
    rsp->Close();
  }
}

void DumpTextReader(TextReader^ tr, TextWriter^ tw)
{
  String^ line;
  int iLine = 0;
  while ((line = tr->ReadLine()) != nullptr)
    tw->WriteLine("Line {0}: {1}", iLine++, line);
}
```

This code uses the abstract class System::Net::WebRequest. Depending on the URL passed, WebRequest::Create returns a new instance of either FileWebRequest, HttpWebRequest, or FtpWebRequest. The abstract class WebRequest has the virtual method GetResponse, which returns a WebResponse^. Using the returned response object, you can retrieve information about the response, such as the content type and the content length, as well as a stream containing the bytes of the request.

WebResponse is an abstract type, too. Depending on the concrete type of the WebRequest, the WebResponse^ returned by GetResponse refers either to an instance of FileWebResponse, HttpWebResponse, or FtpWebResponse. To receive a stream containing the requested resource, GetResponseStream is called on the response object. After that, a StreamReader is instantiated to operate on the response stream.

Casting Managed Types

If you want to find out what concrete kind of request a WebRequest^ variable refers to, you can use the dynamic_cast operator, as follows:

```
WebRequest^ req = GetWebRequestFromSomeWhere();
if (dynamic_cast<FtpWebRequest^>(req) != nullptr)
  Console::WriteLine("The request was an FTP request");
```

The dynamic cast performs a runtime check and returns a `nullptr` if the type of the casted object does not support the target type. Therefore, the preceding code checks if the cast is not `nullptr` to find out if the cast was successful. In the sample code shown here, it is only required to find out if an expression can be casted and the result of a successful cast is not needed. In contrast to other languages, C++/CLI does not support an extra construct for this need. C#, as an example, has the is operator to find out if an expression is castable to a given type.

```
// this is C# code:
if ( req is FtpWebrequest )
  ... variable req can be casted to an FtpWebRequest ...
```

Even though this C# expression appears to be more expensive than the equivalent C++/CLI expression, the same IL instructions are generated for both cases.

The concrete `WebRequest`-derived classes do not support public constructors that could be used to create a new instance. The only way to instantiate an `HttpWebRequest` for a URL is to call `WebRequest::Create` passing an HTTP- or HTTPS-based URL.

In addition to the members of `WebRequest`, `HttpWebRequest` offers many members that are specific for the HTTP protocol (e.g., to specify whether a `GET` or a `POST` request should be made). To access these members, the `WebResponse` handle returned by `WebRequest::Create` must be downcasted to an `HttpWebRequest` handle. There are different options to achieve such a downcast.

As in the sample before, a `dynamic_cast` could be used. The `dynamic_cast` returns `nullptr` either if the input was a `nullptr` or if the cast was not successful. Since it is clear from the context that a `WebRequest::Create` returns a handle to an `HttpRequest` instance when an HTTP-based URL is passed, one could silently omit the checking for the `nullptr`. If the cast unexpectedly returns a `nullptr` because the assumption that was made is not true, the first attempt to access the object via the `nullptr` results in a `NullReferenceException`. In such a situation, it is impossible to conclude from the exception whether the `dynamic_cast` returned a `nullptr` because its input was an unexpected `nullptr` or because its input was of an unexpected type. The `safe_cast` allows a clear differentiation of these two cases. The following code shows how a `safe_cast` can be used:

```
WebRequest^ req = WebRequest::Create("http://www.heege.net");
HttpWebRequest^ httpReq = safe_cast<HttpWebRequest^>(req);
// use HttpRequest specific members here
httpReq->AllowAutoRedirect = true;
```

When the casted variable refers to an object of the wrong type, a `System::InvalidCastException^` is thrown. When the input of the cast operator is unexpectedly a `nullptr`, the result of the cast is also a `nullptr`, and the attempt to use the casted value will cause a `System::NullReferenceException`.

Even the good old C-style cast can be used for downcasting. For casts to tracking handle types, the C-style cast is either mapped to a `safe_cast` or to a `safe_cast` and a `const_cast`.

The `safe_cast` and the `dynamic_cast` are similar in that they both perform a runtime check against the input object. Such a runtime check is helpful to ensure that wrong assumptions have a clear outcome, but they also imply a performance cost. If you are absolutely sure that the cast will succeed, you can use a `static_cast` instead of a `safe_cast`. The `static_cast` omits the runtime check and is therefore faster.

```
WebRequest^ req = WebRequest::Create("http://www.heege.net");
HttpWebRequest^ httpReq = static_cast<HttpWebRequest^>(req);
// use HttpRequest specific members here
httpReq->AllowAutoRedirect = true;
```

However, if you use a static_cast for a downcast even though the casted object does not support the target type, the result of the cast is undefined. The damage caused by an illegal static_cast can easily destabilize the runtime, and therefore the whole process that hosts the runtime. Since a static downcast could also be used to bypass the .NET security system, it cannot be used if you produce verifiable IL code with /clr:safe.

Managed Debug Helpers

Due to the danger of static_cast, it can be helpful to assert that the casted expression is of the expected type during debug sessions. This can be done either with native or with managed assertions. The following line uses the CRT assertion macro _ASSERT from the native header crtdbg.h to achieve this:

```
_ASSERT(dynamic_cast<HttpWebRequest>(req) != nullptr);
```

For managed assertions, the class System::Diagnostics::Debug from the assembly System.dll can be used. It provides certain helper functions for debugging. These include certain overloads for a static function Assert as well as other static helper functions for debugging purposes, such as Fail, WriteLine, and WriteLineIf. The behavior of these functions depends on the trace listeners that are registered. If Assert is called with a false expression, or if Fail is called, the default trace listener shows a typical assertion dialog and writes output either into the debug window (via the Win32 API OutputDebugString) or to a configurable log file.

If you are familiar with these APIs from other .NET languages, you should be aware of an important difference in the way these functions behave in C++/CLI. All of the Debug functions mentioned previously contain a special kind of metadata (the Conditional("Debug") attribute). This information is used by languages like C# and VB .NET to emit code for calling these methods only in debug builds. Release builds will simply ignore all calls to these methods. The C++/CLI compiler ignores this metadata. Therefore, the Debug functions are called in debug *and* release builds. Developers who used to work with the Debug functions in other .NET languages easily write code that contains unintended assertions in the release build. To avoid unintended assertions, C++/CLI programmers have to use the C++ conditional compilation features.

```
#if DEBUG
Debug::Assert(dynamic_cast<HttpWebRequest>(req) != nullptr);
#endif
```

Notice that the DEBUG macro is automatically set for debug builds if you produce your projects with the Visual Studio project wizard. As an alternative, you can also choose the _DEBUG macro, which is automatically set by the Visual C++ compiler if a debug version of the CRT is used.

The call to the Debug functions can be simplified with macros like the one shown here:

```
#if DEBUG
#define DEBUG_ASSERT(x) Debug::Assert(x);
#else
#define DEBUG_ASSERT(x)
#endif
```

Configuration Files

XML-based configuration files are another fundamental .NET concept. Later chapters will explain how configuration files can be used to control various aspects of the CLR. In this chapter, I will give you an overview of configuration files and discuss how they can be used to maintain application-specific configurations.

Configuration files can be machine-wide or application-specific. If the system directory of your Windows installation is C:\WINDOWS, you can find the machine-wide configuration files in a special directory: C:\WINDOWS\Microsoft.NET\Framework\v2.0.50727\config. (The setup-independent variant of the setup location is %FrameworkDir%\%FrameworkVersion%\config, where FrameworkDir and FrameworkVersion are command-line macros automatically set if you use the Visual Studio 2005 command prompt.)

Application configuration files have the same name as the application's .exe file plus the extension .config. For the UrlDumper.exe application, the configuration file would be UrlDumper.exe.config. The following code shows an application configuration file:

```
<configuration>
  <runtime>
    <!-- CLR specific settings go here -->
  </runtime>
  <system.data>
    <!-- ADO.NET specific settings go here -->
  </system.data>
  <appSettings>
    <add key="URL" value="http://www.heege.net"/>
  </appSettings>
</configuration>
```

Every configuration file starts with a root element named configuration. For CLR-specific settings (e.g., regarding garbage collection or assembly loading), there is a child element, runtime. For various areas of the FCL, there are other special sub-elements of configuration (e.g., system.web for ASP.NET and system.data for ADO.NET). Since the .NET configuration infrastructure is pluggable, you can easily implement support for your own sub-element of configuration.

If you simply need a collection of name/value pairs, you can use the appSettings element instead. To read the value for the URL key in the preceding configuration file, you need just a few lines of code:

```
#using "System.dll"
#using "System.Configuration.dll"
```

```
String^ GetUrlFromConfigFile()
{
  using namespace System::Configuration;
  return ConfigurationManager::AppSettings["URL"];
}
```

If you work with Visual Studio, you can add an application configuration file to your project. From the project's context menu, you can choose Add New Item ➤ Utility ➤ Configuration File (app.config). Since .NET expects a file with the name *<MyApplication>*.exe.config, a custom build step is necessary to copy the configuration file to the target directory after a successful build. Unfortunately, Visual C++ does not create these settings for you, but you can easily do this manually. To do so, open the project properties for the app.config file. Make sure you modify the project settings for all configurations.

In the General category, make sure of the following:

- Exclude From Build is set to No.

- Tool is set to Custom Build Tool.

In the Custom Build Step category, do the following:

- Set Command line to type app.config > "$(TargetPath).config".

- Set Description to Updating target's configuration file.

- Set Outputs to (TargetPath).config.

Summary

This chapter has covered various different aspects of managed development with C++/CLI. These include features of the C++/CLI language (such as various casting options and managed exception handling) and features of the FCL (such as stream-based IO, web IO, and support for configuration files). The next chapter will cover various runtime services that the CLR offers you.

■ ■ ■

CHAPTER 4

Assemblies, Metadata, and Runtime Services

Assemblies are a fundamental abstraction of the .NET infrastructure. Developing software based on .NET always implies working with assemblies. To use managed types defined outside of your project, you have to reference the assembly that defines the required types. The target of a build process is an assembly, too. In this chapter, you will learn how assemblies can be uniquely identified and how the runtime searches for an assembly.

Assemblies are containers for metadata. Once an assembly is loaded, the runtime can use this metadata to provide runtime services like garbage collection and JIT compilation. Via a simple API discussed in this chapter, you can consume an assembly's metadata, too. APIs to access metadata are commonly called *reflection* APIs. Runtime metadata access via reflection APIs is one of the central advantages that managed code can give you, because it allows you to implement your own runtime services. As an example, this chapter discusses a simple algorithm for serialization and deserialization of objects.

Assemblies and Metadata

.NET assemblies can be defined as byte streams containing metadata, managed code, and managed resources.[1] The format of the byte stream is an extension of the PE file format (the file format of DLL and EXE files on Windows NT and later Windows operating systems). In fact, most assemblies are stored as files; however, it is also possible to store assemblies in other locations. As an example, assemblies implementing stored procedures can be stored in SQL Server 2005 databases.

All managed services mentioned previously require metadata at runtime. Therefore, metadata is a fundamental and mandatory part of .NET assemblies. Metadata is automatically generated for the assembly itself, for all managed functions, for all managed types, and for all members of managed types.

---

1. In theory, assemblies can consist of more than one of these byte streams. In this case, each byte stream is called a module and the assembly is called a multi-module assembly. However, this feature is used very seldom; therefore, I cover only single-module assemblies in this book.

Different tools can be used to inspect a .NET assembly and its contents. The two most common ones are ILDASM and Reflector. ILDASM is deployed with the .NET Framework SDK. Reflector is a tool written by Lutz Roeder.[2] Both tools have UIs that show the contents on an assembly in a tree structure. For the ILDASM output for the following code, take a look at Figure 4-1.

```cpp
// SampleLib.cpp
// build with: "CL /LD /clr:safe SampleLib.cpp"

namespace MyNamespace
{

public ref class SampleClass
{
  bool SampleField1;
  int  SampleField2;

public:
  SampleClass()
  : SampleField1(true), SampleField2(1234)
  {}

  void SampleMethod() {}
  void StaticSampleMethod() {}
};

} // MyNamespace
```

ILDASM and Reflector both have outstanding features that are worth mentioning here. Using ILDASM's command-line parameter /out:<outfile>, it is possible to produce a text file describing all managed aspects of your assembly. If your .NET assembly contains only managed aspects, you can use a tool called ILASM to produce an assembly out of such source code again. This approach to disassemble, modify, and recompile is sometimes used to make minor changes to assemblies generated by tools.

Reflector is able to reverse-engineer managed code into different .NET languages. Reflector is a pluggable application; you can plug in support for further languages and other metadata-based tools. In addition, it is often more convenient to use than ILDASM. For example, when managed code is displayed in Reflector, the meaning of various elements of the managed code can be displayed in tool tips. Furthermore, you can use hyperlinks in managed code to easily switch to types or functions used in the code.

---

2. It can be downloaded from Lutz Roeder's web site at www.aisto.com/roeder.

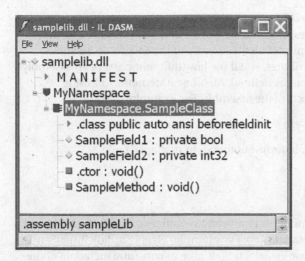

Figure 4-1. *SampleLib.dll in ILDASM*

Assembly Manifests

In addition to the `MyNamespace.SampleClass` type definition, Figure 4-1 also shows a manifest. An assembly manifest is an essential and mandatory part of an assembly. It contains all assembly-specific metadata. This metadata includes information about the assembly's identity and about dependencies to other assemblies and other files. The ILDASM output for `SampleLib`'s assembly manifest is shown here:

```
// Metadata version: v2.0.50727
.assembly extern mscorlib
{
  .publickeytoken = (B7 7A 5C 56 19 34 E0 89 )                 // .z\V.4..
  .hash = (CB 46 AC 1D E2 80 6F A3 04 89 AB BC 78 7C 66 17   // .F....o.....x|f.
           C1 03 B6 06 )
  .ver 2:0:0:0
}
.assembly SampleLib
{
  .hash algorithm 0x00008004
  .ver 0:0:0:0
}
.module SampleLib.dll
// MVID: {8F665591-E900-48AF-9994-7C34E334FF5D}
.imagebase 0x10000000
.file alignment 0x00000200
.stackreserve 0x00100000
.subsystem 0x0002       // WINDOWS_GUI
.corflags 0x00000001    //   ILONLY
// Image base: 0x033C0000
```

In this manifest, the statement `.assembly extern mscorlib` and its contents in curly braces specify that `SampleLib.dll` requires version 2.0.0.0 of `mscorlib` at runtime. The statement `.assembly SampleLib` and its contents define the identity of the `SampleLib` assembly. Later in this chapter, in the context of attributes, you'll see how different parts of an assembly's identity, including the version number, can be defined. All other statements following `.assembly SampleLib` define further aspects of the assembly. For example, the line

```
.corflags 0x00000001    // ILONLY
```

defines that the assembly contains only platform-independent managed code.

Metadata APIs

Metadata isn't only consumed by the runtime and metadata visualizer tools like ILDASM and Reflector; many other tools consume metadata, too. For example, Visual Studio's IntelliSense for managed types is only possible because Visual Studio is able to consume metadata of the assemblies referenced by your projects. Compilers also need to consume metadata of referenced assemblies to ensure that the types and type members used in the source code actually exist. If you want to implement a metadata-driven tool, you need access to metadata, too.

To consume .NET metadata, there are two major reflection APIs. One is a native (COM-based) API called the *Metadata Unmanaged API*. The second alternative is the *Managed Reflection API*, which is part of the FCL. In the next sections, I focus on the Managed Reflection API only, since it is almost as powerful as the Metadata Unmanaged API and much easier to use.

Most types of this API are from the namespace `System::Reflection`. A fundamental type of the Managed Reflection API is the class `System::Reflection::Assembly`, which represents a loaded assembly. To retrieve a handle to the assembly whose code is currently executed, the static function `Assembly::GetExecutingAssembly` can be called. The expression `AppDomain::CurrentDomain->GetAssemblies()` returns an array with one element for every loaded assembly.

In addition to static metadata, `System::Reflection::Assembly` can also provide information about the origin of a loaded assembly. As an example, the property `Location` tells you where in the file system the assembly was found. The property `CodeBase` returns the URL where the assembly was loaded from. This can differ from the location, because assemblies loaded from the Web (e.g., via HTTP-based code bases) are cached on the local hard disk. In this case, the code base is the URL and the location is the path to the cached assembly.

The property `FullName` returns a string containing the assembly's identity. The following code writes the values of the properties `FullName`, `CodeBase`, and `Location` for every loaded assembly to the console:

```
// DumpAssemblyInfo.cpp
// build with "cl /clr:safe DumpAssemblyInfo.cpp"

#using "SampleLib.dll"

using namespace System;
using namespace System::Reflection;
```

```
int main()
{
  MyNamespace::SampleClass^ obj = gcnew MyNamespace::SampleClass();

  for each(Assembly^ a in AppDomain::CurrentDomain->GetAssemblies())
  {
    Console::WriteLine(a->FullName);
    Console::WriteLine("\t" + a->CodeBase);
    Console::WriteLine("\t" + a->Location);
  }
}
```

If you execute this code, you should see an output similar to the following:

```
mscorlib, Version=2.0.0.0, Culture=neutral, PublicKeyToken=b77a5c561934e089
        file:///C:/WINDOWS/Microsoft.NET/Framework/v2.0.50727/mscorlib.dll
        C:\WINDOWS\Microsoft.NET\Framework\v2.0.50727\mscorlib.dll
DumpAssemblyInfo, Version=0.0.0.0, Culture=neutral, PublicKeyToken=null
        file:///C:/tests/DumpAssemblyInfo.exe
        C:\tests\DumpAssemblyInfo.exe
SampleLib, Version=0.0.0.0, Culture=neutral, PublicKeyToken=null
        file:///C:/tests/SampleLib.DLL
        C:\tests\SampleLib.dll
```

Assembly Identity

The preceding output shows that three assemblies have been loaded. All assemblies have an identity (FullName), which consists of the following four parts:

- *Simple name*: The simple name is the name of the assembly without the file extension. (In theory, it is possible to have assemblies with names that differ from the file name, but this aspect is ignored here.)

- *Version*: .NET assemblies have a built-in support for versioning. Therefore, the second part of an assembly name is the version number. It consists of four distinct parts of 16-bit size called major, minor, build, and revision. In many cases, an assembly's version number can be relevant for assembly loading. To specify the version number of an assembly, a line like the one following must be added to your code:

  ```
  [assembly: AssemblyVersionAttribute("1.0.0.0")];
  ```

  In Visual Studio projects, you will find a line like this in a file called AssemblyInfo.cpp. Details of the syntax are discussed later, in the context of attributes.

- Culture: The third part is the Culture. .NET assemblies have a built-in localization support. Assemblies with Culture != neutral should not contain any code, but only localized resources. Assemblies with localized resources are called *satellite assemblies*. For more information on satellite assemblies, consult the MSDN documentation.

- `PublicKeyToken`: The fourth part of an assembly name is called `PublicKeyToken`. It can be either `null` or a 64-bit hexadecimal number. In the preceding sample output, the `PublicKeyToken` for `mscorlib.dll` is `b77a5c561934e089`, whereas the `PublicKeyToken` for `DumpAssemblyInfo` is `null`. Assembly names with `PublicKeyToken != null` are called strong names.

To get a strong name, public-key cryptography is used. Every developer who wants to create assemblies with a strong name can generate a unique pair of a public and a private key. The `PublicKeyToken` is a hash code of the public key. It is used to uniquely identify the developer. The private key is used to sign the assembly. The public key is burned into the assembly's manifest so that the signature can be verified when the assembly is loaded. This provides tamper detection. When an assembly is modified after it has been signed, the verification of the signature will fail.

To create a new key pair, a .NET tool called `SN.EXE` is used. The command-line option `/k` of this tool creates a new key file, as follows:

```
SN -k keyfile.snk
```

Using the linker option `/KEYFILE:<keyfile>`, an assembly can get a strong name. If you want to create a signed `SampleLib.dll` assembly, you can simply rebuild it with the following command lines:

```
CL /c /clr:safe SampleLib.cpp
LINK /DLL /KEYFILE:keyfile.snk SampleLib.obj
```

In Visual C++ projects, there is a special project property for specifying the key file. You can find this setting via Project Properties ➤ Configuration Properties ➤ Linker ➤ Advanced ➤ Key File. If you have multiple projects in your solution, you will likely want all projects to use the same key file. In this case, you should place the key file in the solution directory and set the Key File property of all your projects to `$(SolutionDir)keyfile.snk`.

You should sign all your assemblies apart from simple test applications and libraries like the ones shown so far. Signing assemblies gives you the following benefits:

- If and only if an assembly has a unique name, all types defined in the assembly have a unique name, too.

- Assemblies without a strong name cannot be referenced by strongly named assemblies. As an example, if you try to link `DumpAssemblyInfo.exe` with the command-line option `/KEYFILE`, and the dependent assembly `SampleLib.dll` is not signed, you will get a linker error complaining that the "referenced assembly 'SampleLib' does not have a strong name."

- Assemblies with a weak name can only be installed in the directory where the referencing application is stored or in special subdirectories. For strongly named assemblies, there are more deployment options. These will be discussed in the next section.

- When the runtime searches an assembly, the version number is only relevant for assemblies with a strong name. If the runtime searches a weakly named assembly that is referenced by your project, any available version will be loaded, no matter what version you built your code against.

Assembly Loading and Deployment

Assemblies are usually loaded automatically during JIT compilation, when the first type of an assembly is used in managed code. If you leave the #using "SampleLib.dll" directive as it is, but remove the line that declares the variable obj and instantiates SampleClass, no type from SampleLib is used in the code, and the SampleLib assembly will not be loaded. In this case, the output will contain only two assemblies.

When the JIT compiler decides to load a referenced assembly, it looks into the manifest of the referencing assembly. If the type SampleClass from the SampleLib assembly is used in the source code of the DumpAssemblyInfo application, the manifest of DumpAssemblyInfo.exe contains the following metadata:

```
.assembly extern SampleLib
{
  .ver 0:0:0:0
}
```

This information is just an alternative form of SampleLib's assembly name:

```
SampleLib, Version=0.0.0.0, Culture=neutral, PublicKeyToken=null
```

When an assembly with a strong name is referenced, the assembly extern metadata also contains the PublicKeyToken:

```
.assembly extern SampleLib
{
  .publickeytoken = (65 D6 F5 D1 B5 D4 89 0E)
  .ver 0:0:0:0
}
```

In both cases, the path to SampleLib.dll is not contained in DumpAssemblyInfo's metadata. To determine the path, a special algorithm called *assembly resolution* is used.

If the referenced assembly does not have a strong name, the assembly resolver uses a simplified algorithm. This algorithm depends on the so-called application base directory. The application base directory is the directory in which the EXE file is located (unless you perform special customizations—which is outside of this chapter's scope).

The first location where the assembly resolver looks for an assembly without a strong name is the application base directory itself. If the assembly is not found there, it searches for a subdirectory of the base directory that is named after the simple name of the requested assembly. For the SampleLib assembly, the assembly resolver would try to find the assembly in a subdirectory named SampleLib.

Unless you provide extra configuration, no further subdirectories of the application base directory will be inspected by the assembly resolver. If you need to configure the assembly resolver to search for assemblies in further subdirectories of the application base directory, you can create an application configuration file as follows:

```
<!-- MyApplication.exe.config -->
<?xml version="1.0"?>
<configuration>
  <runtime>
```

```
    <assemblyBinding xmlns="urn:schemas-microsoft-com:asm.v1">
      <probing privatePath="lib;bin" />
    </assemblyBinding>
  </runtime>
</configuration>
```

When a weakly named assembly is found, the assembly loader checks if the simple name, the `Culture`, and the `PublicKeyToken` of the found assembly match the name of the requested assembly. If this is the case, the assembly will be loaded. As mentioned previously, the version number of a weakly named assembly is not relevant for assembly loading. Even if the version number of the found DLL is lower than the requested version number, the assembly will be loaded and used.

For assemblies with a strong name, the version number is *not* silently ignored: you must ensure that the right version of every dependent strongly named assembly can be found. However, for strongly named assemblies, there are further deployment options.

The Global Assembly Cache (GAC)

Assemblies with strong names can be installed in a machine-wide repository for assemblies. This repository is called the *global assembly cache* (GAC). The GAC is the preferred location for assemblies that are used by many different applications. As an example, all assemblies from the FCL are installed in the GAC.

The GAC has the term *cache* in its name because assemblies from the GAC can be loaded faster than strongly named assemblies installed in other locations. This is possible because the signature of an assembly in the GAC is verified when the assembly is placed into the GAC. Since only administrators have write access to the GAC, the runtime considers this one check to be sufficient. The signature is not reverified when the assembly is loaded from the GAC.

Due to the faster assembly loading, the assembly resolver first tries to find a strongly named assembly in the GAC. If an assembly is not found in the GAC, the assembly resolver tries to find the assembly in the application base directory or a subdirectory named after the simple name of the requested assembly.

The GAC is implemented as a special directory structure in the file system. This directory structure supports side-by-side installation of assemblies. Instead of overwriting one version of an assembly with another one, you can install two different versions of an assembly at the same time. To achieve this, mangled directory names are used. If you install `SampleLib.dll` in the GAC, it will end up in the following directory:

```
%systemroot%\assembly\GAC_MSIL\SampleLib\0.0.0.0__656F5D1B5D4890E
```

In this directory specification, `%systemroot%` is the OS name of the system directory (typically `C:\WINDOWS`). The subdirectory `GAC_MSIL` is for platform-neutral assemblies. Assemblies that can only execute on the 32-bit CLR end up in the `GAC_32` subdirectory instead.

The subdirectory below `GAC_MSIL` or `GAC_32` is named after the first part of the four-part assembly name (the simple name). The remaining three parts of the assembly name are mangled into the last subdirectory name `0.0.0.0__656F5D1B5D4890E`. The first underscore (_) separates the version number from the `Culture` specification. Since the `Culture` of the `SampleLib` assembly is `neutral`, the `Culture` specification in the mangled directory name is empty. The second underscore separates the `Culture` specification from the `PublicKeyToken`.

There are various options to install an assembly into the GAC. From the command prompt, you can use a tool called GACUtil.exe. To install an assembly, you can use the command-line argument -i followed by the path to the assembly. To uninstall an assembly, the command-line option -u is used. Notice that this command-line option expects either the assembly's simple name (without the file extension) or the four-part assembly name.

```
gacutil -i SampleLib.dll
gacuitl -u SampleLib, Version=0.0.0.0, Culture=neutral,
    PublicKeyToken=656F5D1B5D4890E
```

Typically, you will want to install assemblies into the GAC as part of an application's setup procedure. Visual Studio supports so-called setup projects to produce MSI files for your assemblies. These setup projects support the GAC as an installation destination for components. For more information, consult the MSDN documentation.

Version Redirections

.NET applications often depend on a large number of other assemblies. As a consequence, bugs in a .NET application are often caused by bugs in dependent components, not the application itself. Instead of recompiling and redeploying an application when a bug-fixed version of a dependent component is available, you can just redeploy the bug-fixed component and provide a configuration so that the assembly resolver looks for the new version of a strongly named assembly.

Configurations that cause a different version to be loaded are called *version redirections*. Version redirections can be defined at three different levels as follows:

- The application level

- The machine level

- The assembly level (via publisher policy assemblies)

The following application configuration file shows a typical version redirection at the application level:

```
<!-- MyApplication.exe.config -->
<configuration>
  <runtime>
    <!-- CLR specific settings go here -->
    <assemblyBinding xmlns="urn:schemas-microsoft-com:asm.v1">
      <dependentAssembly>
        <assemblyIdentity name="SampleLib" publicKeyToken="65d6f5d1b5d4890e" />
        <bindingRedirect oldVersion="0.0.0.0-1.0.0.0" newVersion="1.0.0.0" />
      </dependentAssembly>
    </assemblyBinding>
  </runtime>
</configuration>
```

This configuration file tells the assembly resolver to load the assembly SampleLib, Version =1.0.0.0, Culture=neutral, PublicKeyToken=65d6f5d1b5d4890e when any version between 0.0.0.0 and 1.0.0.0 is requested.

For machine-wide redirections, you must modify a file named machine.config, which can be found in the directory *%frameworkdir%\%frameworkversion%*\config, where *%framewrokdir%* and *%frameworkversion%* should be replaced with the content of the environment variables frameworkdir and frameworkversion.

If you have implemented a .NET assembly that is used by many applications, you will likely prefer version redirections via publisher policy assemblies over application configuration files and machine-wide configurations. Both application and machine configurations would require modifications of configuration files on each of the client machines.

To simplify versioning of libraries, a library developer can deploy two assemblies: the new version of the library, and an assembly that explicitly states that the new version is backward compatible with a set of older versions of the library. Such an assembly is called a *publisher policy assembly*.

When a publisher policy assembly is installed in the GAC, the assembly resolver will load the new version of the assembly when a compatible older version is requested.

To create a publisher policy assembly, you first have to create a configuration file that specifies the version redirection. This configuration file has the same format as the application configuration file shown previously.

Using this configuration file and the key file that was used to sign your library, a tool called *assembly linker* (AL.EXE) can produce a publisher policy assembly. Depending on the target platform of the assembly and the compilation model you have used, different command-line options are needed. The following samples assume that the assembly MyLibrary, which was signed with the key file keyfile.snk, should be configured with a configuration file named MyLibrary.dll.config.

For assemblies built with /clr:safe, you should use the following command line:

```
al /link:MyLibrary.dll.config /platform:anycpu /out:policy.0.0.myLibrary.dll
    /keyfile:keyfile.snk
```

If the assembly is built with /clr or /clr:pure, the command-line options depend on the target platform. For assemblies that depend on the 32-bit CLR, the command line is as follows:

```
al /link:MyLibrary.dll.config /platform:x86 /out:policy.0.0.myLibrary.dll
/keyfile:keyfile.snk
```

For assemblies that depend on the AMD64 CLR, you should use the following command line instead:

```
al /link:MyLibrary.dll.config /platform:x64 /out:policy.0.0.myLibrary.dll
/keyfile:keyfile.snk
```

To apply the publisher policy assembly, you just have to create a deployment package that installs both the new version of the library and the publisher policy assembly. While the publisher policy assembly must be installed in the GAC, the new version can be installed at any location that allows the application to find and load the assembly.

Manual Assembly Loading

It is also possible to load assemblies via explicit APIs. This is especially helpful for applications that support plug-ins. There is a variety of static functions in System::Reflection::Assembly that can be used to load an assembly dynamically. The two most important ones are as follows:

```
Assembly^ Assembly::Load(String^ assemblyName);
Assembly^ Assembly::LoadFrom(String^ url);
```

Assembly::Load expects a string with the four-part assembly name as an argument. To determine the code base to the assembly, the assembly resolution algorithm is used in the same way as it is used for assemblies loaded during JIT compilation.

Assembly::LoadFrom expects a string specifying a file name or a path to the assembly. This API is often used for unit tests. LoadFrom does not simply load the assembly from the specified location. Instead, it first opens the assembly file to determine the assembly's four-part assembly name. This assembly name is then passed to the assembly resolution algorithm. If an assembly is found via assembly resolution, the assembly will be loaded from the resolved location. Otherwise, the assembly will be loaded from the specified path.

Even though this behavior sounds strange, it can prevent two assembly files with the same identity from being loaded. These problems existed in earlier versions of the CLR, in which LoadFrom simply loaded the assembly from the specified location.

Consuming Metadata for Types and Type Members at Runtime

The .NET-specific extensions to the PE format have surprising similarities to databases. Like a normal database, assemblies contain tables. These tables are called metadata tables. Metadata tables exist for type definitions, method definitions, and many other abstractions. Like database tables, each metadata table has a column structure specific for the abstraction. The structures for all tables start with a 32-bit column called a *metadata token*. Such a metadata token can be compared to a primary key in a database table. To establish relationships between the different abstractions stored in metadata tables, an approach similar to using foreign keys in databases is used: the structure of various metadata tables contains columns that store metadata tokens of other tables. As an example, since there is a one-to-*n* relationship between type definitions and methods (a type can have an arbitrary number of methods), there is a column for the parent type in the metadata table for methods.

The Managed Reflection API also contains classes for all kinds of abstractions that can be stored in the metadata of assemblies. These abstractions include type definitions, methods (global functions as well as member functions of a managed type), and fields (member variables). All these types are semantically bound together via "has-a" relationships. An assembly has type definitions, type definitions have fields and methods, methods have parameters, and so on. To navigate from one type to another one, each of these types offers functions with the prefix Get. The following code uses Assembly::GetTypes to iterate through all type definitions of an assembly:

```
// dumpAssemblyTypes.cpp
// build with "CL /clr:safe dumpAssemblyTypes.cpp"

using namespace System;
using namespace System::Reflection;

int main( array<String^>^ args)
{
  for each (String^ url in args)
  {
    Assembly^ a = Assembly::LoadFrom(url);
    Console::WriteLine(a->Location);
    for each (Type^ t in a->GetTypes())
    {
      Console::WriteLine(t);
      Console::WriteLine("Base class: {0}", t->BaseType);
      if (t->IsValueType)
        Console::WriteLine("This is a value type");
    }
  }
}
```

Assembly::GetTypes returns an array of System::Type handles. Instances of System::Type are called type objects. Each handle refers to a type object that describes a public type of the assembly.

System::Type allows you to find out almost everything about a type, including its name, base class, and supported interfaces. When a handle to a type object is passed to Console::WriteLine, then Type's overload for ToString is called. Type::ToString simply returns the namespace-qualified type name. However, the string returned is not a C++-like type name, but a language-neutral type name. Since most .NET languages use the dot character (.) as a namespace separator, Type::ToString does the same.

There are various ways to get a type information object. As mentioned before, System::Object has a function called GetType(). Using this method, you can easily find out the type of any managed object and of any managed value. If the requested type is known at build time, the keyword typeid can be used. The following code checks if an object passed is of type String:

```
bool IsString(Object^ o)
{
  return o != nullptr && o->GetType() == String::typeid;
}
```

If you have a string representing the type's name in the language-neutral form, you can use `Type::GetType(String^)` to retrieve a type information object. As an example, the following expression is true:

```
Type::GetType("System.Int32") ==  int::typeid
```

However, this function is not always as easy to use as it seems, as the following code shows:

```
// GetTypePitfall.cpp
// build with "CL /clr:safe GetTypePitfall.cpp"
using namespace System;

#using <System.dll>

int main()
{
  Console::WriteLine(Type::GetType("System.Int32") == int::typeid);  // writes True
  Console::WriteLine(Type::GetType("System.Uri") == Uri::typeid);   // writes False!
}
```

`Type::GetType` allows you to pass the namespace-qualified type name only if you want to get a type information object for a type defined in the assembly that called `Type::GetType` or if the requested type is defined in `mscorlib`.

For all types in other assemblies, the assembly-qualified name must be passed to `Type::GetType`. As mentioned in the previous chapter, the assembly-qualified name acts as the identifier of a .NET type. It contains the namespace-qualified type name followed by a comma and a space, followed by the name of the assembly that defines the type. `Type::AssemblyQualifiedName` can be used to return this identifier. The expression

```
Uri::typeid->AssemblyQualifiedName
```

evaluates to

```
System.Uri, System, Version=2.0.0.0, Culture=neutral,
    PublicKeyToken=b77a5c561934e089
```

From this type name, you can conclude that `System::Uri` is defined in the assembly `System` (and not in `mscorlib`). If you pass `System::Uri`'s assembly-qualified type name even though the assembly `System` has not been loaded, `Type::GetType` will load the assembly dynamically.

Dynamic Type Instantiation

In addition to retrieving static information about a type, it is possible to instantiate a type dynamically. A typical usage of this feature is the creation of plug-in objects. Since pluggable applications allow a user to configure new plug-ins, a class implementing a plug-in is not known at compile time. Therefore, the operator `gcnew` cannot be used to instantiate the object.

Dynamic instantiation is also helpful if you want to write generic code. As an example, an MFC document/view template is used to create instances of a document class and the document's default view class dynamically. To achieve this, you have to use a set of macros

(DECLARE_DYNCREATE and IMPLEMENT_DYNCREATE). .NET gives you this ability for any type without writing any extra lines of code.

The static method Activator::CreateInstance(Type^) acts as the late-bound alternative to the operator gcnew. To instantiate a type, given its assembly-qualified type name, the following helper function can be used:

```
Object^ CreateInstanceFromTypename(String^ type)
{
  if (!type)
    throw gcnew ArgumentNullException("type");

  Type^ t = Type::GetType(type);
  if (!t)
    throw gcnew ArgumentException("Invalid type name");

  Object^ obj = Activator::CreateInstance(t);
  return obj;
}
```

For simplicity, this function expects the passed type to have a default constructor. Many types, including System::Uri, do not have a default constructor. To instantiate a type via a constructor with parameters, an overload for Activator::CreateInstance exists. This overload allows you to pass constructor arguments as an array of System::Object handles. The next line of code shows you how you can use it:

```
Object^ CreateInstanceFromTypename(String^ type, ...array<Object^>^ args)
{
  if (!type)
    throw gcnew ArgumentNullException("type");

  Type^ t = Type::GetType(type);
  if (!t)
    throw gcnew ArgumentException("Invalid type name");

  Object^ obj = Activator::CreateInstance(t, args);
  return obj;
}
```

In order to instantiate System::Uri with this helper function, you can use the following code:

```
Object^ o = CreateInstanceFromTypename(
            "System.Uri, System, Version=2.0.0.0, "
                "Culture=neutral, PublicKeyToken=b77a5c561934e089",
            "http://www.heege.net"
        );
```

If you don't pass the correct argument types, a System::MissingMethodException will be thrown in Activator::CreateInstance.

Runtime Information About Type Members

The Managed Reflection API gives you access to further metadata. As mentioned previously, there are several one-to-many relationships between abstractions stored in metadata. Most of these relationships are bound to type definitions. A type definition can have many type members of different kinds. These type members include fields (member variables), methods (member functions), properties, events, and nested type definitions.

For each of these different kinds of type members, the Managed Reflection API contains a class that delivers type-specific metadata. These classes are FieldInfo, MethodInfo, ConstructorInfo, PropertyInfo, and EventInfo from the namespace System::Reflection, as well as the class System::Type.

To receive instances for these types, System::Type provides functions with the prefix Get. As an example, for fields, these functions are GetField and GetFields. GetField has a String^ argument that allows you to pass the name of the requested field. It returns a handle to the FieldInfo object describing the requested field, or nullptr if a public field with that name does not exist. GetFields returns an array with one element for each public field.

MethodInfo and ConstructorInfo have a common base class called MethodBase. This base class allows you to determine the parameter list of a method. The following code iterates through all public methods of a type whose type object was passed as an argument to DumpMethods, and writes the method's signature, including the return type and the parameter types, to the console:

```cpp
// DumpMethods.cpp
// build with "CL /clr:safe DumpMethods.cpp"

using namespace System;
using namespace System::Reflection;

void DumpMethods(Type^ t)
{
  Console::WriteLine("Public methods of type {0}:", t->FullName);
  for each (MethodInfo^ mi in t->GetMethods())
  {
    Console::Write("{0} {1}(", mi->ReturnType->FullName, mi->Name);

    bool isFirstParam = true;
    for each(ParameterInfo^ pi in mi->GetParameters())
    {
      if (isFirstParam)
        isFirstParam = false;
      else
        Console::Write(", ");
      Console::Write("{0}", pi->ParameterType);
    }
    Console::WriteLine(")");
  }
}

int main()
{
  DumpMethods(String::typeid);
}
```

Dynamic Member Access

Using the Reflection API, it is also possible to access a type's member dynamically. If you have a handle to a MethodInfo object, you can call the method via MethodInfo::Invoke. A FieldInfo object can be used to read or write the field's value via GetValue and SetValue. For properties and events, similar members exist.

Such runtime-bound dynamic access to type members is obviously much slower than a direct method call or direct field access. (For static and non-static methods without arguments and return values, a call is about 300 times slower. Depending on the signature, the overhead can be multiples of that.) However, dynamic access can be helpful for implementing helper algorithms that can operate on objects even if the objects' type is not known at build time. As an example, a data binding implementation can automatically bind control fields of a dialog to data fields of a data object based on field names.

Before the dialog is displayed, a helper method of the data binding implementation could be called. This method can easily get FieldInfo objects for all fields of the data source class and the dialog class. FieldInfo objects from the data source class and FieldInfo objects from the dialog class with matching field names could be used to automatically read the value of the fields in the data source and to set the control's text in the dialog with these fields. When the OK button of the dialog is clicked, a helper function could be called that dynamically updates the fields from the data source with values dynamically read from the controls' fields.

The following code uses the Managed Reflection API to implement a serialization of objects into streams and a deserialization of objects from streams:

```
// customSerialzation.cpp
// CL /clr:safe customSerialization.cpp

using namespace System;
using namespace System::IO;
using namespace System::Reflection;

ref struct Person
{
  String^ Name;
  int Age;
};

void Serialize(Stream^ strm, Object^ o)
{
  if (!strm)
    throw gcnew ArgumentNullException("strm");
  if (!o)
    throw gcnew ArgumentNullException("o");

  BinaryWriter^ bw = gcnew BinaryWriter(strm);
  try
  {
    Type^ t = o->GetType();
```

```
      bw->Write(t->AssemblyQualifiedName);

      array<FieldInfo^>^ fields = t->GetFields();
      for each (FieldInfo^ fi in fields)
      {
        if (fi->FieldType == int::typeid)
          bw->Write((int)fi->GetValue(o));
        else if (fi->FieldType == String::typeid)
          bw->Write((String^)fi->GetValue(o));
        else
          // for simplicity, other types are not supported here
          throw gcnew NotSupportedException();
      }
    }
    finally
    {
      bw->Close();
    }
}

Object^ Deserialize(Stream^ strm)
{
  if (!strm)
    throw gcnew ArgumentNullException("strm");

  Object^ o;
  BinaryReader^ br = gcnew BinaryReader(strm);
  try
  {
    String^ type = br->ReadString();
    Type^ t = Type::GetType(type);
    o = Activator::CreateInstance(t);

    array<FieldInfo^>^ fields = t->GetFields();
    for each (FieldInfo^ fi in fields)
    {
      if (fi->FieldType == int::typeid)
        fi->SetValue(o, br->ReadInt32());
      else if (fi->FieldType == String::typeid)
        fi->SetValue(o, br->ReadString());
      else
        // for simplicity, other types are not supported here
        throw gcnew NotSupportedException();
    }
  }
  finally
  {
```

```
    br->Close();
  }
  return o;
}

int main()
{
  array<Byte>^ bytes = gcnew array<Byte>(1024);

  Person^ p = gcnew Person();
  p->Name = "Paul";
  p->Age = 35;
  Serialize(gcnew MemoryStream(bytes), p);

  Person^ p2 = (Person^)Deserialize(gcnew MemoryStream(bytes));
  Console::WriteLine(p2->Name);
  Console::WriteLine(p2->Age);
};
```

In this code, serialization and deserialization of objects is done with the methods
Serialize and Deserialize. Serialize expects a handle to the Stream instance into which
the object should be serialized, as well as the object that is to be serialized. To serialize fields
of primitive types, it uses the helper class System::IO::BinaryWriter. Similar to StreamWriter,
this class has helper methods for serializing data into streams. In contrast to StreamWriter,
it does not write its data line by line as text into the stream. Instead of WriteLine, it has various
overloads of the Write methods to write primitive types in a binary format. The overloads used
in this code are Write(String^) (for writing a string in a length-prefixed format) and
Write(int).

First, the object's type is determined, and the assembly-qualified type name is written
into the stream. This allows the deserialization function to instantiate the object dynamically.
After that, the FieldInfo objects for the public fields are determined. After that, a for each
loop iterates through all fields. Every iteration determines the object's value of the current
field. Depending on the type, different overloads of BinaryWriter::Write are used. For simplicity, only fields of type int and String^ can be serialized.

The method Deserialize expects a stream with the serialized data, instantiates an object,
initializes its fields, and returns a handle to that object. To achieve this, Deserialize creates a
BinaryReader that operates on the stream. Using this reader, the data can be read in the same
order as it was written by the Serialize method. The first piece of information that is read via
the reader is the assembly-qualified type name. Using this type name, a handle to the type
object for the serialized data can be requested. Once the type object is available, a new
instance is created via Activator::CreateInstance. To initialize each field,
FieldInfo::SetValue is called for each FieldInfo provided for the type.

Access to Private Members

The algorithms discussed so far are not very usable. For encapsulation reasons, most programmers define their fields as private members of a type. The GetFields method called in

Serialize and Deserialize returns only FieldInfo^ for public fields. However, serialization is an obvious example why dynamic access to private members is useful.

The Managed Reflection API has overloads for the GetFields and the other Get functions. These overloads have an additional parameter of type BindingFlags, which is an enumerator type. You can use this argument to filter out certain members that you are not interested in. By default, non-public members are filtered out, but you can easily change that. The following code shows how to get an array<FieldInfo^> for all public and non-public instance-bound (non-static) fields:

```
array<FieldInfo^>^ publicAndPrivateFields =
    t->GetFields(BindingFlags::Public |
                 BindingFlags::NonPublic |
                 BindingFlags::Instance);
```

If you add the BindingFlags parameter as shown in the preceding code to the GetFields call in Serialize and Deserialize, private fields will be serialized, too.

Attributes

Another useful extension to the serialization method is the exclusion of certain fields; not all fields of a type should be serialized. Like most other .NET languages, C++/CLI does not have a keyword to express that a field should not be serialized. However, .NET allows you to extend languages so that you can provide additional metadata to types, type members, and various other targets of your assembly. This can be done with attributes.

Attributes in .NET languages have a syntax that is very similar to the Interface Definition Language (IDL) syntax for attributes in COM. An attribute is specified within square brackets and (typically) applies to the item that follows the attribute. As an example, the following code could be used to apply a DoNotSerializeThisField attribute to a field.

```
ref struct Person
{
  String^ Name;

  // not everybody wants that his age is stored somewhere
  [DoNotSerializeThisField]
  int Age;
};
```

Supporting such an attribute is quite simple. It only requires a class with the special base class System::Attribute.

```
ref class DoNotSerializeThisFieldAttribute : public Attribute
{};
```

Notice that the DoNotSerializeThisFieldAttribute class follows a common naming convention for attribute classes—it has the suffix Attribute. Due to this naming convention, it is sufficient in C++/CLI and most other .NET languages to write [DoNotSerializeThisField] instead of [DoNotSerializeThisFieldAttribute].

An attribute, as it is defined in the following example, can be applied to many targets. The following code shows some typical examples:

```
using namespace System;
```

```
ref class DoNotSerializeThisFieldAttribute : public Attribute
{};
```

```
[assembly: DoNotSerializeThisFieldAttribute];
```

```
[DoNotSerializeThisField]
ref class ATypeDefinition
{
  [DoNotSerializeThisField]
  int field1;

  [DoNotSerializeThisField]                 // applied to the following method
  [returnvalue: DoNotSerializeThisField]    // applied to return type of method
  int func2() { return 0; }
};
```

Obviously, the DoNotSerializeThisField attribute can only be applied to fields in a useful way. None of the other applications (to the assembly, to the class ATypeDefinition, or to the method func2 and its return value) makes sense. To restrict the usage of the attribute class so that it can only be applied to fields, it can be defined as follows:

```
[AttributeUsage(AttributeTargets::Field, AllowMultiple=false)]
ref class DoNotSerializeThisFieldAttribute : public Attribute
{};
```

In this code, System::AttributeUsageAttribute is applied to the attribute class. Notice that this attribute is applied with further information provided in brackets. In the preceding sample code, AttributeTargets::Field means that the attribute can only be applied to fields, and AllowMultiple = false means that the attribute cannot be applied more than once to a single field.

If the possible targets included type definitions or methods, it could also have been useful to write Inherit = true or Inherit = false within the brackets of the attribute. Using these options, one can specify if the attribute is inherited to derived types or overloaded methods.

AttributeTargets::Field is passed like a function call argument, whereas AllowMultiple=false is passed with an assignment-like syntax. The attribute can be applied like this because it implements a constructor expecting an argument of type AttributeTargets and a Boolean property named AllowMultiple.

To ensure that a field with this attribute is not serialized, the attribute must be discovered at runtime. This can be done with the interface System::Reflection::ICustomAttributeProvider. All classes from the Managed Reflection API that provide metadata for attribute targets implement this interface. These classes include System::Type as well as Assembly, FieldInfo, and MethodInfo from the System::Reflection namespace. ICustomAttributeProvider has the method IsDefined, which can be used to check if an attribute was applied or not. This method returns true if the requested attribute is applied to the target. IsDefined expects a type info object of the requested attribute class and a Boolean parameter that specifies if attributes inherited from a base class or an overridden virtual method should be considered or not. For FieldInfo objects, this second parameter of IsDefined is not relevant.

```
array<FieldInfo^>^ fields = t->GetFields();
for each (FieldInfo^ fi in fields)
{
  if (fi->IsDefined(DoNotSerializeThisFieldAttribute::typeid, false))
    continue;

  … serialization and deserialization logic as before ...
}
```

ICustomAttributeProvider also has two overloads of the method GetCustomAttributes. This method can be used if you are interested in details of the attribute. For attributes that contain additional information passed as constructor arguments or via property assignments (like the AttributeUsage attribute), GetCustomAttributes is typically used. The first overload returns an array with one handle referring to each applied attribute; the second overload expects a type object specifying the requested attribute class, and gives you only handles to attributes of the requested type.

System::Runtime::Serialization

Instead of implementing a serialization algorithm manually, you can use the serialization feature provided by the FCL. This is an API that resides in the namespace System::Runtime::Serialization. It is a much more sophisticated API than the implementation described previously. As an example, it supports many more field types than int and String^. These include all primitive types, as well as tracking handles to serializable objects. Using this serialization implementation, a single serialization operation can persist a complete graph of serializable objects into a stream. System::Runtime::Serialization is also aware of object identities within a serialized stream. Each object of a graph is serialized only once into the stream, even if an object is referenced multiple times within the graph's objects.

System::Runtime::Serialization is attribute-based. To mark a type as serializable, the attribute System::SerializableAttribute must be applied to a class. A field can be excluded from serialization with the attribute System::NonSerializableAttribute. For customizing serialization, a serializable object can also implement the interface ISerializable. The following code uses the less complicated approach with attributes:

```
[Serializable]
ref struct Person
{
  String^ Name;

  [NonSerialized]
  int Age;
};
```

Serializing a graph involves three abstractions: an object representing the root of the graph, a stream, and a formatter. The object specifies *what* should be serialized. Unless you apply the attribute NonSerialized or implement ISerializable, all fields of a serializable type will be serialized. The stream represents the *medium* into which a graph should be serialized. All stream implementations mentioned in the previous chapter can be used. The formatter defines the format in which an object is serialized into a stream.

The FCL provides two formatter implementations as follows: System::Runtime::Serialization::Formatters::Binary::BinaryFormatter and System::Runtime::Serialization::Formatters::Soap::SoapFormatter. For real-life applications, BinaryFormatter is preferable. It is faster, more compact, and can serialize more kinds of types. From the name SoapFormatter, you might conclude that the serialized document is interoperable across platforms, since SOAP is a protocol for interoperable message exchange. However, this conclusion is wrong. You should use the type SoapFormatter only if you want a human-readable, text-based format, as in the sample application that follows, which serializes a Person object to the console's output stream.

```
// FCLSerialization.cpp
// build with "cl /clr:safe FCLSerialization"

using namespace System;
#using <System.Runtime.Serialization.Formatters.Soap.dll>
using namespace System::Runtime::Serialization::Formatters::Soap;

[Serializable]
ref struct Person
{
  String^ Name;

  [NonSerialized]
  int Age;
};

int main()
{
  Person^ p = gcnew Person();
  p->Name = "Bruce";
  p->Age = 57;
  SoapFormatter^ sf = gcnew SoapFormatter();
  sf->Serialize(Console::OpenStandardOutput(), p);
}
```

If you execute this application, the following output will appear on the screen:

```
<SOAP-ENV:Envelope xmlns:xsi="http://www.w3.org/2001/XMLSchema-instance"
xmlns:xsd="http://www.w3.org/2001/XMLSchema"
xmlns:SOAP-ENC="http://schemas.xmlsoap.org/soap/encoding/"
xmlns:SOAP-ENV="http://schemas.xmlsoap.org/soap/envelope/"
xmlns:clr="http://schemas.microsoft.com/soap/encoding/clr/1.0"
```

```
SOAP-ENV:encodingStyle="http://schemas.xmlsoap.org/soap/encoding/">
<SOAP-ENV:Body>
<a1:Person id="ref-1" xmlns:a1="http://schemas.microsoft.com/clr/assem/ser%2C%20
Version%3D0.0.0.0%2C%20Culture%3Dneutral%2C%20PublicKeyToken%3Dnull">
<Name id="ref-3">Bruce</Name>
</a1:Person>
</SOAP-ENV:Body>
</SOAP-ENV:Envelope>
```

Since the graph contains only one object, there is only one XML element in the SOAP body. Notice that this element has the namespace prefix a1, which maps to the XML namespace "http://schemas.microsoft.com/clr/assem/FCLSerialization%2C%20Version%3D0.0.0.0%2C%20Culture%3Dneutral%2C%20PublicKeyToken%3Dnull". This XML namespace contains the name of the assembly in which the Person type is defined. The assembly name is contained in a URL-encoded text format—%2C is the URL-encoded comma (,), %20 is the space character, and so on.

Using this information, assemblies implementing the serialized objects can be loaded dynamically at runtime. Since other platforms like Java are not able to load .NET assemblies, this format is not interoperable. If you need to serialize objects in an interoperable format, consider using the type XmlSerializer, or the type DataContractSerializer, which is introduced in .NET 3.0.

Summary

This chapter has explained how you can give an assembly a unique identity, how assemblies are loaded, and how you can consume the metadata of an assembly. Metadata is burned into the assembly at build time. At runtime, metadata is consumed to provide type-agnostic services. The CLR uses metadata to implement services like garbage collection, JIT compilation, and object graph serialization. Using the Managed Reflection API, you can implement your own metadata-based runtime services. When implementing custom metadata-based runtime services, the amount of system-provided metadata is often not sufficient. By implementing custom attributes, you can define your own metadata. A client using your service can influence the behavior of your service by applying your attributes to definitions in its own code. Most metadata is bound to type definitions. The next chapter discusses how to implement managed types.

CHAPTER 5

■ ■ ■

Defining Managed Types

A primary task of every .NET programming language is to map source files to assemblies with custom managed type definitions. This chapter discusses the C++/CLI language features to define custom managed types.

If you compare the CTS of .NET with the C++ type system, you will find many similarities, but also a bunch of differences. Some features of the C++ type system are not supported by the CTS. These features include multiple inheritance, protected and private inheritance, const member functions, friends, and unions. At the end of the day, it is not very important whether you miss these features or not; as a programmer, you have to use the available features to solve your task.

On the other hand, there are CTS features that are not supported by the C++ type system. These features include new kinds of types, new type members, and refinements of existing constructs.

Figure 5-1 shows a schema for managed type definitions. The keywords class and struct have been extended with a prefix that describes the kind of managed type that is to be defined. A ref class is used to define a custom managed reference type. Managed interfaces are defined with the keyword interface class. The prefix value is used to define custom value types and an enum class defines a managed enumerator type.

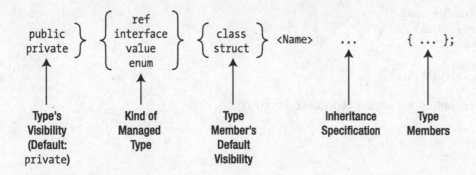

Figure 5-1. *Managed type definitions*

Type Visibility

As shown in Figure 5-1, managed type definitions can have a visibility modifier. In native C++, library developers usually separate type definitions into two kinds of header files: those that are deployed with the library, and those that are only used to build the library. Since the metadata in an assembly contains all the information necessary at build time, there is no need to include a header file, but the assembly must be referenced via the #using directive or the /FU compiler switch, as described in Chapter 3.

An assembly contains metadata describing all types; therefore, it is necessary to distinguish types that can only be used inside an assembly from types that can be used by other assemblies, too. This is done with the visibility modifier. The CTS supports public and private type visibility. The more restrictive modifier (private) is the default value if no visibility modifier is used.

The following code shows two simple reference type definitions: a private one containing an implementation detail (the Pi value), and a public one representing the library's functionality:

```
// SomeReferenceTypes.cpp
// build with "CL /clr:safe /LD SomeReferenceTypes.cpp"

private ref class MathConstants
{
public:
  static const double Pi = 3.141592658;
        // You should not define static const values in your code
        // It is only used here because better solutions have not been covered yet
};

public ref class Circle
{
  double radius;
public:
  Circle(double radius)
  : radius(radius)
  {}

  double CalculateArea()
  {
    return radius * radius * MathConstants::Pi;
  }
};
```

Friend Assemblies

It is also possible to explicitly grant other assemblies access to all private types. This is usually done in unit testing scenarios. The InternalsVisibleToAttribute from the namespace System::Runtime::CompilerServices can be used to specify friend assemblies as shown here:

```
// SomeReferenceTypes2.cpp
// build with "CL /LD /clr:safe SomeReferenceTypes2.cpp"

using System::Runtime::CompilerServices::InternalsVisibleToAttribute;
[assembly: InternalsVisibleTo("SomeReferenceTypes2UnitTests")];

private ref class MathConstants
{
public:
  static double Pi = 3.141592658;
};

public ref class Circle
{
  double radius;
public:
  Circle(double radius)
  : radius(radius)
  {}

  double CalculateArea()
  {
    return radius * radius * MathConstants::Pi;
  }
};
```

To get access to the private members, the as_friend modifier must be applied to the #using declaration.

```
// someReferenceTypes2UnitTests.cpp
// build with "CL /clr:safe someReferenceTypes2UnitTests.cpp"

#using "SomeReferenceTypes2.dll" as_friend

using namespace System;

int main()
{
  // access to private type
  Console::WriteLine("PI = {0}", MathConstants::Pi);
  Circle^ c = gcnew Circle(10);
  Console::WriteLine(c->CalculateArea());
}
```

Value Type Definitions

The CTS allows you to define custom value types. The following code shows an example:

```
public value class Point
{
  int x;
  int y;
public:
  Point(int x, int y);
  void Move(int x, int y);
};
```

In most cases, it is preferable to define a reference type instead of a value type. As discussed in Chapter 2, your clients have to consider various boxing pitfalls when using your value type. Furthermore, there are several restrictions for value type definitions. Value types do not support inheritance. You can neither derive a value type from another type, nor can you use a value type as a base class. Special member functions for value types (e.g., the default constructor, copy constructors, operators for copy assignment, and the destructor) are not supported either.

Copy constructors, copy-assignment operators, and destructors are not supported because there are scenarios in which the compiler cannot guarantee that these functions are called. For example, when a value is boxed, neither would the copy constructor be called to create the boxed value, nor could it be guaranteed that the destructor would be called.

Defining managed value types can be useful when many instances are needed in the same time frame. For value types, multiple instances can be created in one chunk by creating a managed array. When V is a value type, the expression

```
gcnew array<V>(100)
```

allocates the memory for 100 instances of V in one chunk. For a reference type R, however, the expression

```
gcnew array<R^>(100)
```

would allocate memory for 100 tracking handles only. All instances would have to be created manually.

Using value types in this case can also improve the GC performance. For value type arrays, only one managed object needs to be collected, whereas if you create a reference type array with n elements and initialize it so that each element refers to a new instance of the reference type, the GC would have to collect the array as well as each instance individually.

Due to the lack of a default constructor for value types, initializing value type arrays is a fast operation, because it is sufficient to set the whole memory to 0 values. If the element type had a default constructor, this constructor would have to be called for each element of the array.

C++ Managed Extensions (the .NET extensions for Visual C++ 2002 and 2003) supported the definition of custom default constructors for value types. If you compile code based on C++ Managed Extensions with the compiler switch /clr:oldSyntax of Visual C++ 2005, you can still define value types with custom default constructors. However, this can be dangerous, since arrays of such a value type would not be initialized correctly by the C# compiler. C# simply leaves the value type array with zero-initializations for every element, even if the element type supports a default constructor. To perform the initialization correctly, the base class System::Array comes with the Initialize method, which a C# programmer must call explicitly. In contrast to C#, C++/CLI calls this method automatically as part of the array initialization, if the element type has a default constructor.

Managed Enums

Like the C++ type system, the CTS supports enums as a distinct kind of type. To define a managed enum, the keyword enum class is used.

```
enum class Color
{
  Red = 1,
  Blue = 2,
  Yellow = 4
};
```

There are a few differences between managed enums and native enums that you should know. First of all, values of managed enums must be written in a type-qualified way, as shown in the following line:

```
Color c = Color::Red;
```

To achieve a similar type-scoped behavior for native enums, they can be defined as nested types. In this case, the nesting type is the naming scope for the enum literals.

The width of a managed enum value defaults to the width of int, but it can be customized with an inheritance-like syntax. The following code defines an 8-bit-wide managed enum:

```
enum class Color : unsigned char
{ /*...*/ };
```

To define the width of the enum, the type bool, as well as the primitive signed and unsigned integer types, can be used.

In contrast to native enums, managed enums do not have a standard conversion to and from int. Neither does such a conversion exist for the primitive type that specifies the width of the enum type. Instead of standard conversions, casts must be used.

When the C++/CLI compiler generates a managed enum type, it extends a class from System::Enum, which itself derives from System::ValueType. Since a managed enum type is implicitly a value type, it can be instantiated as a value on the stack. This implies boxing when an enum value is casted or converted to a tracking handle type. As an example, when an enum value is passed to Console::WriteLine, the overload WriteLine(Object^) is called. To pass the enum value as an argument, a standard conversion to Object^ is applied, which implies boxing.

To perform the console output, `Console::WriteLine(Object^)` calls `ToString` on the object passed. `System::Enum` implements a special overload for `ToString`. You can use the following application to explore the behavior of `Enum::ToString`:

```
// managedEnum1.cpp
// build with "cl /clr:safe managedEnum1.cpp"

enum class Color : unsigned char
{
  Red = 1,
  Blue = 2,
  Yellow = 4
};

using namespace System;

int main()
{
  Color c = Color::Red;
  Console::WriteLine(c);
  c = Color::Red | Color::Blue;
  Console::WriteLine(c);
}
```

Executing this application causes an output that is probably surprising:

```
Red
3
```

When the value `Color::Red` is passed to `Console::WriteLine`, the literal name `Red` is written to the console. `Enum::ToString` is able to read the literal names from the enum type's metadata. When the value `Color::Red | Color::Blue` is passed instead, the numeric value 3 appears.

In addition to the enum literals, the `ToString` overload is aware of the `System::FlagsAttribute`. This attribute can be applied to a managed enum to express that bitwise-or combinations are valid values. When the attribute is applied to the `Color` type, the expression `(Color::Red | Color::Blue).ToString()` evaluates to `Red, Blue`. Here is a piece of code that uses an enum with the `FlagsAttribute`:

```
// managedEnum2.cpp
// build with "cl /clr:safe managedEnum2.cpp"

using namespace System;

[Flags]
enum class Color
{
  Red = 1,
```

```
  Blue = 2,
  Yellow = 4,
  Orange = Red | Yellow,
  Green = Blue | Yellow,
  White = Red | Blue | Yellow
};

int main()
{
  Console::WriteLine(Color::Red | Color::Blue);        // "Red, Blue"
  Console::WriteLine(Color::Red | Color::Yellow);      // "Orange"
  String^ colorText = "\tBlue,\nYellow";
  Color c = (Color)Enum::Parse(Color::typeid, colorText);
  Console::WriteLine(c);                               // "Green"
}
```

Enum::ToString uses literals for combined values if possible. In this sample, (Color::Red | Color::Yellow).ToString() evaluates to "Orange". Enum::Parse can be used to parse an enum value out of a string. As the preceding sample code shows, even input strings with whitespace are accepted.

Enum::Parse returns an Object^. Since a managed enum is a value type, the parsed enum value is boxed and a tracking handle to the boxed value is returned by Enum::Parse. When the caller casts the boxed object back into a managed enum type, unboxing occurs. As discussed in Chapter 2, a boxed object must be unboxed to the correct type. Even though a managed enum can be explicitly casted to int, the cast of a boxed enum object to int would cause a System::InvalidCastException at runtime.

Type Member Visibility

In managed type definitions, class and struct affect the default visibility of type members. As in native C++, the default visibility is public for struct types and private for classes. To define members with another visibility, the keywords public, protected, and private can be used as usual.

In native type definitions, the concept of friend visibility can be used to define exceptions to the normal visibility rules; friend declarations explicitly allow a set of types or functions in the same project to access members that would otherwise be invisible. The CTS does not have a friend construct, but there are additional visibility alternatives. In C++/CLI, the visibility modifiers internal, public protected, and protected private can be used.

Type members with internal visibility can be accessed by all code in the same assembly. Instead of picking just some special types and functions that get extended access to private members (like the friend construct in C++), all types in the same assembly are allowed to access internal members.

The variant public protected is the union of protected and internal visibility. This combination of the public and the protected keyword has a less restrictive part (public) and a more restrictive part (protected). The less restrictive part describes the visibility inside the assembly. The more restrictive part describes the visibility outside the assembly. Inside the assembly, all types can access public protected members; outside the assembly, only derived types can access public protected members.

The same idea has lead to the visibility modifier protected private. The less restrictive part (protected) means that derived classes in the same assembly can access protected private members. The more restrictive keyword (private) disallows access from outside the assembly. Therefore, protected private is the intersection between internal access and protected access.

Nested classes can access all members of the containing class. The following code shows the member access options within an assembly:

```
// TestVisibility.cpp
// compile with "CL /LD /clr:safe TestVisibility.cpp"

using namespace System;

public ref class Base
{
private:               int iPrivate;
internal:              int iInternal;
protected private:     int iProtectedPrivate;
protected:             int iProtected;
public protected:      int iPublicProtected;
public:                int iPublic;

  ref class Inner
  {
  public:
    void TestVisibility(Base^ base)
    {
      Console::WriteLine("{0}, {1}, {2}, {3}, {4}, {5}",
            base->iPrivate, base->iInternal, base->iProtectedPrivate,
            base->iProtected, base->iPublicProtected, base->iPublic);
    }
  };

  void TestVisibility(Base^ base)
  {
    // all Base members can be accessed here
    Console::WriteLine("{0}, {1}, {2}, {3}, {4}, {5}",
          base->iPrivate, base->iInternal, base->iProtectedPrivate,
          base->iProtected, base->iPublicProtected, base->iPublic);
  }
};

public ref class Derived : Base
{
public:
  void TestVisibility(Base^ base)
  {
    // only internal, public protected and public members can be accessed via Base^
```

```cpp
      Console::WriteLine("{0}, {1}, {2}",
                         base->iInternal, base->iPublicProtected, base->iPublic);
    }
    void TestVisibility(Derived^ derived)
    {
      // all except private members can be accessed via Derived1^
      Console::WriteLine("{0}, {1}, {2}, {3}, {4}",
              derived->iInternal, derived->iProtectedPrivate, derived->iProtected,
              derived->iPublicProtected, derived->iPublic);
    }
};

public ref class Unrelated
{
  void TestVisibility(Base^ base)
  {
    // only internal, public protected and public members can be accesed via Base^
    Console::WriteLine("{0}, {1}, {2}",
                       base->iInternal, base->iPublicProtected, base->iPublic);
  }
};
```

The member visibility outside of an assembly is shown in the next block of sample code, which depends on the previous one:

```cpp
// TestExternalVisibility.cpp
// CL /LD /clr:safe TextExternalVisibility.cpp

#using "TestVisibility.dll"

using namespace System;

public ref class ExternalDerived : Base
{
public:
  void TestVisibility(Base^ base)
  {
    // only public members an be assecced via Base^
    Console::WriteLine("{0}", base->iPublic);
  }
  void TestVisibility(ExternalDerived^ derived)
  {
    // all except private, protected private and internal members
    // can be accessed via ExternalDerived^
    Console::WriteLine("{0}, {1}, {2}",
        derived->iProtected, derived->iPublicProtected, derived->iPublic);
  }
```

```
};

public ref class ExternalUnrelated
{
  void TestVisibility(Base^ base)
  {
    // only public can be accesed via Base^
    Console::WriteLine("{0}", base->iPublic);
  }
};
```

Visibility and Naming Conventions

The code in the samples shown before follows some common naming conventions used for the definition of managed types. These naming conventions depend on type visibility. Type names for public as well as private types use the PascalCase naming convention: The first letter of the name as well as the first letter of each word within the name are uppercase letters, and the remaining letters are lowercase. For managed classes, you should not use the prefix C, as is typically done in MFC- and ATL-based code.

Names for data members do not use type-specific prefixes (Hungarian notation). You should also avoid the prefix m_ for data members. Some coders use the underscore (_) prefix for private members, but it is not a common practice. Public members always use PascalCase, and private members typically use camelCase-based names. In camelCase names, the first letter is lowercase, the first letter of each word within the name is uppercase, and the remaining letters are lowercase. For local variables and parameter names, camelCase is used, too.

In addition, there are some prefixes and suffixes for special cases. As an example, interfaces are named starting with a capital I, immediately followed by a PascalCase name; exception classes have the suffix Exception; and classes for custom attributes have the suffix Attribute.

Methods

In the .NET space, member functions of managed classes are often called methods. To simplify working with methods, C++/CLI has a syntax for method declarations and definitions that is very similar to the C++ syntax for member functions. As an example, in both worlds, there are static member functions. However, there are also some fundamental differences between methods in the C++ type system and methods in the CTS.

To pass managed types by reference, a new kind of referencing type, called a *tracking reference*, exists. Just as native references are defined with the ampersand character (&), tracking references are defined with the percent (%) character. The following code shows by-reference and by-value passing of arguments:

```
#include <iostream>
using namespace std;
using namespace System;
```

```
public ref class MethodSamples
{
public:
  void NativeByValArgs(int i, string str, string* pstr)
  {
    // caller will not see all these changes
    i = 10;
    str = "123";
    pstr = new string("123");    // leaking string object!
  }

  void NativeByRefArgs(int& i, string& str, string*& pstr)
  {
    // caller will see all these changes
    i = 10;
    str = "123";
    pstr = new string("123");    // caller is responsible for deleting pstr
  }

  void ManagedByValArgs(int i, String^ str)
  {
    // caller will not see these changes
    i = 10;
    str = gcnew String('a', 5);    // GC can reclaim memory for String immediately
  }

  void ManagedByRefArgs(int% i, String^% str)
  {
    // caller will see these changes
    i = 10;

    // lifetime of string depends on usage of str outside this function
    str = gcnew String('a', 5);
  }
};
```

To compile existing C++ code to managed code, C-style support for functions with a variable number of arguments still exists; however, if you define a new managed function, you should consider using an alternative concept supported by C++/CLI. The syntax for this alternative is also based on an ellipsis (...), but in addition to the ellipsis, a managed array type is used to define the argument. The following code shows how you can use this new syntax:

```
Object^ CallAnyFunction( Object^ obj, String^ function, ... array<Object^>^ args )
{
  if (!obj)
```

```
        throw gcnew ArgumentNullException("obj");

    // determine the type of the object
    Type^ t = obj->GetType();

    // determine the MethodInfo object for the target method
    MethodInfo^ mi = t->GetMethod(function);
    if (!mi)
        throw gcnew ArgumentException("Function does not exist");

    return mi->Invoke(obj, args);
}
```

For the argument args, zero or more arguments of any tracking handle type and of any managed value type can be passed. Managed values passed will be boxed, and the Object^ element in the args array will refer to the boxed value.

If a function is compiled to native code, or if you want to allow native callers for your function, you have to use the old C-style alternative for vararg functions. For managed functions called only by managed clients, the managed alternative can have several advantages over C-style vararg functions. It is often easier to use than macros like va_start, va_arg, and va_end. In addition to that, this alternative is language interoperable; other .NET languages can seamlessly call a function like CallAnyFunction.

And finally, this approach is typed. Instead of array<Object^>^, any one-dimensional managed array type can be used. The following code defines a function that can take an arbitrary number of int arguments:

```
int Sum(... array<int>^ args)
{
    int result = 0;
    for each (int i in args)
        result += i;
    return result;
}
```

To invoke such a function, only int values or values with a standard conversion to int can be passed.

Default Arguments Are Not Supported

A few features that are supported for member functions of C++ classes are not supported for methods in the CTS. For example, you cannot define a method with default parameters. The following code is illegal:

```
ref class R
{
    void f(int i = 10, int j = 20)
    { /* ... */ };
};
```

To mimic the behavior of default parameters, you have to implement separate functions that forward to the real implementation:

```
ref class R
{
  void f(int i, int j)
  { /* ... */ }

  void f(int i)
  { f(i, 20); }

  void f()
  { f(10, 20); }
};
```

const Methods Are Not Supported

Another restriction you should be aware of is the lack of const methods. It is important to keep this restriction in mind, because it affects other traditional usages of the keyword const. Even though it is possible to define a variable or a parameter of type const T^, it is seldom useful. Due to the lack of const methods, you would not be able to call *any* method on such a variable. Without casting away the const modifier, you would only be able to assign a new reference to the variable, or to read a const member variable. However, in managed types, you should not define const data members, as the next section explains.

Fields

As member functions of managed types are often called methods, data members of managed types are often called *fields*. For most fields, you will likely use exactly the same syntax as for data members in native C++ classes. However, there are additional options for defining fields with read-only semantics. In C++/CLI, you can declare a non-static field as initonly. This allows you to initialize the field in either the member initialization list of the constructor or the constructor's body, but not outside.

An initonly field is language interoperable. Other languages also have support for this construct. As an example, the equivalent C# keyword is readonly. Furthermore, the read-only character of an initonly field can be ensured not only by the compiler, but also by the JIT compiler. C++/CLI and most other .NET languages return compiler errors if you try to modify an initonly field out of the constructor's code. However, using tools like the IL Assembler (ILASM.EXE) or the System::Reflection::Emit API, you can easily bypass this compiler-level safety and generate code that tries to modify an initonly field. Even if you do this, the JIT compiler can detect that illegal attempt and throw a System::Security::VerificationException instead of blindly executing this illegal operation. This aspect can be important in the context of sandboxed execution.

For static fields, there are two read-only concepts. These are literal fields and static initonly fields. A typical usage of these managed concepts would be with the value PI from the MathConstants class shown earlier.

```
ref class MathConstants
{
public:
  literal double Pi = 3.141592658;
  static initonly double Pi2 = 3.14159268;
        // two managed alternatives, which one should be chosen when?
};
```

Distinguishing literal fields and static initonly fields is important in the context of assembly versioning. A literal field can only be a fixed value known at build time. When a literal field is used by a compiler building a client assembly, the compiler burns the field's value into the managed code. This means that the client code needs to be recompiled to achieve that a modified literal value is used.

Fields marked as static initonly are different. Instead of burning the field's value into managed code, IL instructions for accessing the field via its name are emitted. This enables the JIT compiler to determine the value of the static initonly field. When the assembly in which the field is defined is updated so that the static initonly field has a new value, the client will see the new value automatically after the new version is deployed; there is no need to recompile the client.

Notice that despite its versioning benefits, a static initonly field has only a slight impact on the performance of JIT compilation; the JIT-compiled native code is the same as if a literal field had been used instead. Therefore, static initonly fields are often the favored alternative. In the case of natural constants like PI and E, however, a change in the number is not expected. Therefore, the FCL has defined them as literal fields in a class called System::Math.

Bye-Bye const

Even though C++/CLI allows you to define static and non-static const fields, I recommend using initonly fields instead of const fields, and static initonly fields or literal fields instead of static const fields. Since the CTS does not have natural support for const fields, C++/CLI uses special extensibility features of the CTS (so-called optional signature modifiers) if you define a const field. These signature modifiers are ignored by other .NET languages. Furthermore, they are not used during JIT compilation to optimize the generated code or to verify type safety of IL code.

When implementing managed types, the only scenario in which const still makes sense is the definition of const local variables of primitive types. The following code shows an example:

```
void R::f()
{
  const double PISquare = Math::PI * Math::PI;
  // ... do something with PISquare here
}
```

Type Initialization

Since static initonly fields are resolved when the code that uses the field is JIT-compiled, it is not necessary to specify the value of a static initonly field at build time. However, the value of a static initonly field must be determined before the JIT compiler resolves the field. To achieve this, .NET comes with a new construct called a *type initializer*. According to the CLI specification, a type initializer is called by the runtime "at or before first access of any static field of that type." (For details on the timing guarantees for type initialization, please refer to the documentation on the beforefieldinit modifier in the CLI specification.)

Type initializers are sometimes called *static constructors* because many .NET languages, including C++/CLI and C#, allow you to define a type initializer with a constructor-like syntax. The following code shows a static constructor that reads a value from a configuration file:

```
ref class TaxRates
{
public:
  static initonly float GermanVAT;
  static initonly float UKVAT;

  static TaxRates()
  {
    GermanVAT = float::Parse(ConfigurationManager::AppSettings["GermanVAT"]);
    UKVAT = float::Parse(ConfigurationManager::AppSettings["UKVAT"]);
  }
};
```

When static constructors are implemented, exceptions must be considered, too. To discuss exceptions that occur during type initialization, I'll review the static constructor implemented previously. The expression ConfigurationManager::AppSettings["GermanVAT"] evaluates to nullptr when a configuration file like the one following is not found:

```
<configuration>
  <appSettings>
    <add key="GermanVAT" value="0.16"/>
    <add key="UKVAT" value="0.175"/>
  </appSettings>
</configuration>
```

When float::Parse is called with nullptr as an argument, it throws a System::ArgumentNullException. Since the exception is not caught within the constructor, it will be handled by the caller—the runtime. In this case, the type is marked as unusable. The code that caused the JIT compilation will face a System::TypeInitializationException. All further attempts to use the type in any way will also cause a TypeInitializationException to be thrown. Since developers rarely expect such an exception when they instantiate a type or use its static members, you should not allow exceptions to be thrown from a type initializer. The following code shows how an exception can be avoided in the TaxRates type initializer:

```
static TaxRates()
{
  if (!float::TryParse(ConfigurationManager::AppSettings["GermanVAT"], GermanVAT))
    GermanVAT = 0.16;
  if (!float::TryParse(ConfigurationManager::AppSettings["UKVAT"], UKVAT))
    UKVAT = 0.175;
}
```

If a static field or a static initonly field is initialized within the field's declaration, the C++/CLI compiler automatically emits a static constructor that initializes the field. The following class demonstrates this:

```
ref class TaxRates
{
  static float GetConfigValue(String^ key, float defaultValue)
  {
    float value = 0.0f;
    if (!float::TryParse(ConfigurationManager::AppSettings[key], value))
      value = defaultValue;
    return value;
  }

public:
  static initonly float GermanVAT = GetConfigValue("GermanVAT", 0.16);
  static initonly float UKVAT = GetConfigValue("UKVAT", 0.175);
};
```

The CLR is implemented so that static constructors are called in a thread-safe way. For example, if one thread tries to access a static field of a managed type while another thread is currently executing the managed type's initializer, the first thread has to wait.

In rare cases, you may want to ensure that a type initializer is called even though you are not about to use a type directly. You can achieve this by calling System::Runtime::CompilerServices::RuntimeHelpers::RunClassConstructor, passing the type info object for the type you want to preinitialize.

Inheritance

The CTS supports custom inheritance only for reference types and interfaces. As shown in Figure 5-2, custom value types and managed enum types have implicit base classes; custom value types are derived from System::ValueType, and managed enum types inherit System::Enum. However, neither type supports further inheritance—neither custom value types nor managed enum types can be used as a base class.

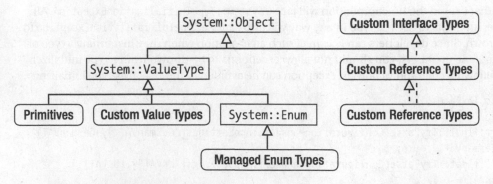

Figure 5-2. *Managed types and inheritance*

For custom reference types, inheritance is mandatory. If the class definition does not contain a base class specification, the type implicitly extends System::Object. Interfaces do not have an implicit base type. A tracking handle of an interface type is either a nullptr or it refers to an object, which implies that the methods of System::Object can be called.

A ref class can inherit one base class and any number of managed interfaces. While base classes are used to reflect *is-a* relationships, base interfaces represent *behaves-as* relationships. Like a COM interface, a managed interface is an abstract type specifying a set of operations. All interface members are implicitly public and abstract. A managed interface can have any number of base interfaces. Interfaces support the design-by-contract approach. A managed class implementing an interface must provide implementations for all members of the interface, including all members of the base interfaces; a user of the class can call all these members.

The following code shows some interface and class definitions:

```
public interface class I2DObject
{
  double CalculateArea();
};

public interface class IVisibleObject
{
  void Draw();
};

public ref class Shape
: public IVisibleObject     // only public inheritance, keyword public optional
{
  /* ... */
};

public ref class Circle
: Shape, I2DObject          // inheritance implicitly public
{
  /* ... */
};
```

The CTS does not support private or protected inheritance. Since public inheritance is the only option for managed types, the keyword public in the inheritance list is optional.

An inheritance modifier can be used to specify inheritance options for a class. A managed class can be defined as abstract even if it does not have a pure virtual function. This can be achieved with the inheritance modifier abstract.

```
public ref class Shape abstract
: public IVisibleObject
{ /* ... */ };
```

The keyword abstract is mandatory if the class has pure virtual functions. A class can also be marked as sealed. In this case, it cannot be used as a base class. This means that further inheritance is forbidden.

```
public ref class Circle sealed
: public Shape, public I2DObject
{ /* ... */ };
```

If neither of the inheritance modifiers is used, the class can be instantiated and inherited. A combination of both inheritance modifiers can be used to define a class that has only static members. Therefore, such a class is often called a static class. In the FCL, the class System::Math, which contains definitions for PI, E, as well as functions sin, cos, and so on, is defined as a static class.

Inheritance and Versioning

Public inheritance implies that a base class developer can influence the public interface of a derived class. A developer of a derived class implicitly allows the base class developer to add functions to the set of operations that a client can call. This must be considered especially in cross-component scenarios in which the base class and the derived class are controlled and versioned by different developers. .NET's ability to use a later version of a component by simply applying a version redirection instead of recompiling existing code can increase the potential for trouble with public inheritance and versioning.

To understand what problems can occur, consider a class library that provides the following base class:

```
public ref class Base
{
public:
  void f();
};
```

A user of the class library could inherit a class Derived, as follows:

```
ref class Derived : public Base
{
public:
  void g();
};

int main()
{
  Derived^ d = gcnew Derived();
  d->f();
  d->g();
};
```

If the next version of the base class library introduces a function void g() in the base class, the compiler is still able to resolve the function calls—but for human beings working with a Derived object, the situation can cause a misunderstanding.

```
Derived^ d = gcnew Derived();
d->g();    // calls Derived::g
Base^ b = d;
b->g();    // calls Base::g, even though the call is made on the same object
```

To make sure that the ambiguity is at least detected when the next version of the derived class is built, the compiler emits a level 4 warning. You can use the keyword new to express that you are aware that you have defined an unrelated function with the same name and signature as in the base class. This avoids the ambiguity warning.

```
ref class Derived : public Base
{
public:
  void g() new;
};
```

Virtual Functions

Extending a base class with virtual functions can cause even more problems. Some of these problems are in the nature of public inheritance; other problems exist because the C++ syntax for virtual functions leaves room for ambiguities. The following code shows an ambiguity that exists in C++ code:

```
class Derived : public Base
{
public:
  void f();
};
```

If you see just this class declaration, you cannot say whether the function f is a virtual function or not. If Base defines or inherits a virtual function f with the same and signature as Derived::f, then Derived::f overrides this virtual function, and therefore, Derived::f is a virtual function, too. This is sometimes called implicit overriding. When overriding a virtual function in C++, the keyword virtual is optional; Derived::f overrides Base::f without explicitly stating this.

To make clear that Derived::f is a virtual function, you could define the function with the keyword virtual. However, in this case, it would not be clear whether Derived overrides Base::f or introduces a new virtual function f.

C++/CLI introduces a new syntax for the declaration of virtual functions. This syntax is mandatory for virtual functions of managed types. If you compile with /clr or /clr:pure, you can also use this syntax for native classes. The new syntax is called explicit overriding. This means that the keyword virtual is no longer optional; whenever you declare a virtual function, you have to use the keyword virtual. (This also means that the lack of this keyword is a sure indicator that the function is not virtual.) In addition to the keyword virtual, the declaration can contain an override modifier. Figure 5-3 shows the syntax for explicitly overriding virtual functions.

$$\texttt{virtual } \textbf{\textit{ReturnType Name(...)}} \left\{ \begin{array}{l} \texttt{new} \\ \texttt{abstract} \\ \texttt{new abstract} \\ \texttt{override} \\ \texttt{= \textbf{\textit{Base::Name}}} \\ \texttt{sealed override} \\ \texttt{sealed = \textbf{\textit{Base::Name}}} \end{array} \right\} \texttt{ ;}$$

Figure 5-3. *Override modifiers*

Declaring a virtual function without an override modifier means that a virtual function is introduced and that no conflicts with a virtual function in the base class are assumed. If the base class has a conflicting virtual function (e.g., because it was introduced by a later version of the base class library), you will get a compiler error. The following code gives an example:

```
ref class Base
{
public:
  virtual void f();
};

ref class Derived : public Base
{
public:
  virtual void f();
        // error C4485: 'Derived::f' : matches base ref class method 'Base::f',
        // but is not marked 'new' or 'override'
};
```

As the error message suggests, there are two options to handle this problem. For one, you can decide that the virtual function in the base class library is unrelated to this virtual function. In this case, you have to use the override modifier new. You can also decide that your implementation of Derived::f shall override Base::f. In this case, the keyword override is necessary.

When you declare your virtual function as unrelated to an inherited virtual function with the same name, you may still want to override the virtual function in the base class. This can be achieved with named overriding:

```
ref class Base
{
public:
  virtual void f();
};
```

```
ref class Derived : public Base
{
public:
  virtual void f() new;

  // Derived::AnyOtherName overrides Base::f
  virtual void AnyOtherName() = Base::f;
};
```

As the following code shows, a programmer inheriting the class `Derived` can even provide a further overriding of `Base::f`:

```
ref class MoreDerived : Derived
{
public:
  virtual void AnyOtherName() override
  { /* ... */ }
};

int main()
{
  Base^ b = gcnew MoreDerived();
  b->f();          // calls MoreDerived::AnyOtherName
}
```

If further overriding is not intended, you can use the keyword `sealed` in conjunction with explicit overriding (`sealed override`) or with named overriding (`sealed = Base::f`).

Since custom value types cannot be used as base classes, it does not make sense to define a new virtual function in a value type. However, it makes sense to override virtual functions inherited from `System::Object`. The following code defines a value type that overrides `Object::ToString`:

```
public value class Point
{
  int x;
  int y;

public:
  Point(int x, int y);

  virtual String^ ToString() override
  {
    return String::Format("({0} : {1})", x, y);
  }
};
```

To define a pure virtual function, you can either use the keyword `abstract`, the C++-like modifier `= 0`, or a combination of both. The override modifier `new abstract` defines an abstract function that is unrelated to an inherited virtual function with the same name. There is a subtle difference between pure virtual functions of native classes and abstract functions of managed classes. A pure vital function of a native class can have an implementation; an abstract function of a managed class must not have an implementation.

Overriding Interface Members

Interfaces form a contract between an implementer and a client. This contract consists of a formal definition and a semantic description of the interface and its members. As an example, consider the interface System::IComparable from the FCL. The following code shows the formal definition in the C++/CLI syntax:

```
public interface class IComparable
{
  int CompareTo(Object^ o);
}
```

The semantic description of IComparable can be found in the MSDN documentation. It specifies that this interface is used to determine the ordering of instances of a type, and that CompareTo must be implemented so that the following requirements are met:

- A System::ArgumentException will be thrown if the argument o refers to an object that is not of the same type as the object that CompareTo was called on.

- A negative value will be returned if the object that CompareTo was called on is less than the object passed as an argument.

- Zero will be returned if both objects are equal or if an object is compared to itself.

- A positive value will be returned if the object that CompareTo was called on is greater than the object passed as an argument, or if a null reference (nullptr) was passed as an argument.

To implement an interface, you must implement all its members as virtual functions. The override modifier override is not allowed (unless a single function acts as an override of a virtual function in a base class as well as an interface implementation). The following class implements IComparable:

```
public ref class Person
: public IComparable
{
  String^ name;
  int age;

public:
  Person(String^ name, int age)
  : name(name), age(age)
  {}
```

```
virtual int CompareTo(Object^ obj)
{
  if (!obj)
    return 1; // by definition, any object compares greater than nullptr

  Person^ person = dynamic_cast<Person^>(obj);
  if (!person)    // Person object is expected
    throw gcnew ArgumentException("obj");

  int res = name->CompareTo(person->name);
  if (res != 0)
    return res;
  return age.CompareTo(person->age);
}
};
```

If you want to prevent less-important functionality from polluting the public interface of a class, you can implement it as a protected or a private function. This means that a client can call the interface members only via an interface reference, not via a reference of the concrete object's type.

To implement interface members with protected functions, the named overriding syntax must be used.

```
public ref class Person
: public IComparable
{
  ... same as before ...
protected:
  virtual int CompareTo(Object^ obj) = IComparable::CompareTo
  {
    ... same as before ...
  }
};
```

A protected implementation allows a derived class to override the implementation of the interface member. A private implementation would not even allow that. To implement an interface with private members only, you have to use named overriding as in the sample before. To express that the function cannot be overridden in a derived class, you also have to use the keyword sealed in your overriding specifier. The following code shows an example:

```
public ref class Person
: public IComparable
{
  ... same as before ...
private:
  virtual int CompareTo(Object^ obj) sealed = IComparable::CompareTo
  {
    ... same as before ...
  }
};
```

However, you should consider that a private implementation of an interface member is not a guarantee that a derived class does not provide a custom implementation of the interface member. By inheriting the interface again, a derived class can reimplement all interface members.

Interfaces Are Immutable

If you are a COM programmer, you surely know the golden rule: COM interfaces are immutable. A COM interface, once deployed, must not be changed. Members must not be removed or modified because clients of the interface may rely on these members. Members must also not be added, because depending on the versions of the components installed on the client machine, clients calling the new members may call a component that provides only the old members. In all these cases, the behavior is undefined.

In .NET, the immutability rule for interfaces is not as well known, which is a pity, because it applies to .NET interfaces equally: *.NET interfaces are immutable*. Do not remove, change, or add members to a deployed managed interface.

For .NET interfaces, the CLR is able to throw a well-defined exception instead of blindly running into undefined behavior. While a managed exception that precisely describes the problem is better than an access violation at a random address, it is still undesired.

To understand why .NET interfaces are immutable, too, it is helpful to reproduce an exception scenario. Consider the following simple interface:

```
// InterfaceLib.cpp
// build with "CL /LD /clr:safe InterfaceLib.cpp"

public interface class ICar
{
  void Drive();
};
```

A client of this library could be implemented as follows:

```
// UsingInterfaceLib.cpp
// build with "CL /clr:safe UsingInterfaceLib.cpp"

#using "InterfaceLib.dll"

ref class Car : public ICar
{
public:
  virtual void Drive() {}
};

int main()
{
  Car car;
}
```

If you build the library and its client, you should be able to execute the application without an exception being thrown.

For the next version of InterfaceLib.dll, assume that a new function is added to the interface.

```
// interfaceLib.cpp
// build with "CL /LD /clr:safe interfaceLib.cpp"

public interface class ICar
{
  void Drive();
  void Refuel();
};
```

Removing the Drive method or modifying its signature would obviously be a breaking change. Adding the new method is a breaking change, too. When the new version of InterfaceLib.dll is loaded by the application built against the old version of the DLL, the TypeLoadException shown following will be thrown:

```
Unhandled Exception: System.TypeLoadException: Method 'Refuel' in type 'Car' from
assembly 'UsingInterfaceLib, Version=0.0.0.0, Culture=neutral,
PublicKeyToken=null' does not have an implementation.
   at main()
```

When main is JIT-compiled, the type Car is used for the first time. Therefore, the type Car must be prepared to be used in managed code. Part of this preparation is the building of the method dispatch tables used when a method is called via an interface. During this preparation, the runtime detects that not all methods of the interface are supported by the class. Therefore, a TypeLoadException is thrown.

To solve this problem in an interface-based design, a new interface definition is necessary. This often leads to interface names with numerical suffixes like ICar2.

Using abstract base classes, you can prevent the versioning difficulties mentioned here from influencing type naming. Equivalent to the first version of the interface, an abstract base class could be defined like this:

```
public ref class ICar abstract
{
public:
  virtual void Drive() abstract;
};
```

When the second version is defined, it can provide a default implementation for all new members.

```
public ref class ICar abstract
{
public:
  virtual void Drive() abstract;
  virtual void Refuel()
  { /* ... default implementation goes here ... */ }
};
```

Since the new members do have an implementation now, the type can be prepared without a `TypeLoadException`. An old client using the new version of the library will automatically use the default implementation.

On one hand, abstract base classes allow you to extend existing types in later versions. On the other hand, the single–base class restriction forces a developer to derive new classes from an abstract base class instead of implementing an interface in an existing class.

In version 2 of the FCL, Microsoft has often favored abstract base classes over interfaces. As an example, ADO.NET 1.0 and 1.1 managed providers defined a set of interfaces like `IDbConnection` and `IDbCommand` that an ADO.NET data provider has to implement; in version 2, you have to extend base classes like `DbConnection` and `DbCommand` to implement an ADO.NET provider.

Has-A Relationships

In addition to is-a relationships (achieved via base classes) and behaves-as relationships (achieved via base interfaces), you can also define has-a relationships between managed types. A has-a relationship can be established simply by adding a field to a managed class.

For encapsulation reasons, it is not recommended to define public fields. However, it is sometimes desirable to expose has-a relationships to clients. To achieve this without using public fields, you can define properties. Properties consist of metadata and either one or two accessor methods. For read access to a property, a *get accessor* method is called. Write access is translated to a call of a *set accessor* method. A property can have either both accessor methods or just one of them. This means that you can define read-only properties and write-only properties, as well as properties that can be read and modified.

In most .NET languages, including C++/CLI, properties can be accessed with a field-like syntax. In the following code, the read-only property `Length` of a managed array is used:

```
void DumpArray(array<Object^>^ arr)
{
  for (int i = 0; i < arr->Length; ++i)
    Console::WriteLine(arr[i]);
}
```

The next block of code shows a managed class, `Person`, with two properties, `Name` and `Age`. For the `Name` property, the accessors are implemented in the class declaration. The accessors of `Age` are just declared in the class and implemented outside. The setter of the `Age` property performs a consistency check; if the assigned value is less than 0 or greater than 150, a `System::ArgumentException` is thrown.

```
public ref class Person
{
  // backing storage for properties
  String^ name;
  int age;

public:
  property String^ Name
  {
```

```
      String^ get()
      {
        return name;
      }
      void set(String^ newValue)
      {
        name = newValue;
      }
    }

    property int Age
    {
      // here, accessor methods are only declared, not implemented
      int get();
      void set(int);
    }
};

// implementation of Age's accessor methods
int Person::Age::get()
{
  return age;
}

void Person::Age::set(int newValue)
{
  if (newValue < 0 || newValue > 150)
    throw gcnew ArgumentException("newValue must be > 0 and < 150.");
  age = newValue;
}
```

For many property implementations, it is sufficient to define a simple backing storage field, a get accessor that returns the backing storage field, and a set accessor that updates the backing storage. C++/CLI simplifies the definition of such a property with the following trivial property syntax:

```
public ref class Person
{
public:
  property String^ Name;
  ... definition of Age property not trivial ...
};
```

Properties can also be declared as virtual. This implies that the accessor functions of the property are virtual functions. In contrast to fields, properties can be members of interfaces.

To handle a one-to-n relationship, a property of a container type is typically used. In the simplest case, such a container type is a managed array, but the FCL comes with a bunch of other container types, too. In the namespace System::Collections, there are several container types. These types include ArrayList, Queue, Stack, SortedList, and HashTable. All these collections can be used to manage elements of type System::Object^. When you use these collections with concrete types, downcasts are necessary. These casts are either dangerous (static_cast) or expensive (safe_cast). When the element types for these collections are value types, using these collections also implies a lot of boxing and unboxing.

Version 2.0 of the FCL also contains the namespace System::Collections::Generic with typed collection classes. These classes are based on *generics*, a template-like .NET feature that allows you to define and use parameterized types. As an example, there is a type List that represents a typed list of a dynamic size. The following code uses the read-only List<Person^> property to establish a one-to-*n* relationship:

```
using namespace System;
using namespace System::Collections::Generic;

public ref class Person
{
  List<Person^>^ friends;

public:
  Person()
  : friends(gcnew List<Person^>())
  {}

  property String^ Name;
  property int Age;

  property List<Person^>^ Friends
  { // since Friends is a read-only property, it can't be a trivial property
    List<Person^>^ get()
    {
      return friends;
    }
  }
};

int main()
{
  Person^ george = gcnew Person();
  george->Name = "George ";
  george->Age = 26;

  Person^ johnny = gcnew Person();
  johnny->Name = "Johnny ";
  johnny->Age = 33;

  george->Friends->Add(johnny);
  Console::WriteLine(george->Friends->Count);
}
```

To retrieve elements from a collection, you can either use the for each construct, as follows:

```
List<Person^>^ friends = george->Friends;
for each (Person^ p in friends)
  DoSomethingWithPerson(p)
```

or an array-like syntax, like so:

```
List<Person^>^ friends = george->Friends;
for (int i = 0; i < friends->Count; ++i)
  DoSomethingWithPerson(friends[i]);
```

The for each iteration is possible because the type List implements the interface IEnumerable. You can find various implementations of this and related interfaces on the Web, so I won't add a further implementation here. An important constraint on the for each construct is that the elements are invariant, so you cannot modify them. For example, the following code compiles, but it does not modify the content of the list:

```
List<Person^>^ friends = george->Friends;
for each (Person^ p in friends)
  p = gcnew Person();
```

Using an array-like syntax on a List<Person^>^ is possible because the type List implements a so-called default indexed property. A default indexed property is the managed equivalent to the subscript operator (operator []). It is a property with the name default and additional arguments provided in squared brackets. If you want to implement your own collection class, you should consider supporting this feature, too. The following code shows a simple class that implements two overloads of a default indexed property:

```
ref class PersonCollection
{
  // internal data storage not relevant here
public:
  property Person^ default[int]
  {
    Person^ get(int i)
    {
      // implementation of getter depends on internal storage
    }
    void set(int i, Person^ newValue)
    {
      // implementation of setter depends on internal storage
    }
  }

  // the second overload is a read-only property
  property Person^ default[String^]
  {
    Person^ get(String^ name)
    {
```

```
      // implementation of getter depends on internal storage
    }
  }
};
```

Notice that the accessor methods have additional arguments analogous to the argument types specified within the square brackets of the property declaration.

Components

Visual C++, as well as other .NET languages integrated into the Visual Studio .NET IDE, have a sophisticated support for software development based on has-a relationships. Using designers, you can easily add a new field to a class by dragging an item from the Toolbox window (which contains a palette of available components) and dropping it onto the designer.

In this context, Visual Studio and the FCL use the misleading term *component*. For most developers, a component is a deployable unit of executable code, like a .NET assembly, a COM server, or a Win32 DLL. In the context of Visual Studio, a component is a class that can be created with a designer or used by a designer. Visual C++ has designer support for general components as well as for Windows Forms UIs. To add a new component to your project, choose Add New Item from the Project menu, and then select Component Class from the Code category, as shown in Figure 5-4.

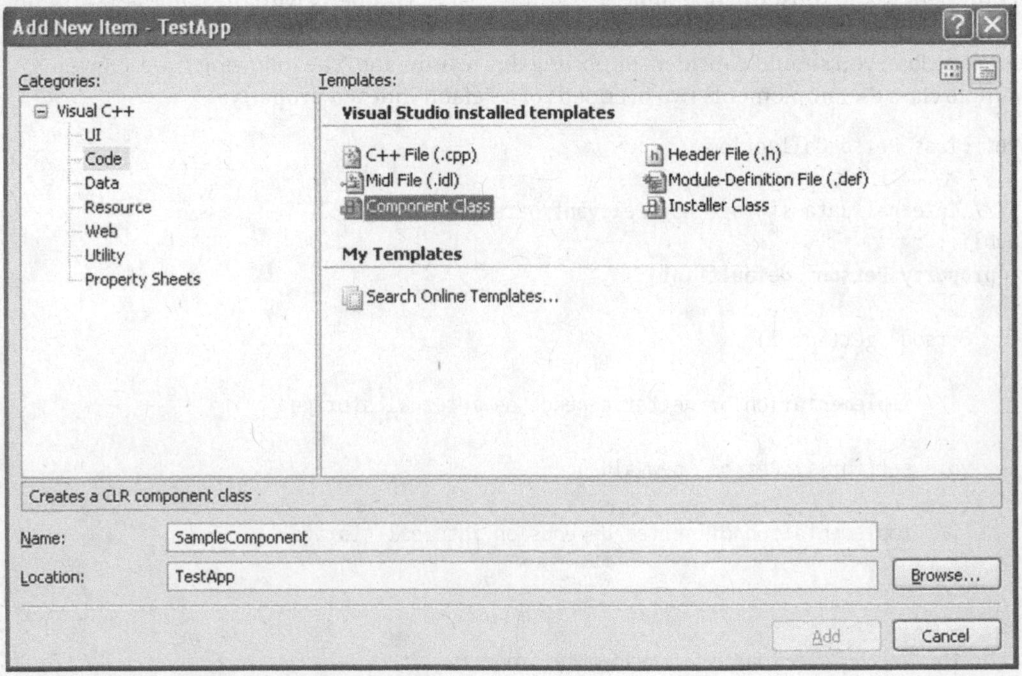

Figure 5-4. *Adding a new component*

When a new component is created, two files are added to your project. For SampleComponent, these files are SampleComponent.h and SampleComponent.cpp. The latter file simply includes the precompiled header file and SampleComponent.h. This ensures that the component class is compiled. SampleComponent.h declares the class SampleComponent in your project's default namespace. All methods generated by the wizards are implemented within the class declaration so that SampleComponent.cpp typically remains untouched.

You can open SampleComponent.h either with the component designer or with the normal text editor. If you browse through SampleComponent.h in the text editor, you will see that the class SampleComponent has a special base class called System::ComponentModel::Component. This base class is required for Visual Studio designer support. The SampleComponent class has a default constructor, which is also a requirement for all Visual Studio components. The default constructor calls a special method, InitializeComponent. This method is responsible for initializing the component and its contained items. For a freshly created component, InitializeComponent is almost empty—however, if you use the designer to modify the component, this method will automatically be filled with initialization code.

The default editor for a component's header file is the component designer. Figure 5-5 shows the component designer for a freshly created SampleComponent.

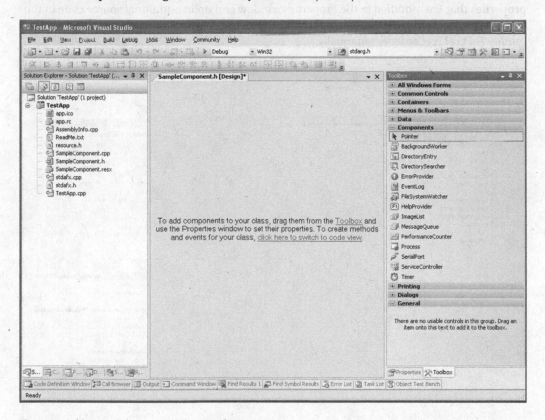

Figure 5-5. *The Visual C++ component designer*

The Toolbox window (on the right of the component designer) contains a range of components from different categories. The Components category includes various helpful types: The BackgroundWorker component is used to simplify the execution of asynchronous operations in Windows-based UIs. Using the EventLog component, you can write entries to the system event log. The ServiceController component can be used to start and stop OS service processes. For non-service processes, the Process component must be used instead.

To add a member variable for one of the component classes in the Toolbox window to your new component class, it is sufficient to just drag the component from the Toolbox window and drop it onto the designer's UI. Once this has happened, a member variable for the component is automatically added to your component class, and in InitializeComponent, a line is added to instantiate the component and assign a reference to it to the member variable.

The member variable for the component instance is represented as an icon on the component designer. Figure 5-6 shows the designer for SampleComponent after the Process component has been dropped onto the designer. Notice that the SampleComponent designer shows an icon for the field process1. On the right side of the Visual Studio window is the Properties window. Instead of writing code to initialize the instance of the Process component, you can simply select the process1 icon and modify the properties in the Properties window. All properties that are modified in the Properties window end up in additional source code in the InitializeComponent method. To avoid conflicts with the component designer, you should not modify InitializeComponent manually.

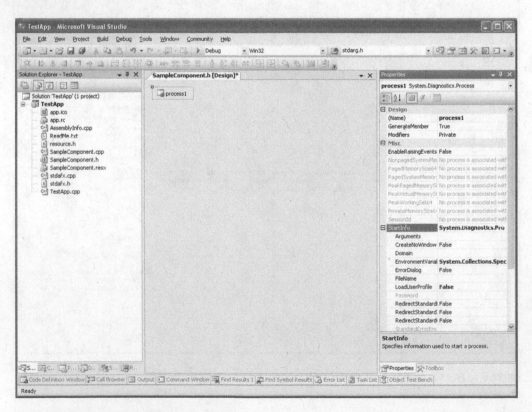

Figure 5-6. *Child components and properties*

Properties are grouped into categories. For the process1 field, the categories Design and Misc are available. *Design* is a general category that exists for all fields added to a component. In this category, you can change the name of the field and the visibility modifier. Changing the name of the field does not automatically modify code that refers to your field. Therefore, it is recommended to change this setting directly after you have dropped a component on the designer.

Apart from the Design category, all categories contain properties defined by the component class. In Figure 5-6, the property StartInfo is of the type ProcessStartupInfo^. Since ProcessStartupInfo is a managed class that has properties itself, you can expand the StartInfo property to modify the child properties. Also notice that a description of the selected property is shown at the bottom of the Properties window. For the property StartInfo, which is selected in Figure 5-6, the description part says

StartInfo
```
Specifies information used to start a class
```

To start a process, you have to set the FileName property and call Start on the Process instance. Setting the FileName property to a path of an EXE file can be done in the designer. To call the Start method, you have to write some code yourself. In the simplest case, this is done in the constructor.

Handling Events of a Component

Public methods and properties of a component allow invocations from a client to an object. A communication in the other direction is often necessary, too. As an example, in the context of starting a process, it can also be interesting to get the information about the termination of the started process. A straightforward approach would be to start a separate thread that waits for the process to terminate and performs a callback from the process component to its client when the process has exited. The process component in fact supports this feature. This feature is not turned on by default, but you can enable it by setting the EnableRaisingEvents property to true.

To perform the callback when the process has exited, the Process component exposes an *event* called Exited. For the events exposed by a component, the Properties window supports a second view. Figure 5-7 shows the event view of the Properties window for the process component.

Switch to properties view   Switch to events view

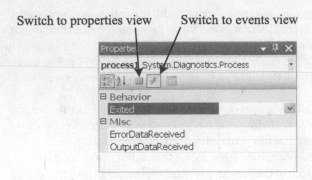

Figure 5-7. *The events view of the Properties window*

To handle an event, you can write the name of an event handler function into the text box of an event and press the Enter key. As an alternative, you can simply double-click in an event's text box. In this case, the name of the event handler will be the name of the component variable, followed by an underscore (_), followed by the name of the event. For the event shown in Figure 5-7, this would be process1_Exited.

When you use the Properties window to handle the Exited event, the designer automatically adds an empty event handler function to your component class. Such an event handler looks like this one:

```
private: void process1_Exited(Object^ sender, EventArgs^ e)
{
}
```

The signature for the event handler function is specified by the event. For different events, there can be different signatures. However, all event handler signatures of the FCL follow a common pattern. Event handler signatures have void as a return type and two arguments. The first argument is always of type Object^. It identifies the instance that has fired the event. This argument is helpful if you handle an event of several child components with the same event handler function. The second argument contains event-specific data. For events that do not require event-specific data (like the Exited event discussed here), the type EventArgs^ is used for the second argument.

Defining Custom Component Classes

By defining your own component classes, you allow programmers to use your classes in Visual Studio designers. You can integrate your component class into Visual Studio .NET so that a user of your class library can benefit from all the features mentioned previously.

For the designer support, Visual Studio .NET uses reflection APIs internally. For instance, Visual Studio retrieves metadata for the properties of the component class to dynamically add items to the Properties window. To allow the integration of a class into the Visual Studio .NET designer, it is often sufficient to derive your class from System::ComponentModel::Component

and to provide additional metadata via custom attributes from the namespace
System::ComponentModel. The following class shows an example:

```
public ref class FileDumper
: public Component
{
  int pagesDumped;

  void DumpPage(StreamReader^ sr, String^% line)
  {
    const int linesPerPage = Console::WindowHeight -1;
    const int charsPerLine = Console::BufferWidth -1;

    for (int i = 0; i < linesPerPage; ++i)
    {
      if (!line)
      {
        line = sr->ReadLine();
        if (!line)
          break; // end of stream
      }
      if (line->Length <= charsPerLine)
      {
        Console::WriteLine(line);
        line = nullptr;
      }
      else
      {
        Console::WriteLine(line->Substring(0, charsPerLine));
        line = line->Substring(charsPerLine);
      }
    }
  }
public:
  [Category("Input")]
  [Description("The name of the file to dump")]
  [DefaultValue("")]
  property String^ FileName;

  [Browsable(false)]
  property int PagesDumped
  {
    int get() { return pagesDumped; }
  }

  void Dump()
  {
    pagesDumped = 0;
```

```
      StreamReader^ sr = gcnew StreamReader(FileName);

      String^ line = nullptr;
      while (!sr->EndOfStream)
      {
        DumpPage(sr, line);
        ++pagesDumped;
        if (!sr->EndOfStream)
          Console::ReadKey();
      }

      sr->Close();
    }
};
```

The component implemented here can be used to dump a file page by page to the console. After each page is written, a key is read from the console to ensure that the user can read each part of the file.

The property FileName has two attributes. The text passed in the attribute Description is shown in Visual Studio's Properties window when the property FileName is selected. The attribute Category defines which category of the Properties window the property appears in.

The attribute Browsable is used to define that the property PagesDumped does not appear in the Properties window.

To use the FileDumper in the component designer, you can select Choose Items from the context menu of the Toolbox window and browse to the assembly defining the FileDumper component class. Once this is done, the FileDumper can be picked from the Toolbox window and dropped on another component, and the property FileName can be set. To dump the file, you have to write some code that calls the Dump method on the FileDumper object. Code using the contained components is typically written in methods of the containing class.

Defining Custom Events

Instead of waiting for a key from the console, the FileDumper can do a callback to leave it up to the client what should happen when a full page has been dumped to the console. To do this, the FileDumper component class can provide a PageDumped event. A client can implement the event handler to wait for a keystroke like before, but it would also be an option to display a message box instead. It would even be possible to not handle the event. In this case, one page after the other would be written to the console without an interruption.

The callback described here is the typical usage scenario for an event. Events are a special kind of type member that is based on delegates. Delegates are a special kind of type in the CTS that has a lot of similarities to function pointers in C++; they can store information that can be used to call a function. However, delegates support various other features that native function pointers do not have. These features include asynchronous method calls, dynamic method calls, and multicasting. Asynchronous method calls and dynamic delegate invocations are used very seldom in conjunction with event implementations. Therefore, these features are not covered here. For more information on these topics, consult the MSDN documentation for "asynchronous delegates" and for "Delegate.DynamicInvoke."

To understand delegates, it is helpful to first concentrate on the similarity to C++ function pointers. In C++, there are two function pointer concepts. From its C roots, C++ inherits the normal function pointer. A typedef for such a function pointer typically looks like this:

```
// PFN is a pointer to a boolean function with an int argument
typedef bool (*PFN)(int);
```

Such a function pointer can target global functions and static functions of native C++ classes. To target non-static functions of native C++ classes, a second pointer concept is necessary, since non-static functions have a hidden argument for the this pointer. This kind of function pointer is called a pointer-to-member function. The following code shows two such pointers, one for member functions of a native type T1 and one for a type T2:

```
// PT1FN is a pointer to a boolean member function of T1 with an int argument
typedef bool (T1::*PT1FN)(int);

// PT2FN is a pointer to a boolean member function of T2 with an int argument
typedef bool (T2::*PT2FN)(int);
```

Delegates unify the concept of C function pointers and C++ pointers-to-member functions. The syntax to define delegates is very similar to the native function pointer syntax.

```
public delegate void SampleDelegate(int);
```

For this one line of code, the C++/CLI compiler generates a type, as shown in Figure 5-8.

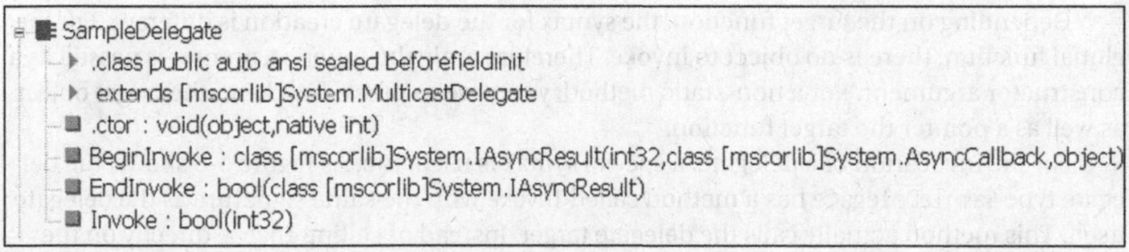

```
SampleDelegate
    .class public auto ansi sealed beforefieldinit
    extends [mscorlib]System.MulticastDelegate
    .ctor : void(object,native int)
    BeginInvoke : class [mscorlib]System.IAsyncResult(int32,class [mscorlib]System.AsyncCallback,object)
    EndInvoke : bool(class [mscorlib]System.IAsyncResult)
    Invoke : bool(int32)
```

Figure 5-8. *A delegate type under the hood*

As this figure shows, the generated SampleDelegate has a constructor (named .ctor) that expects a tracking handle to any object, and a native int (a type of the native pointer size). If the target function is a global function or a static function, a nullptr is expected. For non-static functions, a tracking handle to the target object is expected. The second argument is used to pass a pointer to the target function.

The following code implements a global and a non-static target function and instantiates a delegate for both targets:

```
// delegates.cpp
// compile with "cl /clr:safe delegates.cpp"

public delegate bool SampleDelegate(int);

bool GlobalTargetFunction(int i)
{
```

```
    System::Console::WriteLine("Global target");
    return true;
}

ref class SampleTargetType
{
internal:
  bool TargetMethod(int i)
  {
    System::Console::WriteLine("Non-static target?");
    return false;
  }
};

int main()
{
  SampleDelegate^ d1 = gcnew SampleDelegate(&GlobalTargetFunction);
  SampleTargetType^ targetObj = gcnew SampleTargetType();
  SampleDelegate^ d2 = gcnew SampleDelegate(targetObj,
                                            &SampleTargetType::TargetMethod);


  // ... delegate invocation discussed next ...
}
```

Depending on the target function, the syntax for the delegate creation is different. For the global function, there is no object to invoke. Therefore, only the function pointer is passed as a constructor argument. For a non-static method, you have to pass a handle to the target object as well as a pointer the target function.

For the invocation of a delegate, a special syntax is used, too. As Figure 5-8 shows, the delegate type SampleDelegate has a method called Invoke with the same signature as the delegate itself. This method actually calls the delegate target. Instead of calling Invoke directly on the delegate, an alternative language syntax adapted from the syntax for function pointer invocations is preferred:

```
bool res = d1(10);
bool res2 = d2->Invoke(10);  // possible in VC2005, but not recommended
```

As mentioned previously, delegates support multicasting. For delegate definitions, C++/CLI defines classes that are derived from System::MulticastDelegate, which itself extends System::Delegate. System::MulticastDelegate acts as a linked list of delegates. System::Delegate provides methods that can be used to create and control multicast delegates. As an example, you can combine two delegates into a multicast delegate:

```
SampleDelegate^ dCombined;
dCombined = safe_cast<SampleDelegate^>(Delegate::Combine(d1, d2));
```

Another option to combine delegates is to use the += operator:

```
SampleDelegate^ dCombined2 = nullptr;
dCombined2 += d1;
dCombined2 += d2;
```

When the += operator is used, the C++/CLI compiler generates IL code that calls Delegate::Combine to combine both delegates and assigns the result to the left-hand side of the operation. In a similar way, the -= operator calls Delegate::Remove to remove a delegate from the invocation list of a multicast delegate.

When a multicast delegate like dCombined is invoked, both targets are invoked sequentially. The return value and output arguments of a multicast invocation are determined by the last invocation; however, you should not make assumptions about the invocation order. If you are interested in the outcome of every single invocation, call the helper function GetInvocationList, which the delegate type inherits from its base class, System::Delegate. GetInvocationList returns an array of single-cast delegates—one for every target of the multicast delegate.

Event Handler Delegates

Before an event can be defined, you must either choose an existing event handler delegate or define a new one. The choice of an event handler delegate depends on the information that should be passed with the callback. If no special information is passed, the delegate System::EventHandler can be used:

```
public delegate void EventHandler(Object^ sender, EventArgs^ ea);
```

The type EventArgs does not have instance-specific properties or fields. Therefore, no information is passed with an EventArgs object. Its only purpose is to ensure that the EventHandler delegate follows the common pattern for event handler delegates.

If you want to support a cancellation option, you can use the System::ComponentModel::CancelEventHandler instead:

```
public delegate void CancelEventHandler(Object^ sender, CancelEventArgs^ ea);
```

It is a common pattern to define a new type XXXEventArgs that is derived from System::EventArgs for a delegate named XXXEventHandler. The type CancelEventArgs follows this pattern because it is used in the signature of the CancelEventHandler delegate. The CancelEventArgs class has the Boolean property Cancel, which can be set to true in an event handler implementation to indicate that an operation should be canceled.

For the PageDumped event, there should be a cancellation option, and the current page number should be passed. Therefore, a custom event handler delegate can be defined as follows:

```
public ref class PageDumpedEventArgs
: public CancelEventArgs  // property Cancel inherited
{
  int pagesDumped;
internal:
  PageDumpedEventArgs(int _pagesDumped)
  : pagesDumped(_pagesDumped)
  {}
public:
  property int PagesDumped
  {
    int get() { return pagesDumped; }
```

```
    }
};

public delegate void PageDumpedEventHandler(Object^ sender,
                                            PageDumpedEventArgs^ ea);
```

The delegate `PageDumpedEventHandler` has two characteristic arguments: an `Object^` for the sender and an event-specific argument of type `PageDumpedEventArgs^`. The type `PageDumpedEventArgs` contains all information passed between the code that fires the event and the code that handles the event.

The class `PageDumpedEventArgs` inherits the read/write property `Cancel` from its base class, `CancelEventArgs`. `PageDumpedEventArgs` itself defines the read-only property `PagesDumped`. The event's target function can use the `PageDumpedEventArgs` argument to read the `PagesDumped` property and to modify the `Cancel` property. The code that fired the event can see this modification. In general, information passed by value to the event handler should end up in a read-only property, whereas information passed by reference should be a read/write property of the `EventArgs`-derived type.

When delegates are used for event handling, it is the client's job to instantiate a delegate and pass it to the component. The component can store a handle to the delegate object in a member variable and use it for the callback when the event needs to be fired.

So far, we have not discussed how a client can pass a delegate. The CTS introduces a new kind of type member especially for the passing of event handler delegates. This type member is called *event*. The following code defines a `PageDumped` event in the `FileDumper` component:

```
public ref class FileDumper
: public Component
{
  int pagesDumped;

  void DumpPage(StreamReader^ sr, String^% line)
  { /* ... same as before ... */ }
public:
  [Category("Input")]
  [Description("The name of the file to dump")]
  [DefaultValue("")]
  property String^ FileName;

  [BrowsableAttribute(false)]
  property int PagesDumped
  {
    int get() { return pagesDumped; }
  }

  [Category("Output")]
  [Description("Event is fired when a full page has been dumped")]
  event PageDumpedEventHandler^ PageDumped;

  void Dump()
  { /* ... discussed later ... */ }
};
```

For this new member in the source code, the C++/CLI compiler emits five new members in the managed FileDumper class. First of all, a private backing storage field is defined. This field is a tracking handle to the event handler delegate. Since the event is defined as a public event, there are two public accessor methods defined. These are called add_PageDumped and remove_PageDumped. The first function registers an event handler delegate by adding it to the invocation list; the latter one removes an event handler delegate from the invocation list to unregister it. To fire the event, a third accessor method, raise_PageDumped, is added to the FileDumper class. This method is protected because it should only be possible to fire the event within the implementation of the FileDumper class or a derived class.

Finally, there is the event metadata that binds all the accessor methods together:

```
.event specialname SampleLib.PageDumpedEventHandler PageDumped
{
  .addon instance void SampleLib.FileDumper::add_PageDumped(
      class SampleLib.PageDumpedEventHandler)
  .removeon instance void SampleLib.FileDumper::remove_PageDumped(
      class SampleLib.PageDumpedEventHandler)
  .fire instance void SampleLib.FileDumper::raise_PageDumped(
      object, class SampleLib.PageDumpedEventArgs)
}
```

To call the raise_PageDumped method, you can simply use the delegate invocation syntax:

```
void Dump()
{
  pagesDumped = 0;
  StreamReader^ sr = gcnew StreamReader(FileName);

  String^ line = nullptr;
  while (!sr->EndOfStream)
  {
    DumpPage(sr, line);
    ++pagesDumped;
    if (!sr->EndOfStream)
    {
      PageDumpedEventArgs^ ea = gcnew PageDumpedEventArgs(pagesDumped);
      PageDumped(this, ea); // calls raise_PageDumped(this, ea)
      if (ea->Cancel)
        break;
    }
  }

  sr->Close();
}
```

The metadata of the event, including the Category and Description attributes, is read by Visual Studio to display the event in the events view of the Properties window, as Figure 5-9 shows.

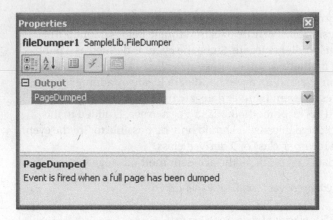

Figure 5-9. *The PageDumped event in the Properties window*

Double-clicking the `PageDumped` event adds a new event handler function to the hosting component. This event handler has the signature specified by the event handler delegate type.

```
private:
  void fileDumper1_PageDumped( System::Object^ sender,
                               SampleLib::PageDumpedEventArgs^  ea)
{
}
```

In addition to that, the wizard adds code to `InitializeComponent` so that the event handler function is registered with the event:

```
void InitializeComponent(void)
{
  this->fileDumper1 = (gcnew SampleLib::FileDumper());
  //
  // fileDumper1
  //
  this->fileDumper1->FileName = "C:\\data\test.txt";
  this->fileDumper1->PageDumped +=
        gcnew SampleLib::PageDumpedEventHandler(this,
                 &SampleComponent::fileDumper1_PageDumped);
}
```

If you use the `FileDumper` class without the component designer, you have to write the event handler function as well as the registration code manually.

Nontrivial Events

The event syntax discussed so far is called *trivial event*. Similar to the trivial properties syntax, the compiler provides the backing storage field and the accessor methods automatically.

There is also a nontrivial event syntax that allows the manual definition of accessor methods. The add and remove accessors are mandatory, but the raise accessor is optional.

Nontrivial events are often used in Windows Forms controls. Even a simple control like System::Windows::Forms::Button has 69 different events. Most clients are only interested in one of these events—the Click event. If all these events were implemented as trivial events, there would be 69 tracking handle fields for the backing storage of the different events in the class. To avoid this overhead, a customized backing storage can be used. Like FileDumper, the Button class is (indirectly) derived from System::ComponentModel::Component. In addition to the designer features discussed previously, this base class provides such custom backing storage for events. Using this backing storage, an event can be implemented as follows:

```cpp
public ref class FileDumper : public Component
{
  // this is a dummy object identifying the event member
  static initonly Object^ eventPageDumped = gcnew Object();

  int pagesDumped;

  void DumpPage(StreamReader^ sr, String^% line)
  { /* ... as before ... */ }
public:
  event PageDumpedEventHandler^ PageDumped
  {
    void add(PageDumpedEventHandler^ handler)
    {
      Component::Events->AddHandler(eventPageDumped, handler);
    }
    void remove(PageDumpedEventHandler^ handler)
    {
      Component::Events->RemoveHandler(eventPageDumped, handler);
    }
    void raise(Object^ sender, PageDumpedEventArgs^ ea)
    {
      PageDumpedEventHandler^ handler =
          (PageDumpedEventHandler^)Component::Events[eventPageDumped];
      if (handler != nullptr)
        handler(sender, ea);
    }
  }

  void Dump()
  { /* ... as before ... */ }
};
```

Summary

If you use .NET to define a system of type definitions that maps your problem domain, you must be aware of the features that .NET's CTS offers you. Many of the CTS features allow you to define relationships between the types you define. Using inheritance, you can define is-a relationships. Interfaces allow different types to support the same operations (behaves-as relationships). Fields can establish has-a relationships. In the next chapter, you will learn how to implement special member functions like constructors and destructors.

■■■

CHAPTER 6

Special Member Functions and Resource Management

The previous chapter discussed how to implement different kinds of managed types and relationships between types. In this chapter, I will focus on the implementation of special member functions for custom managed types. Like in the C++ type system, these special member functions are used to integrate a type's behavior into language and runtime constructs. As an example, constructors and destructors allow you to integrate your type in the object creation and destruction infrastructure.

C++/CLI allows you to implement constructors and destructors for managed types with a language syntax that is very similar to the equivalent syntax for native class definitions. However, in this chapter you will also learn significant differences between constructors and destructors of managed and native types. Being aware of these differences is required to implement special member functions of managed types correctly.

There are several typical C++ features based on special member functions like copy constructors and assignment operators. C++/CLI has adopted most of them for managed types as well. However, these special member functions are not language interoperable. Therefore, you should not define them in public types. Nevertheless, many of these features can be powerful implementation helpers.

Object Construction

Like constructors of C++ classes, constructors of managed types can have a member initialization list and a body. The following code shows both options:

```
ref class FileDumper
{
  FileStream^ fs;
  StreamReader^ sr;

public:
  FileDumper(String^ filename)
  : fs(gcnew FileStream(filename, FileMode::Open))     // member initialization list
  {
```

```
    // rest of initialization is done in constructor's body
    sr = gcnew StreamReader(fs);
  }


  /* remaining functions elided for clarity */
};
```

It is also possible to catch exceptions thrown during member initialization or in the constructor's body with the following C++-like function-try block syntax:

```
FileDumper::FileDumper(String^ filename)
try
: fs(gcnew FileStream(filename, FileMode::Open))
{
  sr = gcnew StreamReader(fs);
}
catch (FileNotFoundException^ ex)
{
  /* ... clean up intermediate resources and handle exception here ... */
}
```

Like in C++, exceptions handled in a catch block of a function-try block are automatically rethrown if the catch block does not throw another exception. You should use function-try blocks to translate a caught exception to an exception that your constructor is supposed to throw.

When defining your own constructors for a custom managed type, you must be aware of the following two significant differences:

- Virtual functions that are called on an object while it is constructed are dispatched differently.

- The order in which dependent constructors are called is different.

Virtual Functions Called on an Object During Construction Time

To understand the difference in the way virtual functions are dispatched on an object while it is constructed, it is necessary to understand the details of virtual function calls on C++ classes and managed classes. Since the CTS does not support multiple inheritance, I will ignore complex multiple inheritance scenarios in the discussion of native virtual functions here.

Virtual functions of native classes are dispatched via the famous vtable (virtual function table). A *vtable* is an array of pointers to virtual functions that a class introduces, inherits, or overrides. In the following code, the class Derived inherits two virtual functions (f1 and f2); one of them is overridden (f2). Furthermore, it introduces the virtual function f3:

```
class Base                 // Base does not inherit virtual functions
{
public:
```

```
  virtual void f1();    // Base introduces the virtual functions f1 ...
  virtual void f2();    // ... and f2
};

class Derived
: public Base          // Derived inherits f1 and f2 from Base
{
public:
  virtual void f2();    // Derived overrides f2
  virtual void f3();    // Derived introduces f3
};
```

For every type that introduces or overrides at least one virtual function, the compiler generates a vtable. For every virtual function that has been inherited or introduced, there is one pointer in the vtable. In the preceding code, Base does not inherit a virtual function, but it introduces f1 and f2. Therefore, its vtable has two pointers. Since Derived inherits two virtual functions (f1 and f2) and introduces a further one (f3), the Derived class's vtable has three pointers.

Pointers in the vtable appear in the order in which they are declared, from the original base class via all other base classes to the class itself. This ensures that a vtable of a derived class starts with pointers for the same virtual functions as the vtable of its base class. These function pointers are either pointers to inherited virtual functions or pointers to overrides. Due to the compatibility of a vtable for a derived class with the vtable of its base class, a derived class's vtable can be treated as a specialization of its base class's vtable. Figure 6-1 shows two classes and their vtables.

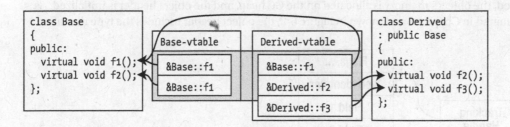

Figure 6-1. *Classes and vtables*

Every instance of a class that has at least one virtual function contains a pointer to a vtable (vptr). When a virtual function is called via a pointer or a reference, this vtable pointer is used to determine the address of the most derived function at runtime. This implementation ensures that overrides provided by a derived class are called.

However, virtual functions called on partially constructed objects are not always resolved to the most derived override. To understand this, it is necessary to discuss the construction order of native classes.

Every constructor first calls its base class constructor until the root of the object hierarchy is reached. Instead of initializing the vtable pointer once to refer to the vtable of the most derived class, each base class constructor in the object hierarchy initializes the vtable pointer to refer to the vtable of its class. For the classes Base and Derived, the compiler would automatically generate default constructors. Since Base is the root of the inheritance hierarchy, there are no further base class constructors to call. Therefore, the constructor of Base would only initialize the vtable pointer so that it refers to the vtable of Base. The Derived constructor would first call the Base constructor and then initialize the vtable pointer to the Derived vtable.

The vtable of a native class only knows functions defined either in the class itself or its base classes. Virtual functions called from a constructor or from a function that is directly or indirectly called from a constructor are dispatched to virtual functions known by the constructor's class, even if the class that is actually instantiated provides an override. For example, assume that Base has the following constructor:

```
Base::Base()
{
  f2(); // virtual function call
}
```

Even if the Base constructor is created during the construction of a Derived instance, the function Base::f2 is called—not the more derived function Derived::f2.

At first view, this may seem strange, because it is the intention of virtual functions to call specialized implementations if a derived class provides them. However, if the most derived virtual function (e.g., Derived::f2) were called during construction time, it would be possible for overriding methods to be called even though the constructor of the derived class that provides the override has not been executed yet. This could easily cause access to an uninitialized state of the derived class.

The CTS uses a different approach to instantiate a managed class. Before a constructor is called, the object's memory is allocated on the GC heap, and the object header is initialized. As explained in Chapter 2 and shown in Figure 6-2, the object header includes the type identifier.

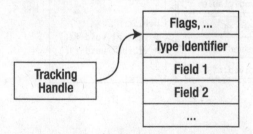

Figure 6-2. *A tracking handle referring to a managed object*

The type identifier is initialized to the concrete type of the new instance before any constructors are called. This implies that the most derived virtual functions are called even during construction time. As a consequence, an overriding function can access uninitialized fields because the constructor of the overriding class has not finished yet. The following code shows how virtual function calls on partly constructed managed types can cause a problem:

```
// ctorVirtCall.cpp
// cl /clr:safe ctorVirtCall.cpp
```

```
using namespace System;

public ref class Base abstract
{
public:
  Base()
  {
    Dump();
  }
  virtual void Dump()
  {
    // this function is not called when a Derived instance is created
  }
};

public ref class Derived : Base
{
  int x;
public:
  Derived()
  {
    x = 42;
  }
  virtual void Dump() override
  {
    Console::WriteLine("x = {0}", x);
  }
};

int main()
{
  gcnew Derived(); // output: x = 0
}
```

Even though x is initialized to 42 in the Derived constructor, Derived::Dump writes the text x = 0 to the console. When a new Derived object is created, the body of the Base constructor is executed before the body of the Derived constructor. When Derived::Dump is called in the Base constructor, x has not yet been initialized to 42, and its default initialized value is 0.

Order of Calls to Dependent Constructors

To reduce the risk of accessing uninitialized state, the construction order for managed types has been changed. For native classes, the base class constructor is called first, followed by the field constructors, in the order of the field declarations. Base class initializations and field initializations can be influenced with the member initialization list. Fields of managed classes are also initialized in declaration order, but in contrast to the initialization of native classes, field initialization is done *before* the base class constructor is called. The following code shows the initialization order of ref class types:

```cpp
// InitOrder.cpp
// CL /clr:safe InitOrder.cpp

using namespace System;

int f(String^ str, int i)
{
  Console::WriteLine(str);
  return i;
}

ref class Base
{
private protected:
  Base()
  {
    Console::WriteLine("executing Base::Base");
  }
};

ref class Derived : Base
{
  int i;
  int j;

public:
  Derived()
  : Base(),
    j(f("initializing Derived::j", 42)),
    i(f("initializing Derived::i", 42))
  {
    Console::WriteLine("executing Derived::Derived");
  }
};

int main()
{
  gcnew Derived();
}
```

When you execute this code, the following output will appear:

```
initializing Derived::i
initializing Derived::j
executing Base::Base
executing Derived::Derived
```

As the output shows, the fields are initialized first. If Base and Derived were native classes, then Base::Base would be executed before the fields are initialized. As in the C++ type system, member variables are initialized in declaration order. Since the field i is declared before j, it is initialized first, even though j appears first in the member initialization list.

To avoid the problems discussed here, two rules should be considered as follows:

- Try to ensure that you don't call virtual functions on partially constructed objects. Calling virtual functions on partially constructed objects is the root of all the evil discussed here. Sometimes, virtual functions are called indirectly, which makes it difficult to detect such a call. For example, if your constructor calls Console::WriteLine passing this as an argument, the virtual function ToString is called internally. If a constructor adds an entry to a hash table using this as a key, GetHashCode and Equals are called internally.

- Prefer using the member initialization list over initializations in the constructor's body. This can reduce the risk of accessing uninitialized state. To solve the problem in the preceding sample code, you can simply modify the Derived constructor's code from the following variant:

```
Derived()
{
  x = 42;
}
```

to this one:

```
Derived()
: x (42)
{}
```

Object Destruction

There are also significant differences in the way objects are destroyed. In C++, object destruction and memory reclamation are coupled. For a native pointer p, the C++ compiler translates the statement

```
delete p;
```

into native code that checks whether p is not a null-pointer, and calls the destructor, followed by the delete operator. The delete operator can then hand the object's memory back to the heap so that this memory can be used for later memory allocations.

Since managed objects are always allocated on the garbage-collected heap, the GC is responsible for the memory cleanup. The timing of this memory cleanup is up to the GC. This is often called nondeterministic cleanup, because a programmer should not make assumptions about the point in time when an object is garbage-collected.

In addition to managed memory, objects on the GC heap often contain further resources. For example, a FileStream internally wraps a native file handle. For resources other than memory on the GC heap, it is often necessary to ensure deterministic cleanup.

In native classes, destructors play an important role for ensuring deterministic cleanup. C# and C++ Managed Extensions support a destructor-like syntax for managed types; however, in both languages, these special functions do *not* support deterministic cleanup. Instead of that, they can be used to provide nondeterministic cleanup by implementing a so-called finalizer. Due to its nondeterministic character, this finalizer concept is fundamentally different from the concept of destructors in native types. Since finalizers should only be implemented in special cases, I defer that discussion to Chapter 11.

The CTS does not have a concept for destructors, but you can implement a special .NET interface to support a destructor-like deterministic resource cleanup. This interface is called System::IDisposable. The following code shows how it is defined:

```
namespace System
{
  public interface class IDisposable
  {
    void Dispose();
  };
}
```

IDisposable is implemented by classes containing non-memory resources. Many types in the FCL implement this interface. System::IO::FileStream—.NET's wrapper around the Win32 File API—is one example.

For a user of a class library, the implementation of IDisposable provides the following two pieces of information:

- It acts as an indicator that instances should be cleaned up properly.

- It provides a way to actually do the cleanup—calling IDisposable::Dispose.

As a C++/CLI developer, you seldom work with the IDisposable interface directly, because this interface is hidden behind language constructs. Neither is IDisposable implemented like a normal interface, nor is its Dispose method called like a normal interface method.

Destructors of the C++ type system and implementations of IDisposable::Dispose in managed classes are so comparable that the C++/CLI language actually maps the destructor syntax to an implementation of IDisposable::Dispose. If a ref class implements a function with the destructor syntax, C++/CLI generates a managed class that implements IDisposable so that the programmer's destructor logic is executed when IDisposable::Dispose is called.

The following code shows a simple ref class with a destructor:

```
public ref class AManagedClassWithDestructor
{
  ~AManagedClassWithDestructor()
  { /* ... */ }
};
```

The following pseudocode shows that this ref class is complied to a managed class that implements IDisposable:

```
ref class ManagedClassWithDestructor : IDisposable
{
public:
```

```
  virtual void Dispose() sealed
  {
    Dispose(true);

    // Remainder of Dispose implementation will be discussed in Chapter 11
  }

protected:

  virtual void Dispose(bool disposing)
  {
    if (disposing)
      ~ManagedClassWithDestructor (); // call destructor
    else
      // non-disposing case will be discussed in Chapter 11
  }

private:
  ~ManagedClassWithDestructor ()
  {
    /* destructor code provided by the programmer*/
  }

  // other members not relevant here
}
```

The compiler-generated IDisposable implementation follows a common pattern for deterministic cleanup. This pattern is used to implement finalizers as well as the IDisposable interface. Aspects of this pattern are related to finalization and will be discussed in Chapter 11. In this chapter, I will cover how this pattern supports implicit virtual destruction.

Even though the destructor of the managed class is not marked as virtual, it has the same behavior as a virtual destructor of a native class—it is automatically ensured that the most derived destructor is called even if the object is deleted via a tracking handle of a base class type.

Key to the virtual destruction of managed classes is the Dispose function that takes a Boolean parameter. Notice that this function is a *virtual* function. If you derive a class from ManagedClassWithDestructor and implement a destructor in the derived class as well, the compiler will generate a managed class that inherits the IDisposable implementation from ManagedClassWithDestructor, instead of implementing IDisposable again. To override the destruction logic, the compiler overrides the virtual function void Dispose(bool), as shown in the following pseudocode:

```
// pseudocode
ref class DerivedFromManagedClassWithDestructor : ManagedClassWithDestructor
{
protected:
  virtual void Dispose(bool disposing) override
  {
```

```
    if (disposing)
    {
      try
      {
        ~DerivedFromManagedClassWithDestructor(); // call destructor
      }
      finally
      {
        // call base class constructor even when an exception was thrown in
        // the destructor of the derived class
        ManagedClassWithDestructor::Dispose(true);
      }
    }
    else
      // non-disposing case will be discussed in Chapter 11
  }

private:
  ~DerivedFromManagedClassWithDestructor()
  {
    /* destructor code provided by the programmer*/
  }

  // other members not relevant here
}
```

Disposing Objects

From the client perspective, IDisposable is hidden behind language constructs, too. There are different options to call IDisposable::Dispose. If you have a tracking handle, you can simply use the delete operator. This does not free the object's memory on the GC heap, but it calls IDisposable::Dispose on the object. The next block of code shows how the delete operator can be used:

```
// deletingObjects.cpp
// compile with "CL /clr:safe deletingObjects.cpp"

int main()
{
  using System::Console;
  using namespace System::IO;

  FileStream^ fs = gcnew FileStream("sample.txt", FileMode::Open);
  StreamReader^ sr = gcnew StreamReader(fs);
  Console::WriteLine(sr->ReadToEnd());
  delete sr;    // calls Dispose on StreamReader object
  delete fs;    // calls Dispose on FileStream object
}
```

Similar to native pointers, you can use the delete operator on a nullptr handle. The C++/CLI compiler emits code that checks if the tracking handle is nullptr before calling IDisposable::Dispose.

Notice that you can use the delete operator on any tracking handle expression. It is not a requirement that the tracking handle is of a type that actually implements IDisposable. If the type of the tracking handle passed does not support IDisposable, it is still possible that the handle refers to an object of a derived type that implements IDisposable. To handle such a situation, the delete operator for tracking handles can check at runtime whether the referred instance can be disposed. Figure 6-3 shows this scenario.

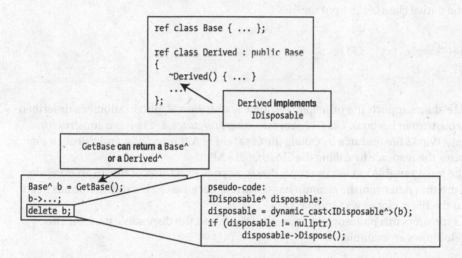

Figure 6-3. *Deleting handles of types that do not support IDisposable*

If the type of the expression that is passed to the delete operator implements IDisposable, then the compiler will emit code that does not perform an expensive dynamic cast, but a static cast, as Figure 6-4 shows.

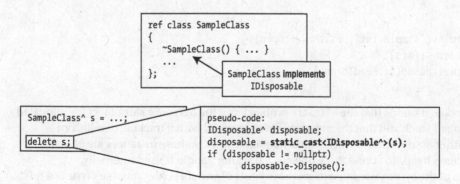

Figure 6-4. *Deleting handles of types that support IDisposable*

The static_cast operator used here does not perform a runtime check. Instead, it assumes that the referred object supports the target type (in this case, IDisposable). If this assumption is not true (e.g., because the type of the deleted tracking handle is a type from another assembly and the next version of the assembly does not implement IDisposable anymore), the CLR will throw a System::EntryPointNotFoundException when Dispose is called.

Cleanup for Automatic Variables

There is a second option for calling IDisposable::Dispose. This alternative is adapted from the lifetime rules of variables in C++. A C++ variable lives as long as its containing context. For local variables, this containing context is the local scope. The following code uses a local variable of the native class CFile from the MFC:

```
{
  CFile file("sample.txt", CFile::Open);
  file.Read( ... );
}
```

The CFile class supports the principle "resource acquisition is initialization," as described by Bjarne Stroustrup in his book *The C++ Programming Language*. CFile has a constructor that allocates a Win32 file resource by calling the CreateFile API internally, and a destructor that deallocates the resource by calling the CloseHandle API.

When the local variable has left its scope, due to normal execution or due to an exception, you can be sure that deterministic cleanup has occurred, because CFile's destructor has been called so that the file is closed via CloseHandle.

C++/CLI transfers this philosophy to managed types and the disposable pattern. The following code shows an example:

```
// automaticDispose.cpp
// compile with "CL automaticDispose.cpp"

using namespace System;
using namespace System::IO;

int main()
{
  FileStream fs("sample.txt", FileMode::Open);
  StreamReader sr(%fs);
  Console::WriteLine(sr.ReadToEnd());
}
```

In this code, it seems that the FileStream object and the StreamReader object are allocated on the managed stack and that the objects are not accessed with a tracking handle, but directly. Neither assumption is true. Like all managed objects, these instances are allocated on the managed heap. To access these objects, a tracking handle is used internally.

Because of the syntax used to declare these kinds of variables (the variable's type is a reference type without the ^ or the % specifier), they are sometimes called *implicitly dereferenced* variables.

For implicitly dereferenced variables, the principle "resource acquisition is initialization" is applied in the same way as it is applied for variables of native types. This means that at the end of the variable's scope, IDisposable::Dispose is called on the FileStream object and the StreamReader object in an exception-safe way.

To understand how this automatic cleanup is achieved, it is helpful to find out what the compiler has generated. Instead of showing the generated IL code, I will show you pseudocode in C++/CLI that describes what is going on during object construction and destruction. This pseudocode does not precisely map to the generated IL code, but it is simpler to understand, as the generated IL code uses constructs that are not very common and handles cases that are not relevant here.

```
int main()
{
  FileStream^ fs = gcnew FileStream("sample.txt", FileMode::Open);
  // start a try block to ensure that the FileStream is
  // deleted deterministically (in the finally block)
  try
  {
    StreamReader^ sr = gcnew StreamReader(fs);
    // start a try block to ensure that the StreamReader instance is
    // deleted deterministically
    try
    {
      Console::WriteLine(sr->ReadToEnd());
    }
    finally
    {
      delete sr;
    }
  }
  finally
  {
    delete fs;
  }
}
```

Similar to the delete operator, implicitly dereferenced variables can be used for types that do not support IDisposable. When an implicitly dereferenced variable is of a type that does not support IDisposable, no cleanup code is emitted at the end of the scope.

Obtaining a Tracking Handle from an Implicitly Dereferenced Variable

To initialize the local variables of type FileStream and StreamReader, the entry point of the preceding sample application contains the following code:

```
FileStream fs("sample.txt", FileMode::Open);
StreamReader sr(%fs);
```

Notice that the argument passed to the StreamReader constructor is the expression %fs. In this expression, % is used as a prefix operator. This operator has been introduced in C++/CLI to obtain a tracking handle encapsulated by an implicitly dereferenced variable. This operator is similar to the & prefix operator (the address-of operator) for native types.

Automatic Disposal of Fields

The concept of automatic disposal is also applied if you define managed classes with implicitly dereferenced member variables. The following code defines a managed class FileDumper with two fields of type FileStream and StreamReader:

```
public ref class FileDumper
{
  FileStream fs;
  StreamReader sr;

public:
  FileDumper(String^ name)
  : fs(name, FileMode::Open),
    sr(%fs)
  {}

  void Dump()
  {
    Console::WriteLine(sr.ReadToEnd());
  }
};
```

For these fields, the compiler generates a constructor that ensures construction of the member variables and an IDisposable implementation that calls the destructors for the member variables. Both construction and destruction of the sub-objects is done in an exception-safe way. The following pseudocode describes what the compiler generates for the FileDumper constructor:

```
FileDumper::FileDumper(String^ name)  // pseudocode
{
  // instantiate the first sub-object
  FileStream^ fs = gcnew FileStream(name, FileMode::Open);

  // if successful ...
  try
  {
    // ... assign tracking handle of new object to member variable
    this->fs = fs;

    // initialize second sub-object
    StreamReader^ sr = gcnew StreamReader(fs);
```

```
  // if successful ...
  try
  {
    // ... assign tracking handle of new object to member variable
    this->sr = sr;

    // call base class constructor
    Object::Object();

    // code for the constructor's body goes here
  }
  // if base class constructor has failed
  catch (Object^ o)
  {
    // ... "undo" initialization of second sub-object
    delete sr;
    // ... rethrow for further undoings
    throw;
  }
}
// if base class constructor or initialization of second sub-object failed ...
catch (Object^ o)
{
  // ... "undo" initialiization of first sub-object
  delete fs;

  // rethrow exception to the code that tried to instantiate FileDumper
  throw;
}
}
```

The code shown here ensures that in case of an exception thrown during object construction, all sub-objects created so far will be deleted. This behavior is analogous to the C++ construction model.

The following pseudocode shows the implementation of the destruction logic:

```
public ref class FileDumper : IDisposable  // pseudocode
{
public:
  virtual void Dispose()
  {
    Dispose(true);

    // Remainder of Dispose implementation will be discussed in Chapter 11
  }
```

```
protected:
  virtual void Dispose(bool disposing)
  {
    if (disposing)
    {
      try
      {
        // dispose 2nd sub-object first
        sr->Dispose();
      }
      finally
      {
        // dispose 1st sub-object even if destructor of
        // the second object has thrown an exception
        fs->Dispose();
      }
    }
    else
      // non-disposing case will be discussed in Chapter 11
  }

  // other members not relevant here
};
```

Analogous to the destruction code that is generated for base classes and members of native classes, the destruction code for managed types is performed exactly in the reverse order of its construction code.

Access to Disposed Objects

Like the native address-of operator (&), the prefix operator % can be misused. The following code shows an obvious example:

```
FileStream^ GetFile()
{
  FileStream fs("sample.txt", FileMode::Open);
  return %fs;
}
```

This function defines a local FileStream variable and returns the tracking handle wrapped by that variable. When that function returns, the local variable leaves its scope, and the FileStream's Dispose method is called. The tracking handle that is returned to the caller refers to an object that has just been disposed.

Accessing an object whose destructor has just been called is obviously not a good idea. This is true for native as well as managed objects. However, access to a destroyed native object typically has more undesired effects than access to a destroyed managed object.

For native objects, destruction and memory deallocation are strictly coupled. For example, when an instance on the native heap is deleted, its destructor is called and the heap can use the object's space for other further allocations. Therefore, reading fields from the deallocated object will likely read random data. Modifying fields from the deallocated object can be even worse, because it can change other objects randomly. This typically causes undefined behavior that is often detected millions of processor instructions later. These scenarios are often difficult to debug, because the source of the problem (an illegal pointer) and the symptoms (undefined behavior because of inconsistent state) often appear unrelated.

Accessing managed objects that have been disposed does not cause access to deallocated memory. The GC is aware of the tracking handle referring to the disposed object. Therefore, it will not reclaim its memory as long as a tracking handle can be used to access the object.

Nevertheless, even with this additional protection level, access to a disposed object is unintended. A caller expects a called object to be alive. To ensure that access to a disposed object is detected, the type System::IO::FileStream (as well as many other disposable reference types) throws an ObjectDisposedException if a method is called on an object that has already been disposed. Throwing a well-defined exception when a disposed object is accessed prevents the possibility of undefined behavior.

For your own classes, you should consider supporting this pattern, too. The following code shows how you can use a simple helper class to protect instances of the FileDumper class against calls after disposal:

```
ref class DisposedFlag
{
  bool isDisposed;
  String^ objectName;
public:
  DisposedFlag(String^ objectName)
  : isDisposed(false),
    objectName(objectName)
  {}

  ~DisposedFlag()
  {
    isDisposed = true;
  }

  // support cast to bool
  operator bool()
  {
    return isDisposed;
  }

  void EnsureObjectIsNotDisposed()
  {
    if (isDisposed)
      throw gcnew ObjectDisposedException(objectName);
  }
};
```

```
public ref class FileDumper
{
  FileStream fs;
  StreamReader sr;

  DisposedFlag disposedFlag;

public:
  FileDumper(String^ name)
  : fs(name, FileMode::Open),
    sr(%fs),
    disposedFlag("FileDumper")
  {}

  void Dump()
  {
    disposedFlag.EnsureObjectIsNotDisposed();

    Console::WriteLine(sr.ReadToEnd());
  }

  void CheckDisposed()
  {
    if (disposedFlag)
      Console::WriteLine("FileDumper is disposed");
    else
      Console::WriteLine("FileDumper is not disposed");
  }
};
```

In this code, the managed class DisposedFlag wraps a simple Boolean variable. In its constructor, this variable is set to false, and the DisposedFlag destructor sets it to true. Since DisposedFlag is used to define an implicitly dereferenced variable in FileDumper, the DisposedFlag constructor is implicitly called by the FileDumper constructor, and the DisposedFlag destructor is implicitly called by the FileDumper destructor.

To throw an ObjectDisposedException if a call is made after the FileDumper is disposed, Dump simply calls EnsureObjectIsNotDisposed on the implicitly dereferenced DisposedFlag field. EnsureObjectIsNotDisposed simply throws an exception if the wrapped Boolean variable is set to true in the DisposedFlag destructor.

Requirements for Destructors of Managed Types

In the MSDN documentation for IDisposable, you can read the following: "If an object's Dispose method is called more than once, the object must ignore all calls after the first one. The object must not throw an exception if its Dispose method is called multiple times. Instance methods other than Dispose can throw an ObjectDisposedException when resources are already disposed."

Since it is legal to call Dispose multiple times on a single object, you must implement managed classes to support multiple destructor calls on a single object. This requirement does not exist for destructors of native classes.

In the FileDumper sample shown previously, no special handling for this case is done. When Dispose is called a second time, it calls Dispose on its child objects again and relies on them to ignore this second Dispose call. If your destructor contains cleanup code, you have to ensure explicitly that cleanup is not done twice. The helper type DisposedFlag can be useful for this problem, too. The next block of code shows how a destructor for FileDumper could be implemented:

```
FileDumper::~FileDumper()
{
  if (disposedFlag)    // already disposed?
    return;            // ignore this call

  /* do your cleanup here */
}
```

The implementation discussed so far is not thread safe. If your class provides thread safety, you must also handle the case in which two threads call Dispose simultaneously. I will address this question in the context of reliable resource cleanup in Chapter 11.

Even though the documentation does not explicitly disallow throwing exceptions other than System::ObjectDisposedException in IDisposable::Dispose, you should not throw exceptions in your destructor function. To understand this restriction, consider the following code:

```
void f()
{
  FileDumper fd("sample.txt");
  DoSomething();
}
```

When an exception is thrown in DoSomething, the FileDumper object will be disposed because it leaves scope before the exception is handled. If the destructor of FileDumper also throws an exception, the caller of f will see the last exception that was thrown, not the exception thrown in DoSomething, which is the one that actually caused the problem.

auto_handle

When the implicitly dereferenced syntax is used, the compiler automatically generates code for creating and disposing an instance. Such a strict coupling of variable declaration and object creation is not always desired. If you want to provide deterministic disposal for an object that is not instantiated by you, but passed to you by foreign code as a return value of a function or in any other way, the implicitly dereferenced syntax cannot be used. The following expression cannot be compiled:

```
FileStream fs = *GetFile();
```

Trying to compile this code fails because the FileStream class (like all other public FCL classes) does not have a copy constructor. Even if there were a copy constructor, the expression would end up in two FileStream objects, and the lifetime rules would be even more complicated.

Visual C++ comes with a special helper template, msclr::auto_handle, which can provide a solution to this problem. This template is defined in the header file msclr/auto_handle.h. The auto_handle template provides exactly the same service to tracking handles that the STL's auto_ptr provides for native pointers. Both helpers provide a scope-based deletion of an object. The STL's auto_ptr can automatically delete objects on the native heap, whereas auto_handle is used for objects on the managed heap. Like auto_ptr, the auto_handle template is only useful in special use cases. To use auto_handle correctly, it is necessary to know these use cases and understand the philosophy of this helper.

The following code shows the most obvious use case for auto_handle:

```
{ // a new scope starts here

  // auto_handle variable wraps tracking FileStream reference
  auto_handle<FileStream> fs = GetFile();

  // ...use auto_handle here

} // when auto_handle leaves scope, FileStream object will be disposed
```

msclr::auto_handle<T> is a template for a ref class that wraps a tracking handle of type T^. In its destructor, it deletes the managed object that the wrapped tracking handle refers to. Here is an extract of this template that shows how the automatic destruction is implemented:

```
namespace msclr
{
    template<typename T>
    ref class auto_handle
    {
        // the wrapped object
        T^ m_handle;

        bool valid()
        {
            // see if the managed resource is in the invalid state.
            return m_handle != nullptr;
        }

    public:
        ... other members ...

        ~auto_handle()
        {
            if( valid() )
            {
                delete m_handle;
```

```
      }
    }
  };
} // namespace msclr
```

The `auto_handle` template implements a special constructor that expects a T^ parameter.

```
auto_handle( T^ _handle )
: m_handle( _handle )
{
}
```

In the sample code just shown, this constructor is used to initialize a new `auto_handle` from the `FileStream^` tracking handle returned by the function `GetFile`.

```
msclr::auto_handle<FileStream> fs = GetFile();
```

Once you have created an `auto_handle`, you will likely want to operate on the wrapped tracking handle. To obtain the wrapped tracking handle from an `auto_handle`, you can call the get function:

```
{
  msclr::auto_handle<FileStream> ah = GetFile();
  FileStream^ fs = ah.get();
  long long fileLength = fs->Length;
}
```

Using the handle returned from get can be dangerous. When the `auto_handle` destructor is executed before you access the wrapped object via the handle returned by get, you will likely access a disposed object.

The `auto_handle` template overloads the member selection operator (operator ->), which allows you to access members of the wrapped object. Instead of calling get to receive the wrapped tracking handle, as in the preceding code, you could also write this more simple code:

```
{
  msclr::auto_handle<FileStream> fs = GetFile();
  long long fileLength = fs->Length;
}
```

Not only is this code more elegant, but using the member selection operator also reduces the risk of accessing a disposed object. If you call get to store the wrapped tracking handle in a variable that is defined in another scope than the `auto_handle` variable, it is possible that the tracking handle will be used after the `auto_handle` is destroyed. In contrast to that, the member selection operator can only be used while the `auto_handle` variable is in scope.

auto_handle and cleanup

`auto_handle` overloads the assignment operator, which allows you to change the wrapped handle. When the wrapped handle is not `nullptr`, and a different handle is to be assigned, the assignment operator first deletes the old tracking handle.

To save the wrapped handle from being deleted by the destructor or the assignment operator, you can call release on the auto_handle. It sets the wrapped handle to nullptr and returns the old handle. It is the caller's responsibility to care about the cleanup of the returned handle.

If you want to find out whether an auto_handle refers to an object, you can use the logical-not operator (operator !). It is overloaded so that it returns false if the wrapped tracking handle is nullptr; otherwise, it returns true.

To avoid double cleanup, the implementation of auto_handle tries to ensure that at most one auto_handle instance refers to a single object. When an auto_handle is assigned to another auto_handle, the wrapped tracking handle moves from the right-hand side of the assignment to the left-hand side. Assume the following code:

```
{
  auto_handle<FileStream> fs1 = GetFile();
  {
    auto_handle<FileStream> fs2;
    fs2 = fs1;
    // fs2 now refers to the FileStream instance, fs1 wraps a nullptr handle

    // ... use fs2 here ...
    // ... don't use fs1 here, its wrapped tracking handle is nullptr ...

  } // the FileStream is disposed here

  // ... don't use fs1 here ...

} // the FileStream is not disposed a second time here
```

When fs1 is assigned to fs2, fs1's wrapped handle is set to nullptr. The auto_handle variable fs2, which was the target of the assignment, holds the wrapped handle now.

The auto_handle template has a copy constructor, which is implemented to support the concept of a single valid auto_handle, as described previously. After a new object is created via the copy constructor, the source auto_handle (the one passed to the copy constructor) no longer refers to an object.

To avoid unintended use of an auto_handle that wraps a nullptr handle, it is necessary to be aware of the typical scenarios in which the compiler implicitly invokes the copy constructor. Even though the rules are very similar for managed types and native types, it is helpful to discuss them.

In the following code, three instances of a managed type T are created, one with the default constructor and two with the copy constructor:

```
T t;            // instance created via default constructor
T t1(t);        // instance created via copy constructor
T t2 = t;       // instance created via copy constructor
```

This code implies that a default constructor and a copy constructor for T exist. Without these constructors, compiler errors would occur. The last line is an example of an implicit call to a copy constructor, even though the syntax looks like an assignment.

Copy constructors are often called implicitly to pass method arguments. As an example, assume the following method:

```
void f(auto_handle<T> t);
```

The following code can be used to call f:

```
auto_handle<T> t = gcnew T();
f(t);
```

Before f is called, the parameter t is copied on the stack via the copy constructor. Since auto_handle's copy constructor is implemented so that only one auto_handle refers to an object, an auto_handle variable will wrap a nullptr handle after it is passed into a function call to f. You should define functions with auto_handle parameters *only* if you intend to pass the responsibility for cleaning up the wrapped object from the calling method to the called method.

It is also possible to define methods that return an auto_handle type. To understand the use case for auto_handle return types, it makes sense to review the GetFile function in the sample code shown previously.

```
FileStream^ GetFile()
{
  return gcnew FileStream("sample.txt", FileMode::Open);
}
```

GetFile expects the caller to dispose the returned FileStream object. However, there is nothing in the signature of this function that can be seen as a hint to this fact. In order to find this out, you have to look into the documentation or, in the worst case, you have to reverse-engineer the GetFile function with ILDASM or another tool. If you don't make sure you know about the semantics of the functions you call, you will likely end up disposing expensive objects either twice or not at all. Neither situation is desired. The following code shows how the GetFile method can be modified so that its signature clearly states that the caller is supposed to do the cleanup:

```
auto_handle<FileStream> GetFile()
{
  FileStream^ fs = gcnew FileStream("sample.txt", FileMode::Open);
  return auto_handle<FileStream>(fs);
}
```

In this version of GetFile, the return type is an auto_handle. If you see such a function, it is unambiguous that the caller of GetFile is responsible for disposing the wrapped object. The constructor of the auto_handle is called to build the auto_handle object that is returned.

For methods that are used only inside your assembly (methods of private classes or methods of public classes with private, internal, or private protected visibility), it is recommended to use the auto_handle as a return type if the caller is supposed to dispose the returned object. However, it must also be mentioned that you cannot use this pattern across assembly boundaries. You can use auto_handle in method signatures only if the calling function and the called function are in the same assembly. For methods that can be called outside the assembly, you must use a tracking handle type instead of an auto_handle, even though this is less expressive.

Copy Constructors and Assignment Operators

The CLR implicitly provides a bitwise initialization and assignment behavior for managed values. When a tracking handle is initialized from another tracking handle, the source handle's binary data (the pointer referring into the object's header) is just copied to the target. This is shown in the following code:

```
FileStream^ fs = GetFile();
    // no copy constructor called - handle itself is just copied
FileStream^ fs2 = fs;

FileStream^ fs3;
    // no assignment operator called - handle itself is just copied
fs3 = fs2;
```

If you just stick with tracking handles and managed values for value type instances, you will never have to use a copy constructor or an assignment operator. Copy constructors and assignment operators of managed types are used only in the context of the implicitly dereferenced syntax.

The copy constructor of a ref class R is only called when an implicitly dereferenced variable of type R is initialized with an expression of the same type or of type R%. The following code shows the first case:

```
// construct a new auto handle from a tracking handle
auto_handle<FileStream> fs = GetFile();

// copy constructor called
auto_handle<FileStream> fs2 = fs;
```

This sample uses the implicitly dereferenced syntax to define the two variables fs and fs2 of the ref class auto_handle<FileStream>. To initialize fs2 with the implicitly dereferenced variable fs, the copy constructor of auto_handle<FileStream> is called. Since the implicitly dereferenced syntax is a special feature of C++/CLI, copy constructors and assignment operators are not language interoperable. However, they are necessary to implement helper classes like auto_handle. To explain these special member functions in a concrete context, I will discuss how they are implemented in the auto_handle template.

A copy constructor of a native type N must have exactly one argument of either N& or const N&. Likewise, a copy constructor of a ref class R must have an argument of type R% or const R%. auto_ptr's copy constructor is implemented as follows:

```
auto_handle(auto_handle<_element_type> % _right )
    : m_handle( _right.release() )
{
}

_element_type ^ release()
{
    _element_type ^_tmp_ptr = m_handle;
    m_handle = nullptr;
    return _tmp_ptr;
}
```

When the copy constructor executes, it calls the `release` function on the `auto_handle` that was passed as a constructor parameter. As explained previously, `release` is used to remove the wrapped handle from an `auto_handle` by just setting the wrapped handle to `nullptr` and returning the old wrapped handle. The handle returned by `release` is then used to initialize the handle of the new instance.

To define an assignment operator, you have to use tracking references in the method declaration, too. The following code shows how the assignment operator of `auto_handle` is defined:

```
auto_handle< _element_type> % operator=(
    auto_handle< _element_type> % _right )
{
    reset( _right.release() );
    return *this;
}

void reset( _element_type ^ _new_ptr )
{
    if( m_handle != _new_ptr )
    {
        if( valid() )
        {
            delete m_handle;
        }
        m_handle = _new_ptr;
    }
}
```

Like the copy constructor, the assignment operator calls `release` on the argument it gets. This ensures that the right-hand side wraps a `nullptr` handle after the assignment. The released handle is passed as an argument to the `reset` function, which deletes the current tracking handle before it assigns the new one.

Summary

This chapter has discussed how you can implement special member functions for managed types. Even though many special member functions of managed types have similar counterparts in the native world, there are subtle but significant differences. At construction time, virtual methods of managed objects are dispatched to overridden implementations even though this can cause access to parts of an object that are not yet initialized. To reduce this danger, constructors for fields of managed types are called before the base class constructor is called.

There are also differences regarding object destruction. The GC is responsible for reclaiming memory. Since its timing is nondeterministic, cleanup of the resources held by an object is decoupled from memory cleanup. To implement code that cleans up an object's resources in a deterministic manner, C++/CLI allows you to implement a destructor. This destructor is mapped to an implementation of the IDisposable interface. C++/CLI provides different alternatives to ensure that IDisposable::Dispose is called. The delete operator can be used to explicitly ensure the Dispose call. The implicitly dereferenced syntax provides a cleanup option that is adopted from the C++ principle "resource acquisition is initialization."

This chapter completes the discussion of the language features that were introduced with C++/CLI. The next chapter explains what you have to consider before you can use these language features to extend C++ projects with managed code.

■ ■ ■

CHAPTER 7

Using C++/CLI to Extend Visual C++ Projects with Managed Code

One of the most important use cases for C++/CLI is the extension of existing projects with managed features. Even if you do not plan to rewrite your complete project purely with managed code, chances are good that your application will need to call managed libraries like the .NET Framework 3.0 APIs—Windows Presentation Foundation (WPF), Windows Communication Foundation (WCF), Windows Workflow Foundation (WF), and Windows CardSpace (WCS). The interoperability features of C++/CLI can provide a perfect solution to this requirement, because you can mix managed and native code into a single assembly, and you can define precisely when a transition from managed code to unmanaged code and vice versa is done.

This chapter first discusses important aspects that you have to consider before you start using C++/CLI to migrate an existing project to .NET. After that, it provides a set of step-by-step instructions for reconfiguring a Visual C++ 2005 project so that you can extend it with managed code. Finally, it gives you recommendations for writing source code that should be compiled to managed code.

Up-Front Considerations

Before you start modifying project settings and adding code, it is necessary to consider what C++/CLI interoperability means for your project, especially for the execution and deployment of your assemblies. Chances are good that the issues I address here are solvable for your concrete project. Nevertheless, to avoid bad surprises, you should know about potential problems before you start migrating a project.

In Chapter 1, I mentioned that Visual C++ provides three compilation models for C++/CLI, which can be chosen with the compiler switches /clr, /clr:pure, and /clr:safe. As soon as you use any of these command-line options (or their equivalent Visual Studio project settings), your code requires that a .NET runtime is installed on the target machines. Precisely spoken, such a .NET runtime is an implementation of the CLI. As mentioned in Chapter 1, the most important CLI implementation is the CLR.

C++/CLI's interoperability features pretty much bind you to the CLR. No other CLI implementation supports the features required for executing mixed-code assemblies. Since most Visual C++ developers build code for Windows desktop and server operating systems, a dependency to the CLR is typically not a problem. However, if you want to migrate projects created in eMbedded Visual C++, you cannot use C++/CLI. This restriction exists because the Compact Framework (the CLI implementation for Windows CE–based platforms) is not capable of executing managed code generated by /clr and /clr:pure. At the time of this writing, it is unclear whether a future version of the Compact Framework will support all the features required by C++/CLI interoperability.

Without a CLR installed on the client machine, your application startup will fail, and you'll get the message shown in Figure 7-1.

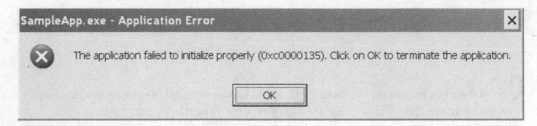

Figure 7-1. *Startup failure of a C++/CLI app executed without the CLR installed*

You must also be aware that assemblies built with C++/CLI require version 2.0 of the CLR. Figure 7-2 shows the failure dialog that appears if only an older version of the CLR is installed on the target machine.

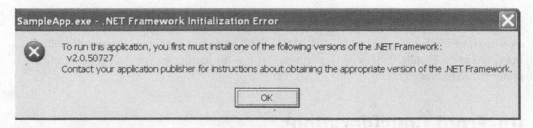

Figure 7-2. *Startup failure of a C++/CLI app executed with only .NET version 1.1 installed*

The Visual Studio project wizard for setup applications and other common setup products automatically creates an installation package that installs the .NET 2.0 redistributable on demand so that you don't have to face the two dialogs just shown.

Nevertheless, considering CLR versioning issues is a must. Even though you can install different versions of the CLR side by side on a single machine, each process can start only one version of the CLR. For example, after a process has started version 1.1 of the CLR, it cannot start version 2.0 or any other version. Even if a CLR version currently running in a process is stopped, it is not possible to start another version of the CLR. (It is not even possible to restart the same version.)

Awareness of CLR versioning issues is especially important when you build mixed-code DLLs. If you want to load a mixed-code DLL implemented with C++/CLI, you must ensure that the process loading the DLL has either started CLR 2.0 (or higher) or that no CLR version has been started in the process so far. In that case, CLR 2.0 will be delay-loaded and automatically started just before the first managed code is executed.

If an earlier version of the CLR has been loaded already into the client process, trying to load an assembly built with C++/CLI will cause a System::BadImageFormatException. To ensure that no other version than version 2.0 of the CLR will be loaded by an application, even if the EXE file does not depend on any version of the CLR or the EXE was built against an earlier version of the CLR, you can use the following application configuration file:

```
<!-- yourapp.exe.config -->
<configuration>
  <startup>
    <requiredRuntime version="v2.0.50727"/>
    <!-- if your app works with a later version of the CLR, add an entry here -->
  </startup>
<configuration>
```

For C++/CLI projects that don't build DLLs, but EXE files, the situation is less complex. EXE projects built with Visual C++ 2005 and C++/CLI automatically load and start version 2.0 of the CLR during application startup. However, you still have to ensure that all assemblies you use can run under .NET 2.0. If you have implemented a dependent assembly for an earlier version of the CLR and want to ensure that it can execute in a .NET 2.0 environment, check the list of breaking changes in .NET 2.0, which is part of the MSDN documentation.

Which Compilation Model Should You Choose?

Whenever you use C++/CLI, whether it is for migrating projects, wrapping native libraries, or other reasons, the choice of the compilation model is probably the most important choice. You should have a detailed knowledge about each compilation model and its advantages, restrictions, and usage cases.

At first glance, the compilation models /clr and /clr:pure seem similar. Both give you backward compatibility with C++. Using both compilation models, you can compile existing code to managed code. Also, both compilation models support the full native type system.

However, there are important differences that make each compilation model the tool of choice for a distinct set of use cases. Table 7-1 shows how you can mix the compilation models at link time. Notice that the compilation model /clr:pure cannot be combined with the compilation model /clr or the native compilation model. This enables the compilation model /clr:pure to ensure that assemblies contain only managed code. Also notice in Table 7-1 that the compilation model /clr is link-compatible with the native compilation model.

Table 7-1. *Mixing Compilation Models*

	/clr	/clr:pure	/clr:safe	Without /clr[:*]
/clr	Yes	No	Yes	Yes
/clr:pure	No	Yes	Yes	No
/clr:safe	Yes	Yes	Yes	Yes
Without /clr[:*]	Yes	No	Yes	Yes

When you extend an existing project with managed code, I recommend minimizing the changes to your existing code. Object file compatibility allows you to keep the native compilation model for all source files that do not benefit from one of the managed compilation models. Since object file compatibility is not supported by /clr:pure, /clr is the compilation model of choice for extending projects with managed code.

Compiling only those files to managed code that benefit from managed execution can very effectively minimize overhead of managed execution. This overhead has various forms, including additional metadata for every native function that is called from managed code, for every managed function that is called from native code (Chapter 9 will cover details about metadata for function calls across managed-unmanaged boundaries), and for every type that is used in managed code (metadata for native types is discussed in Chapter 8). All this additional metadata increases the size of the generated assembly, the amount of memory needed to load the assembly, and the assembly's load time.

Furthermore, managed code is less compact than IA32 assembly code—especially when managed types are used in native code. This can again increase the assembly size and load time. Managed code needs to be JIT-compiled before it can be executed.

Making the wrong choice for the compilation models of your files adds a lot of hidden overhead to your solution. Compiling only those files to managed code that use managed types, however, can be a powerful optimization option.

Load-Time Dependencies to Other DLLs

Since assemblies built with /clr:pure do not have native code, dependent DLLs are loaded differently. This difference is another aspect that must be considered when choosing a compilation model. To get some more information about this difference, consider the following simple application:

```
// DependentDLLs.cpp
// compile with "CL /clr DependentDLLs.cpp"
// or with "CL /clr:pure DependentDLLs.cpp"

// by including windows.h, the function Beep is declared
#include <windows.h>

// this line adds kernel32.lib (the import lib for kernel32.dll)
// the list of linker inputs
#pragma comment(lib, "kernel32.lib")

int main()
{
  Beep(440, 100);
}
```

If you compile this file to native code or choose the compilation model /clr, DLLs like kernel32.dll end up as load-time dependencies of the application. You can easily inspect this using the command-line option /imports from the tool dumpbin.exe. For the application compiled with /clr, the dumpbin output is as follows:

```
Microsoft (R) COFF/PE Dumper Version 8.00.50727.42
Copyright (C) Microsoft Corporation.  All rights reserved.


Dump of file DependentDLLs.exe

File Type: EXECUTABLE IMAGE

  Section contains the following imports:

    MSVCR80.dll
                ... further information about MSVCR80.dll skipped for clarity
here ...

    KERNEL32.dll
                403000 Import Address Table
                4066F8 Import Name Table
                     0 time date stamp
                     0 Index of first forwarder reference

        Import functions table for KERNEL32.dll:
                1F      Beep
                ... remainder of list of imported functions from kernel32.dll
                    is skipped for clarity here ...


    msvcm80.dll
                ... further information about msvcm80.dll skipped for clarity here ...

    mscoree.dll
                4030A8 Import Address Table
                4067A0 Import Name Table
                     0 time date stamp
                     0 Index of first forwarder reference

        Import functions table for mscoree.dll:
                5A      _CorExeMain
```

For the application compiled with /clr:pure, the dumpbin output shows only one
dependency:

```
Microsoft (R) COFF/PE Dumper Version 8.00.50727.42
Copyright (C) Microsoft Corporation.  All rights reserved.


Dump of file DependentDLLs.exe
```

```
File Type: EXECUTABLE IMAGE

  Section contains the following imports:

    MSCOREE.DLL
                402000 Import Address Table
                406270 Import Name Table
                     0 time date stamp
                     0 Index of first forwarder reference

        Import functions table for KERNEL32.dll:
                0         _CorExeMain
```

Generally, an assembly built with /clr:pure has only one load-time dependency, which is always mscoree.dll. For now, it is sufficient to know that the DLL mscoree.dll implements the startup logic of the CLR. (Details of CLR startup will be discussed in Chapter 12.)

Even though only mscoree.dll is listed as a load-time dependency, the other DLLs are still needed to run the application. However, they are loaded on demand at runtime. Chapter 9 discusses how this is done. Loading the dependent DLLs on demand causes changes in the order in which the DLLs are loaded and initialized. This can easily create unintended side effects. Again, this is a good reason to choose /clr instead of /clr:pure.

For extending DLL projects, you are forced to compile with /clr, because /clr:pure does not support exporting functions. Consider the following source code:

```
__declspec(dllexport) void f()
{ /* ... */ }
```

When you try to compile this source code with /clr:pure, you will get a compiler error stating that __declspec(dllexport) cannot be used with /clr:safe or /clr:pure. In general, functions compiled with /clr:pure or /clr:safe cannot be called by a native caller. Details of this restriction will be discussed in Chapter 9.

Why Should You Use /clr:pure at All?

After all these arguments against /clr:pure, you probably want to ask the question, "Why should /clr:pure be used at all?" Well, there are two special restrictions of mixed-code assemblies that can be bypassed with /clr:pure. These restrictions are as follows:

- Mixed-code assemblies must be stored in files.

- Mixed-code EXE files cannot be loaded dynamically into a process.

At first glance, both restrictions sound strange. It seems to be obvious that all assemblies are stored in files. However, it is in fact possible to use assemblies that are stored in different locations. For example, assemblies can be loaded from a byte array containing the assembly's data. For that purpose, Assembly::Load has an overload with an argument of type array<System::Byte>^.

Furthermore, a process can customize the CLR so that assemblies can be found in and loaded from custom locations. For example, SQL Server 2005 customizes assembly loading. Assemblies implementing managed stored procedures for SQL Server are stored in databases instead of files. As a consequence, you cannot use mixed-code assemblies to implement SQL Server stored procedures—only assemblies compiled with /clr:pure or /clr:safe can be used for that purpose.

To store a .NET assembly in a SQL Server database, you have to use the SQL DDL command CREATE ASSEMBLY. Once an assembly is installed in the database, static functions of a managed class can be exposed as stored procedures via the CREATE PROCEDURE command. However, for assemblies created with /clr:pure, some additional steps are necessary. Read the accompanying sidebar for the necessary instructions.

Mixed-code assemblies cannot be loaded from non-file locations because they must be loaded by the operating system's loader for DLLs and EXEs. This is a requirement for mixed-code assemblies because the OS loader has to prepare the native code in a mixed-code assembly for execution. This preparation implies loading imported DLLs and resolving imported functions from the dependent DLLs. Without these steps, the native code parts of a mixed-code DLL will fail to call another DLL.

INSTALLING A /CLR:PURE ASSEMBLY IN SQL SERVER 2005

Installing a verifiable assembly in a SQL Server 2005 database can be done by using a new command named CREATE ASSEMBLY. Installing assemblies compiled with /clr:pure is more complicated because /clr:pure assemblies are unverifiable. This sidebar describes all the necessary steps.

To install an unverifiable assembly in a SQL Server 2005 database, you first need to create an asynchronous key that describes the public key of your assembly:

```
USE master
GO

IF EXISTS (SELECT * FROM sys.asymmetric_keys
          WHERE name=N'MyAssemblyStrongName')
       DROP ASYMMETRIC KEY [MyAssemblyStrongName]
GO

CREATE ASYMMETRIC KEY [MyAssemblyStrongName]
       FROM EXECUTABLE FILE='c:\ MyUnverifiableAssembly.dll'
GO
```

Once you have done that, you can create a new login from the new asymmetric key:

```
IF EXISTS (SELECT * FROM sys.server_principals
          WHERE name = N'MyStrongNamedAssemblies')
       DROP LOGIN [MyStrongNamedAssemblies]
GO

CREATE LOGIN [MyStrongNamedAssemblies]
       FROM ASYMMETRIC KEY [MyAssemblyStrongName]
```

```
GO
```

Make sure that the login you just created has the UNSAFE ASSEMBLY permission:

```
GRANT UNSAFE ASSEMBLY TO [MyStrongNamedAssemblies]
GO
```

Once you have created the login, you are able to create a new unverifiable assembly in your database:

```
USE pubs
GO

IF EXISTS (SELECT * FROM sys.assemblies WHERE name=N'MyUnverifiableAssembly')
        DROP ASSEMBLY MyUnverifiableAssembly
GO

CREATE ASSEMBLY [MyUnverifiableAssembly]
        FROM 'c:\ MyUnverifiableAssembly.dll'
        WITH PERMISSION_SET=UNSAFE
GO
```

Keep in mind that you can only add assemblies created with /clr:pure. If you try to install an assembly that was compiled with /clr, the following error message will occur:

```
"CREATE ASSEMBLY for assembly 'MyUnverifiableAssembly' failed because assembly
'MyUnverifiableAssembly' failed verification. Check if the referenced assemblies
are up-to-date and trusted (for external_access or unsafe) to execute in the
database. CLR Verifier error messages if any will follow this message."
```

The second restriction sounds at least as strange as the first one: it is not possible to load a mixed-code EXE assembly dynamically into a process. Typically, an EXE file is automatically loaded when a process is started. In this case, there is no need to load the EXE file dynamically. However, the Assembly::Load and Assembly::LoadFrom APIs (discussed in Chapter 4) support loading not only DLL assemblies, but also EXE assemblies. Loading an assembly dynamically allows you to reflect on the managed types defined in the assembly. Attempting to load a mixed-code EXE file via an assembly loading API causes a FileLoadException with the following message:

```
Error: Attempt to load an unverifiable executable with fixups (IAT with more than
2 sections or a TLS section.) (Exception from HRESULT: 0x80131019)
```

When the step-by-step approach for project reconfiguration is covered later in this chapter, you will meet such an exception in a concrete context.

Several tools that come with the .NET Framework SDK load assemblies dynamically. As an example, a tool called XSD.EXE loads an assembly dynamically to produce an XML schema containing XML types for managed types defined in the assembly. This tool, as well as all other tools that load an assembly dynamically, cannot be used with mixed-code EXE files. (Notice that this restriction applies only to mixed-code EXE files. It does not to apply to mixed-code DLLs, nor to EXE files built with /clr:pure or /clr:safe.)

The component designers in Visual Studio also try to load the project output dynamically. Since this is not supported for mixed-code EXE files, the component designers have limited functionality if you try to edit components in mixed-code EXE projects. However, instead of compiling an existing project with /clr:pure, you should consider factoring the code that requires the component designer out into a separate DLL.

Compilation Models and .NET Security

.NET introduces a new security model called Code Access Security (CAS). Like garbage collection and JIT compilation, CAS is a .NET feature that cannot be turned off (apart from a debugging option that I will explain later in this chapter). Therefore, you must consider how CAS influences the execution of your code. Failing to consider impacts of CAS up front will likely cause unhappy surprises for your project. For example, if you extend your application with managed features, you can no longer run it from a network share unless you change the default CAS configuration on the client machines!

To understand how CAS impacts the loading and execution of assemblies created with /clr or /clr:pure, you have to take a look at the compilation model that has been silently ignored so far: /clr:safe.

This compilation model is fundamentally different from /clr and /clr:pure because it supports neither the C++ type system nor source code compatibility. If you try to compile the DependentDLLs sample application that I used previously to describe the difference between /clr and /clr:pure with /clr:safe, you will harvest some thousand compiler errors—one for every pointer type and every C++ class, struct, enum, and union used in the header windows.h and all headers indirectly included by windows.h. To compile this application, you can use managed types only. Notice that the following code uses the managed wrapper Console::Beep from the FCL instead of the native function Beep from kernel32.dll:

```
// SafeCode.cpp
// build with "CL /clr:safe SafeCode.cpp"

using namespace System;

int main()
{
  Console::Beep(440, 100);
}
```

Sacrificing the native type system gives you one benefit in return. You can execute your code with restricted CAS permissions. Managed libraries can define CAS permission classes. Instances of permission classes can describe security-relevant operations that can be performed with the managed library. For example, accessing the file system is a security-relevant operation. For the FCL class FileStream, there is also a FileIOPermission class. CAS permissions can be very specific. An instance of the FileIOPermission can, for example, describe read access to a subdirectory named info in your application's base directory.

A set of permissions can be used to define a restricted environment for an assembly. Such a restricted environment specifies how that particular assembly can use types from managed libraries to access security-relevant resources. A restricted environment valid for an assembly is sometimes called a *sandbox* in which an assembly executes. If an assembly that has only the FileIOPermission to read the info directory tries to read the root directory, a System::Security::SecurityException will be thrown by the FileStream class. Each assembly loaded by an application can be executed in its own sandbox of CAS permissions.

Since permissions are granted to types, type safety is a prerequisite for CAS. If you were able to perform an illegal type cast, for example, it would be easy to bypass the security system. To avoid bypassing CAS in this way, IL code can be verified for type safety. Code verification can identify IL code that breaks the rules of the type system. For example, if you push an int on the stack and call a function that expects a System::String^ argument instead, the code verifier will complain.

Pointer-based access to virtual memory could also be used to bypass the security system. For example, an instruction like stind.i4, which can be used to modify virtual memory via a pointer, could be misused to change the state of private variables or even to overwrite return addresses or code. Therefore, the IL code verifier will complain if it finds an instruction like stind.i4.

Using a command-line tool called PEVerify.exe, you can manually verify an assembly. (*PE* stands for portable executable, which is the binary file format of DLLs and EXE files.) If you try to verify an application built with /clr:pure, you will harvest a bunch of verification errors. For applications and DLLs built with /clr, the PEVerify tool gives you an even more rigid reply:

```
C:>PEVerify MixedCodeApp.exe
```

```
Microsoft (R) .NET Framework PE Verifier.  Version  2.0.50727.42
Copyright (c) Microsoft Corporation.  All rights reserved.

[MD]: Unverifiable PE Header/native stub.
1 Error Verifying autoPInvoke.exe
```

Only assemblies built with /clr:safe can be successfully verified using PEVerify. Assemblies built with /clr or /clr:pure implicitly require features that are not verifiable. For example, to use native types, the C++/CLI compiler emits IL instructions that use pointers for read and write access to virtual memory.

In addition to verifying code with PEVerify, code can be verified on the fly during JIT compilation. However, this feature is only turned on if you execute in a sandbox. If an assembly cannot be verified, this does not imply that the assembly does bad things, it only means that the code verifier cannot *guarantee* that it *does not do bad things*. On the one hand, code verification is a requirement for sandboxed execution; on the other hand, assemblies built with /clr and /clr:pure fail to pass code verification. Even if you do not use unverifiable features in your source code, assemblies built with /clr or /clr:pure are not verifiable, because unverifiable features are used during assembly startup.

In order that CAS problems with /clr and /clr:pure assemblies are uncovered as soon as possible, these assemblies refuse to load if they would end up in a sandbox that has turned on code verification during JIT compilation. You can verify this by inspecting an assembly's manifest. If you find metadata like the following (shown in bold), you are likely looking at an assembly built with /clr or /clr:pure:

```
.assembly MixedCodeAssembly
{
  .permissionset reqmin
              = {[mscorlib]System.Security.Permissions.SecurityPermissionAttribute =
                    {property bool 'SkipVerification' = bool(true)}}

  // ... other assembly related metadata elided for clarity ...
}
```

CAS was introduced with .NET so that assemblies that come from partially trusted locations like network shares and the Web are automatically executed in restricted environments. CAS grants permissions to an assembly depending on its origin. The rules according to which permissions are granted can be configured with so-called security policies. When the default security policies of .NET 2.0 are used, permissions are granted based on zones specified in the Internet options on your machine (choose Internet Options from the Control Panel, and select the Security tab to configure these zones).

- Assemblies loaded from the local intranet zone execute with restricted permissions. For example, there are no permissions to use the File IO APIs (FileStream, File, Path, etc.) from the FCL. There are also no permissions to call native code (which could be used to bypass File IO APIs).

- Assemblies from the Internet zone or from the trusted zone execute with even more restricted permissions. For example, they cannot use certain parts of the Windows Forms API.

- Assemblies from the restricted zone are granted no permissions at all (not even the permission to execute code).

- Assemblies directly loaded from a local drive execute with no CAS restrictions. In the CAS terminology, this is called execution with full-trust permissions.

When the default .NET security policy is valid, all your mixed-code or /clr:pure assemblies will be loaded into a sandbox with restricted permissions if they come from another location than a local drive. All these sandboxes imply code verification. Since assemblies built with /clr or /clr:pure refuse to load if they are executed in a sandbox with code verification, you can only load them from a local drive unless you modify the default security policy!

To check if a problem is related to CAS, you can turn off CAS temporarily with the following command line:

```
CasPol.exe -s off
```

As a result, you will see the following output:

```
Microsoft (R) .NET Framework CasPol 2.0.50727.42
Copyright (c) Microsoft Corporation.  All rights reserved.

CAS enforcement is being turned off temporarily. Press <enter> when you want to
restore the setting back on.
```

Notice that CAS is turned on again as soon as you press Enter. Terminating the application any other way will automatically turn on CAS, too. You should also be aware that you need administrator privileges to turn off CAS.

Adapting the Security Policy for Assemblies Using C++/CLI Interoperability

If you want to enable your assemblies built with /clr or /clr:pure to be loaded and executed from network shares or other partially trusted sources, you have to grant these assemblies full-trust permissions independent of their location. However, you should grant full-trust permissions only to signed assemblies. As mentioned in Chapter 4, signing can ensure that modifications made to the assembly after it was signed are detected. If a hacker patches the assembly to inject malicious code, the modification is detected before the assembly is executed in a full-trust environment.

There are different options to reconfigure the CLR so that all assemblies signed with a special public/private key pair execute with full-trust permissions, even if they are loaded from a source other than the local hard disk (e.g., a network share). For example, you can use a command-line tool called CASPOL.EXE. The following command line shows how you can modify the default .NET security policy so that the assembly MyAssembly.dll and all assemblies signed with the same public and private keys are always executed with full-trust permissions no matter where they have been loaded from.

```
CASPOL.EXE -machine -addgroup 1. -strong -file MyAssembly.dll -noname -noversion
FullTrust -name MyCodeGroupName
```

The CASPOL.EXE tool is a .NET application that uses reflection to load the assembly so that it can extract the public key. However, if the assembly you pass is an EXE file created with /clr, loading the assembly will fail because, as discussed previously, EXEs built with /clr cannot be loaded dynamically.

You can also implement your own code to update the .NET security policy. Appendix A contains a sample application that shows how you can achieve this.

Compatibility with Other Compiler Switches

A few compiler switches are incompatible with managed compilation models. Other compiler switches must be set when /clr[:*] is used. These incompatibilities may also influence the way you migrate a project.

Managed Compilation and the C/C++ Runtime Library

Since the compiler switch /clr:safe does not support native types, safe assemblies do not depend on the C/C++ runtime library (CRT) at all. For the compilation models /clr and /clr:pure, only the DLL variants of the CRT are supported. Table 7-2 shows the compiler switches for choosing a variant of the CRT.

Table 7-2. *C/C++ Runtime Variants*

Compiler Switch	DLL or Static Lib	Debug	Compatible with /clr or /clr:pure?	Remarks
/MT	Static lib	No	No	Default setting when no /clr:* option is used
/MTd	Static lib	Yes	No	
/MD	DLL	No	Yes	Default setting when /clr or /clr:pure is used
/MDd	DLL	Yes	Yes	

Understanding the dependency between the C/C++ runtime and the managed compilation options is important because all linker inputs must either use the CRT in a consistent way or be independent of the CRT. You cannot combine linker inputs that have been compiled with different compiler switches for the CRT. If the project you want to migrate uses the DLL variant of the CRT already, there is no need to reconfigure that part of your project. When this is not the case, you have to touch all linker inputs that depend on the CRT. These linker inputs can either be object files or static libraries. To ensure that your object files don't cause trouble, compile all of them with /MD[d]. To ensure that the correct variants of static libraries are used, you have to modify the linker settings. Usually, all linker inputs except import libraries for DLLs depend on the CRT. Therefore, switching the CRT dependency can be a certain amount of work. If the static libraries your project depends on do not exist in variants that depend on the DLL variant of the CRT, you should leave your project as a native project and provide managed code extensions via a mixed-code DLL that you call from your native project.

Managed Compilation and Exception Handling (/EHa)

When the compiler switches /clr or /clr:pure are used, three exception models must be considered. Obviously, managed exceptions can be thrown when managed code is executed. Native functions called from managed code may throw either C++ exceptions or Win32 structured exception handling (SEH) exceptions. C++/CLI supports handling all of these exceptions in managed code. This will be discussed later in this chapter. The compiler switches /EHs and /EHa can be used to turn on exception handling capabilities. The /EHs switch turns on only C++ exception handling. When you use /EHa, C++ exceptions and Win32 SEH exceptions are supported. The /EHa switch is required for managed compilation with /clr and /clr:pure. Using /EHs causes a compiler error.

Features Incompatible with C++/CLI

Edit and Continue is a controversial feature of Visual C++ and some other languages. It allows you to apply source code modifications during debug sessions. Before the debugger hands control to the debugged application, it checks whether the source files are modified. If this is the case, the compiler and the linker try to ensure that the debugged application is adapted according to the modifications of the source file. Many developers question this feature because it supports the "code first, think later" approach, and often results in incomplete and unrepeatable tests.

If there is at least one file in your project that is compiled with /clr or any of its variants, you cannot use Edit and Continue anymore. In native projects, Edit and Continue requires special debug information, which can be generated with the /ZI command-line option. This switch is incompatible with managed compilation. Instead of the /ZI switch, you should use the /Zi switch. This switch creates debug information without support for Edit and Continue.

Another feature that is not supported for the managed compilation model is runtime checking of code, which can emit extra code to avoid certain pitfalls that are typical for unmanaged code. Runtime checks can be turned on at various levels with the command-line options /RTCu, /RCTc, and /RTCcsu. All these flags are incompatible with managed compilation.

The compiler option /Gm is not compatible with managed compilation, either. This switch can reduce the rebuild time by avoiding recompilations of source files that are not affected by modifications in the included header files. The lack of this switch for managed compilation can reduce the compilation speed; however, if you use the managed compilation models only when they are needed, this overhead can be ignored in many projects.

Reviewing Compilation Models

Before I continue with the discussion of the step-by-step migration, take a look at Table 7-3, which summarizes all the differences between the managed compilation models that I have discussed here.

Table 7-3. *Comparing the Compilation Models*

	/clr	/clr:pure	/clr:safe
Can C++ source code be compiled to managed code?	Yes	Yes	No
Can source code use native types?	Yes	Yes	No
Can generated object files be linked with native object files to produce a mixed-code assembly?	Yes	No	Yes, but at the expense of the benefits of /clr:safe
Can managed code in the resulting assembly be verifiably type safe? (Required if assembly should execute with restricted .NET permissions)	No	No	Only if all linker inputs are compiled with /clr:safe
Can the resulting assembly be loaded from a network share?	Only if the default security settings are adapted	Only if the default security settings are adapted	Only if all linker inputs are compiled with /clr:safe

	/clr	/clr:pure	/clr:safe
Must the assembly be loaded by the OS loader for all dependent DLLs to be loaded correctly?	Yes	No	No, unless you produce a mixed-code assembly, because of other linker inputs that were compiled with /clr or to native code
Can the assembly be loaded via System::Reflection::Assembly::Load[From]?	DLL: Yes EXE: No	Yes	Yes, unless you produce a mixed-code EXE
Does the resulting assembly depend on the C/C++ runtime DLLs?	Yes	Yes	No, unless you produce a mixed-code assembly
Can the compilation model be used for extending existing projects with .NET features?	Yes	No	No
Can the assembly export functions to native clients?	Yes	No	No
Can the compilation model be used for wrapping native libraries?	Yes, unless you want to host in customized CLR environments like SQL Server 2005, or unless you have to execute in restricted CAS environments	Yes, but it makes sense only in rare scenarios	Yes, but it can be a lot of work and makes sense only if the assembly is executed in a restricted CAS environment

Step by Step

The next sections introduce a step-by-step approach that I recommend for reconfiguring a project for C++/CLI. This approach has several goals as follows:

- Partial migration and short iterations—in this context, iteration is the timeframe from one buildable and testable state of your project to the next. Shorter iterations give you more options to test your project's output. If a test fails, it is likely caused by changes made since the last iteration. This can simplify the error tracking significantly.

- Minimizing impact on existing code.

- Minimizing overhead of managed execution.

Step 1: Modifying Settings at the Project Level

To migrate to managed compilation, you should start by modifying properties at the project level. Project-level properties are inherited by all project items (source files); however, for a project item, you can explicitly overwrite inherited settings. The very first setting that you should look at is the choice of the CRT variant. Figure 7-3 shows how you can find and modify this setting.

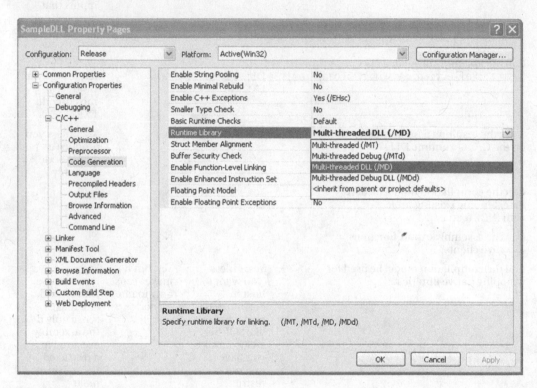

Figure 7-3. *Project properties*

As discussed previously, it is a requirement to ensure that the DLL variant of the CRT is used. Therefore, modifying this setting can require modifications of the linker settings, too.

Typically, you choose /MDd for the debug configuration and /MD for the release configuration. In contrast to the CRT choice, all other settings for projects and project items that are mentioned here should be specified equally for the build and the release configuration (and all other configurations you may have defined in your solution).

My personal preference is to turn off generation of debug symbols with information for Edit and Continue at the project level, too. It does not make sense to generate debug symbols with Edit and Continue information for any of the source files—whether they are compiled to native or managed code. This extra information would be an overhead without benefit, because Edit and Continue is not supported for managed and mixed-code assemblies—

neither in managed nor native debug sessions. To turn on the /Zi switch, open the project properties dialog, select the property Configuration Properties ➤ C/C++ ➤ General ➤ Debug Information Format, and set it to Program Database (/Zi).

I do not recommend setting /clr or /clr:pure at the project level. To avoid unnecessary overhead, you should retain the native compilation model for all existing source files and add new files that are compiled to managed code. This minimizes the impact on your existing code, and can significantly reduce the overhead that comes with managed code, especially the overhead for metadata and JIT compilation.

Step 2: Creating a Second Precompiled Header

Before starting to write code that uses managed types and constructs, I recommend further preparation steps. If your project has a precompiled header (typically called stdafx.pch), you will not be able to use that one for files compiled to managed code. A source file can only use a precompiled header that was created with the same compilation model. Since stdafx.pch was created without any of the /clr switches, it can only be used by files compiled to native code.

To create a second precompiled header, add a new source file to your project. Name it stdafx_clr.cpp. Add just one line of code to that file:

```
#include "stdafx.h"
```

Set the following properties for stdafx_clr.cpp:

- *C/C++ ➤ Precompiled Headers ➤ Create/Use precompiled headers*: Set this property to *Create precompiled header /Yc*.

- *C/C++ ➤ Precompiled Headers ➤ Precompiled header file*: Set this property to *$(IntDir)\$(TargetName)_clr.pch*.

- *C/C++ ➤ Precompiled Headers ➤ Create/Use PCH Through file*: Set this property to *stdafx.h*.

- *C/C++ ➤ General ➤ Compile with CLR Support*: Set this property to *Common Language Runtime Support /clr*.

- *C/C++ ➤ Code Generation ➤ Basic Runtime Checks*: Set this property to *Default*.

- *C/C++ ➤ Code Generation ➤ Enable Minimal Rebuild*: Set this property to *No*.

- *C/C++ ➤ Code Generation ➤ Enable C++ Exceptions*: Set this property to *Yes with SEH exceptions /EHa*.

Again, make sure you specify these settings for debug, release, and any other configurations that you may have defined.

When you expect that the managed code you intend to write needs other types than your native code, you may consider creating a stdafx_clr.h file to build the precompiled header. In this case, you have to modify the *C/C++ ➤ Precompiled Headers ➤ Create/Use PCH Through file* property to *stdafx_clr.h*.

Step 3: Building and Testing

Your project is now configured to produce a mixed-code assembly. If you build a mixed-code EXE file and the linker property *Configuration Properties* ➤ *Linker* ➤ *General* ➤ *Register Output* is set to *true*, your project will fail with the following error message:

```
Registering output...
RegAsm : error RA0000 : Attempt to load an unverifiable executable with fixups
(IAT with more than 2 sections or a TLS section.) (Exception from HRESULT:
    0x80131019)
Project : error PRJ0050: Failed to register output. Please ensure you have the
appropriate permissions to modify the registry.
```

As the error message says, this error occurs when the EXE file is registered. In native projects, the Register Output linker property is used to register COM servers via the COM registration tool RegSvr32.exe. However, since the EXE file is a .NET assembly, this linker property causes a managed tool called RegAsm.exe to be started instead. RegAsm.exe is a tool that is supposed to register managed types as COM types so that native clients can use these types. To perform the COM registration, RegAsm.exe uses the .NET Reflection API. When it tries to load the mixed-code EXE assembly via Assembly::LoadFrom, it fails, because mixed-code EXE files cannot be loaded dynamically, as discussed earlier in this chapter. This problem can simply be resolved by setting the *Register Output* linker property to *false*.

When you have successfully rebuilt the project, the generated DLL or EXE file is a mixed-code assembly. This significantly changes the startup and the shutdown. Therefore, you should do some tests with your mixed-code assembly. These tests should be run on a developer machine as well as on typical client machines. These tests should also include execution of some native and some managed code parts. If your application uses COM, you should especially step through the code that performs the COM initialization via CoInitialize, CoInitializeEx, or OleInitialize, because there is a certain chance that COM has been initialized during the initialization of the CLR. If COM initialization in your application's code fails because the CLR has initialized the wrong COM apartment type, you should touch the linker property Configuration Properties ➤ Linker ➤ Advanced ➤ CLR Thread Attribute.

If you fear that your existing code might conflict with some services of the CLR, you should do some extra tests. For example, many C++ developers have concerns that the GC could have negative impacts on the responsiveness of the application. To experience the impacts of garbage collection on your code, you can write a few lines of test code that starts a thread to periodically create new managed objects. If this thread is started when the application starts, garbage collections will periodically be done while your native code is executed. Watching or measuring the application's responsiveness can give you useful information. To receive statistics about a running application, the performance monitor shipped with the Windows operating systems (PerfMon.exe) can be used. A performance object called *.NET CLR Memory* provides various performance counters that are useful for this case. Figure 7-4 shows how you can inspect statistics about .NET garbage collection in PerfMon.exe.

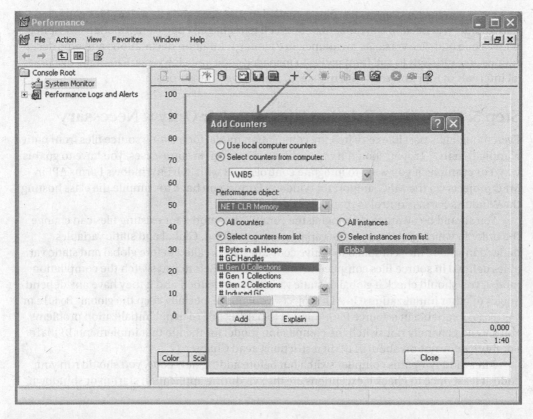

Figure 7-4. *Choosing performance counters from the .NET CLR Memory performance object*

In case you experience other problems with assembly startup, you will likely find useful information in Chapter 12.

Step 4: Adding Additional Source Files Compiled with /clr

To actually implement code that uses managed constructs, you should add another source file and set the following compiler switches:

- *C/C++ ➤ Precompiled Headers ➤ Create/Use precompiled headers*: Set this property to *Use precompiled header /Yu*.

- *C/C++ ➤ Precompiled Headers ➤ Precompiled header file*: Set this property to *$(IntDir)\$(TargetName)_clr.pch*.

- *C/C++ ➤ General ➤ Compile with CLR Support*: Set this property to *Common Language Runtime Support /clr*.

- *C/C++ ➤ Code Generation ➤ Basic Runtime Checks*: Set this property to *Default*.

- *C/C++ ➤ Code Generation ➤ Enable Minimal Rebuild*: Set this property to *No*.

- *C/C++ ➤ Code Generation ➤ Enable C++ Exceptions*: Set this property to *Yes with SEH exceptions /EHa*.

Once you have a project with files compiled to managed code as well as files compiled to native code, you need to call functions compiled to managed code from functions compiled to native code and vice versa. As mentioned in Chapter 1, function declarations and type declarations are sufficient to call from native to managed code and vice versa. Chapter 9 discusses all internals of function calls with managed/unmanaged transitions.

Step 5: Compiling Existing Files with /clr Only If Necessary

Even though it is possible to switch the compilation model for existing source files from native compilation to /clr, you should try to avoid this. However, in some cases, you have to go this way. For example, if you want to integrate controls built with .NET's Windows Forms API in MFC projects via the MFC support for Windows Forms, you have to compile the class hosting the Windows Forms control to managed code.

You should be aware that changing the compilation model for existing files can change the order in which global and static variables are initialized. Global and static variables defined in source files compiled to native code are always called before global and static variables defined in source files compiled to managed code. Before you switch the compilation model, you should check if global or static variables are defined and if they have any dependencies to other initializations. In ATL projects, you must especially keep the global _Module or _AtlModule variable in a source file compiled to native code to avoid initialization problems. You should generally not switch the compilation model for the file that implements DllMain. For more information about DllMain restrictions, read Chapter 12.

After modifying this compiler switch but before adding new code, you should run your code at least once to check if exceptions are thrown during application startup or shutdown.

Handling Exceptions Across Managed-Unmanaged Boundaries

When you mix native and managed code, you often face the situation that an exception thrown in native code must be handled in managed code and vice versa. In native code, there are two exception models: C++ exception handling and Win32 SEH. In mixed code, you also have to care about managed exceptions. The exception handling architecture in .NET has remarkable similarities to the Win32 SEH model. This enables managed code to catch native C++ exceptions as well as SEH exceptions. In addition to these features, native exceptions can also be mapped to managed exceptions if this is required.

Let's start with Win32 SEH exceptions. Even though the following code uses SEH exceptions, it can be compiled with /clr:

```
// ExceptionHandling1.cpp
// compile with "cl /clr ExceptionHandling1.cpp"

#include <excpt.h>
#include <windows.h>

// As I will discuss later, #pargma managed is not recommended; it is
// only used to show exceptions thrown across managed / unmanaged boundaries
// without using two source files
```

```
#pragma managed (push, off)
int f()
{
  int i = 1;
  return 1 / --i;
}
#pragma managed (pop)

int main()
{
  __try
  {
    f();
  }
  __except(GetExceptionCode() == EXCEPTION_INT_DIVIDE_BY_ZERO ?
           EXCEPTION_EXECUTE_HANDLER :
           EXCEPTION_CONTINUE_SEARCH)
  {
    System::Console::WriteLine("Divide by zero exception");
  }

  return 0;
}
```

This code shows the three parts of Win32 SEH: a try block, an exception filter, and an exception handler. When an exception is thrown in the try block, the exception filter is evaluated. This exception filter is an expression that is used to determine how the exception handling proceeds. If it returns EXCEPTION_EXECUTE_HANDLER, then the handler is executed. EXCEPTION_CONTINUE_SEARCH means that the exception is not handled and other filters on the call stack are checked. The IL code generated from the preceding C++/CLI code shows how main is separated into the try block, exception filter, and exception handler.

```
.method assembly static int32
        modopt([mscorlib]System.Runtime.CompilerServices.CallConvCdecl)
        main() cil managed
{
  .maxstack  2
  .locals (int32 filterResult)
begin_:
  call        int32
              modopt([mscorlib]System.Runtime.CompilerServices.CallConvCdecl) f()
  pop
  leave       return_

theFilter_:
  pop

// GetExceptionCode() == EXCEPTION_INT_DIVIDE_BY_ZERO ?
//               EXCEPTION_EXECUTE_HANDLER :
```

```
//              EXCEPTION_CONTINUE_SEARCH
  call          int32
                [mscorlib]System.Runtime.InteropServices.Marshal::GetExceptionCode()
  ldc.i4        0xc0000094     // EXCEPTION_INT_DIVIDE_BY_ZERO
  bne.un        notIntDivByZeroException_
  ldc.i4        1              // EXCEPTION_EXECUTE_HANDLER
  stloc         filterResult
  br        filterReturn_
notIntDivByZeroException_:
  ldc.i4        0              // EXCEPTOIN_CONTINUE_SEARCH
  stloc         filterResult
filterReturn_:
  ldloc         filterResult
  endfilter

theHandler_:
  pop

// Console::WriteLine("Divide by zero exception");
  ldstr         "Divide by zero exception"
  call          void [mscorlib]System.Console::WriteLine(string)

  leave         return_

return_:
// return 0;
  ldc.i4.0
  ret

  .try begin_ to theFilter_    filter theFilter_    handler theHandler_ to return_
} // end of method 'Global Functions'::main
```

Despite all the similarities, there are differences between SEH in managed and native code. As an example, there are differences in the behavior if an exception is thrown inside an exception filter. If you automatically translate Win32 SEH exceptions to C++ exceptions by registering a translator function via _set_se_translator, you should be aware that this affects only catches in unmanaged code. To find more information on exception handling differences, search the MSDN documentation for the article "Differences in Exception Handling Behavior Under /CLR."

Mapping SEH Exceptions to .NET Exceptions

Win32 SEH exceptions can also be caught as .NET exceptions. In the following code, a managed function (main) calls a native function (f), which throws the SEH exception EXCEPTION_INT_DIVIDE_BY_ZERO. In main, this exception is caught in a catch block that handles exceptions of type System::Exception^.

```
// ExceptionHandling2.cpp
// compile with "cl /clr ExceptionHandling2.cpp"
```

```
// As I will discuss later, #pargma managed is not recommended; it is only
// used to show exceptions thrown across managed / unmanaged boundaries
// without using two source files
#pragma unmanaged
int f()
{
  int i = 1;
  return (1 / --i);
}
#pragma managed

int main()
{
  try
  {
    f();
  }
  catch (System::Exception^ ex)
  {
    System::Console::WriteLine(ex->GetType()->FullName);
  }
}
```

If you compile and execute this application, the type name System.DivideByZeroException will be written in the catch block. Most SEH exception codes will be mapped to the type System::Runtime::InteropServices::SEHException. The mapping to System.DivideByZeroException is one of the few special cases. Table 7-4 shows the SEH exceptions for which a special mapping exists.

Table 7-4. *Mapping SEH Exceptions to Managed Exceptions*

Win32 Exception Code	Hex Value	Managed Exception
EXCEPTION_ACCESS_VIOLATION	C0000005	System::AccessViolationException
EXCEPTION_NO_MEMORY	C0000017	System::OutOfMemoryException
EXCEPTION_ARRAY_BOUNDS_EXCEEDED	C000008C	System::IndexOutOfRangeException
EXCEPTION_FLT_DENORMAL_OPERAND	C000008D	System::FormatException
EXCEPTION_FLT_DIVIDE_BY_ZERO	C000008E	System::DivideByZeroException
EXCEPTION_FLT_INEXACT_RESULT	C000008F	System::ArithmeticException
EXCEPTION_FLT_INVALID_OPERATION	C0000090	System::ArithmeticException
EXCEPTION_FLT_OVERFLOW	C0000091	System::OverflowException
EXCEPTION_FLT_STACK_CHECK	C0000092	System::ArithmeticException
EXCEPTION_FLT_UNDERFLOW	C0000093	System::ArithmeticException
EXCEPTION_INT_DIVIDE_BY_ZERO	C0000094	System::DivideByZeroException
EXCEPTION_INT_OVERFLOW	C0000095	System::OverflowException
EXCEPTION_STACK_OVERFLOW	C00000FD	System::StackOverflowException
All other SEH exceptions		System::Runtime::InteropServices::SEHException

As Table 7-4 shows, an access violation (0xC0000005) is automatically mapped to a System::AccessViolationException. This exception type has been introduced in .NET 2.0. In earlier versions of .NET, a System::NullReferenceException is thrown instead. Since this is a breaking change, you can switch back to the old behavior with the configuration file shown here:

```
<configuration>
  <runtime>
    <legacyNullReferenceExceptionPolicy enabled="1"/>
  </runtime>
</configuration>
```

Catching C++ Exceptions

Usually, native C++ exception handling is used much more often than Win32 SEH. C++/CLI allows you not only to catch C++ exceptions in managed code, but also to mix C++ exception handling with managed exception handling. A single try block can have catch blocks for C++ exceptions as well as managed exceptions, as the following code shows:

```
// CPlusPlusExceptions.cpp
// compile with "cl /clr CPlusPlusExceptions.cpp"

using namespace System;

// As I will discuss later, #pargma managed is not recommended; it is only
// used to show exceptions thrown across managed / unmanaged boundaries
// without using two source files
#pragma managed(push, off)
void f()
{
  throw 4;
}
#pragma managed(pop)

int main()
{
  try
  {
    f();
  }
  catch (int i)
  {
    Console::WriteLine("int exception, value={0}", i);
  }
  catch (Exception^ ex)
  {
    Console::WriteLine(ex->GetType()->FullName);
  }
}
```

The first catch block in this code catches C++ exceptions of type int, and the second one catches any CTS-compliant managed exceptions. When a C++ exception of a type other than int is thrown, the CLR's exception mapping mechanism will detect this and map the exception to a managed exception. Since the SEH exception code of a C++ exception (0xE06d7363) is not handled specially, the runtime maps it to an SEHException.

You should always catch C++ exceptions before you catch managed exceptions of type System::Object^, System::Exception^, System::SystemException^, System::Runtime::InteropServices::ExternalException^, and System::Runtime::InteropServices::SEHException^. The first four types mentioned are base classes of SEHException. If a C++ exception is thrown and a catch block for one of the exceptions mentioned here is found, the runtime will map the exception to an SEHException. In the following code, the exception handler for int would never be executed:

```
int main()
{
  try
  {
    f();
  }
  catch (Exception^ ex)
  {
    Console::WriteLine(ex->GetType()->FullName);
  }
  catch (int i)
  {
    Console::WriteLine("int exception, value={0}", i);
  }
}
```

Catching Managed Exceptions in Native Code

Even though it is possible to catch managed exceptions in native code, it is seldom useful. Since native code cannot use any managed types, your exception handler cannot get information about the managed exception that it catches. Managed exceptions are caught as Win32 SEH exceptions with the exception code 0xE0434F4D. The following code catches a System::Exception in native code:

```
// ExceptionHandling3.cpp
// compile with "cl /clr ExceptionHandling3.cpp"

#include <excpt.h>
#include <windows.h>
#include <iostream>
using namespace std;

void f()
{
  throw gcnew System::Exception("Managed exception thrown to native code");
}
```

```
// As I will discuss later, #pargma managed is not recommended; it is only
// used to show exceptions thrown across managed / unmanaged boundaries
// without using two source files
#pragma managed (push, off)
int main()
{
  __try
  {
    f();
  }
  // ('àCOM') evaluates to 0xE0434F4D
  __except(GetExceptionCode() == ('àCOM') ?
           EXCEPTION_EXECUTE_HANDLER :
           EXCEPTION_CONTINUE_SEARCH
    )
  {
    cout << "Managed Exception caught in native code" << endl;
  }

  return 0;
}
#pragma managed (pop)
```

General Hints for Mixed Compilation

The rest of this chapter covers the potential as well as the limits and dangers of certain
features related to mixed-code development.

Avoid #pragma (un)managed

Visual C++ allows you to change the compilation model even within a single file. If you compile
with /clr, you can use #pragma unmanaged to specify that the methods following that directive
should be compiled to native code. Consequently, #pragma managed marks the beginning of a
section of functions compiled to managed code.

```
void fManaged()    // managed compilation is the default if /clr is used
{ /* ... */ }

#pragma unmanaged    // can only be used if you compile with /clr

void fUnmanaged()
{ /* ... */ }

#pragma managed
```

```
void fManaged()
{ /* ... */ }
```

In some other code samples, you may also find the following slightly different approach:

```
void fManaged()    // managed compilation is the default if /clr is used
{ /* ... */ }

#pragma managed(push, off)    // can also be used with native compilation

void fUnmanaged()
{ /* ... */ }

#pragma managed(pop)

void fManaged2()
{ /* ... */ }
```

The option to mix the compilation model within a source file is used to implement certain managed parts of the CRT. For other scenarios, I do not recommend using this feature, because it can cause access to uninitialized global or static variables. If you implement DLLs, you should especially avoid this approach. Chapter 12 provides more information on this topic.

Automatic Choice of Compilation Model: Avoid Warning 4793!

There is another option to mix compilation models within a single source file that is also not recommended—functions that use Visual C++ language features that cannot be mapped to IL code are automatically compiled to native code. Code that uses inline assembly, like the one following, is an obvious example for code that is not mappable:

```
__asm mov eax, 0;
```

Since the IL instruction set does not know about the eax register, the complier cannot map these instructions to IL instructions. A few other language features of Visual C++ cannot be mapped to IL, either. These include setjmp, longjmp, and processor intrinsics like _ReturnAddress and _AddressOfReturnAddress. When the compiler automatically switches to the native compilation model, it reports warning 4793. You should handle this warning by moving the function to a source file that is compiled to native code.

Predefined Macros for Compilation Models

Visual C++ has some predefined macros that allow you to check the compilation model. Using these macros, it is possible to cause a compiler error when a header file is included in a source file compiled to native code, as the following code shows:

```
#ifndef _MANAGED
#error Header xyz.h requires managed compilation.
#endif
```

Table 7-5 shows the different macros and their values depending on the compilation model:

Table 7-5. *Predefined Macros for Managed Code*

Compilation Model	__cplusplus_cli	_M_CEE	_M_CEE_PURE	_M_CEE_SAFE	_MANAGED
Native	Not defined	Not defined	Not defined	Not defined	Not defined
/clr	200406	1	Not defined	Not defined	1
/clr:pure	200406	1	1	Not defined	1
/clr:safe	200406	1	1	1	1
/clr:oldsyntax	Not defined	1	Not defined	Not defined	1

As the following sample shows, checking the different compilation models using these macros is possible—however, not in an elegant way:

```
#ifndef _MANAGED
#pragma message("Native compilation model chosen")
#endif
#if (defined(_M_CEE) && !defined(_M_CEE_PURE) && !defined(_M_CEE_SAFE))
#pragma message("compiling with /clr")
#endif
#if (defined(_M_CEE) && defined(_M_CEE_PURE) && !defined(_M_CEE_SAFE))
#pragma message("compiling with /clr:pure")
#endif
#ifdef _M_CEE_SAFE
#pragma message("compiling with /clr:safe")
#endif
```

Compilation Models and Templates

C++ templates require special attention in mixed-code projects. Templates are typically defined in header files. Before you can use a template type, you have to include the header defining the template type and its members. When a template is used in a file that is compiled to native code, the member functions of the template type are compiled to native code, too. When a source file using a template is compiled to managed code, the template's members are compiled to managed code.

When two source files in your project use the same template and both are compiled with different compilation models, the linker will get two variants of the template's functions: one compiled to managed code and one compiled to native code. In this case, it is up to the linker to decide which version should be chosen. To avoid unnecessary method calls across man-aged-unmanaged boundaries, the linker chooses the native variant of a function if the caller is a native function, and the managed variant if the caller is a managed function. This means that you will likely have both variants of the function in your DLL or EXE file.

Sometimes it is argued that #pragma unmanaged should be used to ensure that a template is compiled to native code even though it is called from managed code. As mentioned before,

#pragma unmanaged is not recommended. In the context of templates, they are often even more misleading. The following code shows a typical attempt to compile a template to native code even though it is used by managed code:

```
// templatesAndPragmaUnmanaged.cpp
// build with: cl /clr templatesAndPragmaUnmanaged.cpp

#pragma managed (push, off)
#include <vector>
#pragma managed (pop)

using namespace std;

int main()
{
  vector<int> vi;
  vi.push_back(5);
}
```

If you build this application, members of the template std::vector such as the push_back function will be compiled to native code. However, if there is a second source file in the project that compiles vector<int>::push_back to managed code, the linker will choose the managed variant instead of the native one when it generates the code for main. Even though you have included the vector in a native section of your source file, the managed variant will be chosen. If you want to ensure that a template is compiled to native code, make sure that you call it from a source file compiled to native code.

Summary

Before you start migrating a native project so that you can extend it with managed types, you should consider what impacts this has. Using managed constructs in your project implies that your code depends on the CLR 2.0 at runtime and that the managed code parts are executed under the CLR's control. All services of the CLR can be beneficial if you know how to use them, but if you are not aware of these services, they can also imply pitfalls. For example, CAS may prevent you from running your code via a network share. In most cases, these pitfalls can be avoided (e.g., by modifying the .NET security configuration).

Once you have finished these up-front considerations, you should follow the step-by-step instructions described in this chapter to migrate the project. Testing is an essential part of this migration because it allows you to detect scenarios that you have not considered up front.

Once the project is migrated, C++/CLI's interoperability features allow you to call managed functions from native functions and vice versa. The functions used so far have had void as a return type, and no arguments. The next chapter covers how and why you can also use complex native types at the migration boundary.

CHAPTER 8

∎∎∎

Mixing the Managed and the Native Type System

Using the step-by-step approach explained in Chapter 7, you can inject managed code parts into a C++ project. Due to the source code compatibility, you can easily call from native code to managed code by just declaring the functions you want to call. However, in the samples discussed so far, the managed functions called from native code and the native functions called from managed code have had void as a return type, and no arguments. For nontrivial scenarios, functions with less simplistic signatures are obviously needed.

The first important thing you have to understand is that if you compile to native code, your source code *cannot* use managed types at all. Just as C doesn't know anything about C++ classes, C++ doesn't know about managed types. In the other direction, the situation looks better. Source code compiled to managed code can use all native types as well as all managed types, just as C++ code can use C structs, enums, and unions, as well as C++ classes. To say this in other words, the C++ type system is the lowest common denominator between sources compiled to native code and sources compiled to managed code.

This means that you have to restrict yourself to the C++ type system if you define methods that act as migration boundaries—all managed functions that should be callable from native code and all native functions that should be callable from managed code can use only native types. However, *any* kind of native type can be used in the method signature. You can use native classes, structs, unions, enums, pointers of any level of indirection, references, and const variants of all native types.

To call a native function or use a native class, you simply include the native header with the function or the class declaration. To define a managed function that native code can call, just make sure that you use only types that C++ understands.

This chapter first covers how C++/CLI maps native C++ types to managed types, which explains why this type compatibility is possible and what happens under the hood. After that, it discusses conversions between managed and native types. Despite the ability to use the C++ type system on both sides, you often have to convert a native type to a managed type and vice versa. For example, if your function has a native string argument so that native clients can call you, you often have to convert that argument to a managed string so that you can pass it into a managed API. Finally, this chapter discusses how managed classes can use fields of native types and how native types can have data members referring to managed objects.

Using Native Types in Managed Code

Even though the C++/CLI compiler silently maps all usages of native types in your source code to functioning IL code, it makes sense to have a closer look at the internals. Let's begin with a simple function:

```
int f(double d);
```

Since all numeric primitives—like int and double—have counterparts with the same binary layout in the managed type system, the C++/CLI compiler simply considers equivalent managed and native primitives as one type. To the C++/CLI compiler, the following declaration is equivalent to the preceding one:

```
System::Int32 f(System::Double d);
```

However, the Visual C++ compiler supports two 32-bit signed integer types: int and long. As a C++ programmer, you can write the following two overloads of the function f:

```
void f(int i)
{ /* ... */ }

void f(long l)
{ /* ... */ }
```

Both int and long should be mapped to System::Int32. However, there must be an option to differentiate both functions. To achieve this, the compiler uses a *signature modifier*. The signature for the function with the int argument just uses the IL keyword for System::Int32, which is int32:

```
.method assembly static void f(int32 i) cil managed
```

The method with the long argument has an int32 argument with a signature modifier to express that the parameter type should be mapped to the native type long instead of int:

```
.method assembly static void f(
            int32 modopt([mscorlib]System.Runtime.CompilerServices.IsLong) l
        ) cil managed
```

At first glance, signature modifiers have a lot of similarities to .NET attributes that are applied to a parameter. Both represent metadata that provides extra information about an argument of a function. However, in contrast to attributes, signature modifiers are part of the method's signature and therefore part of the method's identity. The runtime can differentiate between both overloads when they have different signature modifiers, even if the rest of the functions are the same.

Managed code can also use functions that have native pointer types as arguments, like the function shown here:

```
void f(int* pi);
```

The C++/CLI compiler translates this function into the following IL method:

```
.method assembly static void f(int32* pi) cil managed
```

Most .NET languages do not use this feature, but for C++/CLI interoperability, this feature is essential. IL supports pointers of any type and any level. For example, the C++ type double*** would be mapped to the IL type float64***. To perform read and write operations via a pointer, the IL instruction set has special instructions. To understand these instructions, assume that f is implemented as follows:

```
void f(int* pi)
{
  *pi = 42;
}
```

To map this C++ source code to IL, the C++/CLI compiler generates the following code:

```
// *pi = 42;
ldarg.0        // Push the first argument (int* pi) on the stack
ldc.i4 42      // Push 42 as a 4-byte integer value on the stack
stind.i4       // Pop the top two elements of the stack,
               // store the value in the top element in the address specified by
               // the top - 1 element on the stack
```

The instruction stind.i4 (store a 4-byte integer indirectly) allows managed code to operate on the virtual memory of the running process. Whenever a 4-byte integer value needs to be stored at an arbitrary address in virtual memory, this IL instruction is used. The next code sample combines a read and a write operation:

```
void f(int* pi)
{
  *pi += 42;
}
```

To map this C++ source code to IL, the C++/CLI compiler generates the following code:

```
// *pi += 42;
ldarg.0        // Push the first argument (pi) on the stack (it will be needed
               // by the stind.i4 instruction at the end of this code sample)
dup            // Push it again
               // (it will also be needed by the following instruction)
ldind.i4       // Consider the top of the stack to be a virtual address to a
               // 4-byte integer. Replace the top of the stack with
               // the value that the address refers to
ldc.i4    42   // Push the 4-byte integer value 42 on the stack
add            // Consider the top two elements of the stack to be two 4-byte
               // integer values. Replace these two elements with one element
               // whose value is the sum.
stind.i4       // Store the value on the top of the stack at the address specified
               // by the top - 1 stack element (which is the element pushed in the
               // first instruction of this code sample)
```

In addition to the `stind.i4` instruction, this code contains the `ldind.i4` instruction (load a 4-byte integer indirectly). This instruction can be used to read a 4-byte integer value at a given virtual memory address.

To completely support the C++ type system, C++/CLI must also be able to map C++ reference arguments and arguments with const modifiers to IL code. The following function shows an example of a function with a reference argument:

```
void f(int& i)
{
  i = 42;
}
```

Since a C++ reference has the same binary layout as a native pointer (both simply store addresses), the C++/CLI compiler maps an `int&` to the IL type `int32*`. To differentiate the C++ types `int&` and `int*`, a signature modifier is used again:

```
.method assembly static void
    f(int32*
      modopt([mscorlib]System.Runtime.CompilerServices.IsImplicitlyDereferenced) i)
    cil managed
```

Signature modifiers are also used to differentiate between the functions `void f(int&)` and `void f(const int&)`:

```
.method assembly static void
    f(int32 modopt([mscorlib]System.Runtime.CompilerServices.IsConst)*
      modopt([mscorlib]System.Runtime.CompilerServices.IsImplicitlyDereferenced) i)
    cil managed
```

Notice that pointers, even though they are supported by the IL, are not first-class managed types, because they do not fit into the picture of a single rooted type system with `System::Object` as the ultimate root. For example, the following code does not compile:

```
using namespace System;

int main()
{
  int i = 42;
  int *pi = &i;
  Console::WriteLine("pi = {0}", pi); // this line will cause a compiler error
}
```

The C++/CLI compiler will refuse to compile this code because no matching overload of `Console::WriteLine` could be found. One might expect that the overload `Console::WriteLine( String^ formatString, Object^ arg )` should match, because the first argument passed matches `String^` and the type of the second argument is `Object^`, which is known as the ultimate root. However, there is no standard conversion from `int*` to `Object^`. Trying to use a cast to `Object^` will also fail:

```
  Console::WriteLine("pi = {0}", (Object^)pi);
    // error: cannot convert from int* to Object^
```

As discussed in Chapter 2, a variable of type Object^ is a reference to a managed object on the GC heap. Apart from a few rare cases, native pointers refer to native memory, not into the managed heap. Therefore, it makes sense that a conversion cannot be done. If a native pointer were a value type, it would be boxed so that an Object^ could refer to a new managed object that contains the native pointer value. Native pointers are not treated like value types, but there is a special managed value type that encapsulates native pointers: System::IntPtr.

To pass a pointer to WriteLine, you can wrap it in System::IntPtr, as shown in the following code:

```
Console::WriteLine("pi = {0}", IntPtr(pi)); // this code works
```

Since System::IntPtr is a managed value type, it can be boxed to be passed as an Object^. Just as the IL uses the keyword int32 for System::Int32, the keyword native int is used for the type System::IntPtr.

Using C Structures in Managed Code

To properly use native structures and classes in managed code, the C++/CLI compiler generates managed proxy types. As an example, consider the following function from the Win32 API:

```
HWND GetDesktopWindow(VOID);
```

The return type HWND is defined by the Win32 API as a pointer to a structure named HWND__:

```
typedef struct HWND__ *HWND
```

The structure HWND__ is defined as follows:

```
struct HWND__
{
 int unused;
};
```

To use the return type HWND of the function GetDesktopWindow in managed code, the C++/CLI compiler generates a managed proxy type:

```
.class private sequential ansi sealed beforefieldinit HWND__
     extends [mscorlib]System.ValueType
{
 .size 4

 // [NativeCppClassAttribute]
 .custom instance void
     [mscorlib] System.Runtime.CompilerServices.NativeCppClassAttribute::.ctor() =
     ( 01 00 00 00 )

 // other attributes are elided for clarity
}
```

The proxy type generated by the C++/CLI compiler for the native structure HWND__ has the attribute NativeCppClassAttribute, which the C++/CLI compiler needs to differentiate between these proxy types and other managed types.

Notice that the managed proxy type does not contain information about the field members of the native type. To understand how fields of a native class are accessed in managed code, consider the function GetWindowRect from the Win32 API:

```
bool GetWindowRect(HWND hwnd, PRECT pRect);
```

The argument type PRECT is defined as follows:

```
typedef struct tagRECT
{
  LONG left;
  LONG top;
  LONG right;
  LONG bottom;
} RECT, *PRECT;
```

The managed proxy type for tagRECT looks very similar to the proxy type for HWND__:

```
.class private sequential ansi sealed beforefieldinit tagRECT
       extends [mscorlib]System.ValueType
{
  .size 16

  // attributes elided for clarity here
}
```

Notice that both proxy types for HWND__ and tagRECT are defined as value types (they extend System::ValueType). However, the only information specifying the binary layout of the type is the size. For the HWND__ type, the metadata .size 4 is used because this type contains one 4-byte data member named unused. Since tagRECT has four data members of 4 bytes in length, you can see that the metadata is .size 16. Using this metadata, the JIT compiler knows how much memory to allocate on the stack for each local variable and each parameter.

A value type instance on the stack does not have an object header or any other runtime predefined data. All bytes of a value on the stack can be gotten and set with IL instructions. This allows the C++/CLI compiler to ensure that local variables and parameters of this proxy type have the same binary layout as a local variable of the equivalent native type. Since managed local variables and parameters are not relocated on the stack (in contrast to instances on the GC heap), an address to a local variable or parameter of this managed proxy type can be treated as a pointer to the equivalent native type.

The following program uses the RECT structure as a local variable and passes an address to this variable to GetWindowRect:

```
// GetDesktopResolution.cpp
// build with "cl /clr GetDesktopResolution.cpp"

#include <windows.h>
```

```
using namespace System;

#pragma comment (lib, "user32.lib")

int main()
{
  RECT rect;
  GetWindowRect(GetDesktopWindow(), &rect);

  int pixelsX = rect.right;
  int pixelsY = rect.bottom;
  Console::WriteLine("Resolution of desktop: {0} x {1}", pixelsX , pixelsY);

  return 0;
}
```

The following listing shows the IL code generated from the preceding source (with a few modifications to increase readability):

```
.method assembly static int32
            modopt([mscorlib]System.Runtime.CompilerServices.CallConvCdecl)
        main() cil managed
{
  .vtentry 1 : 1
  .maxstack  3

  .locals (    int32 pixelsY,
               int32 pixelsX,
               valuetype tagRECT rect)

// GetWindowRect(GetDesktopWindow(), &rect);
  call          valuetype HWND__* GetDesktopWindow()
  ldloca        rect
  call          int32 GetWindowRect(valuetype HWND__*, valuetype tagRECT*)
  pop

// pixelsX = rect.right;
  ldloca        rect
  ldc.i4        8
  add
  ldind.i4
  stloc         pixelsX

// pixelsY = rect.bottom;
  ldloca        rect
  ldc.i4        12
  add
  ldind.i4
  stloc         pixelsY
```

```
// Console::WriteLine("Resolution of desktop: {0} x {1}", pixelsX , pixelsY);
  ldstr       "Resolution of desktop: {0} x {1}"
  ldloc.1
  box             [mscorlib]System.Int32
  ldloc.0
  box         [mscorlib]System.Int32
  call        void [mscorlib]System.Console::WriteLine(string, object, object)

// return 0;
  ldc.i4.0
  ret
}
```

Due to the .locals section at the beginning of main, the runtime will allocate 24 bytes on the stack for the three variables: 4 bytes for each of the two integers pixelsX and pixelsY, and 16 bytes for the variable rect.

To pass the address of the rect variable, the ldloca instruction (load a local variable's address) is used:

```
  call        valuetype HWND__* GetDesktopWindow()
  ldloca      rect
  call        int32 GetWindowRect(valuetype HWND__*, valuetype tagRECT*)
```

The value of rect.right is retrieved indirectly. First, the address of rect.right is calculated by adding the offset of right in the RECT structure to the address of the rect variable. In this case, the offset of right in the RECT structure is 8, because right is the third of the four LONG variables, which implies that two variables of 4 bytes are located before right. After determining the address, the ldind.i4 instruction uses this address to load the rect.right value:

```
  ldloca      rect
  ldc.i4      8
  add
  ldind.i4
```

For the rect.bottom variable, the same approach is used. Here, the offset is 12 because bottom is the last of the four LONG variables in the RECT structure:

```
  ldloca      rect
  ldc.i4      12
  add
  ldind.i4
```

Using C++ Classes in Managed Code

The RECT structure discussed so far comes from the C-based Win32 API. If you work with C++-based APIs, structures and classes can obviously be more complex. Nevertheless, everything I have discussed for C structures applies to C++ classes equally. Like C structures, C++ classes define the binary layout of instances. For access to data members of C++ classes, ldind and stind instructions are used in the same way as they're used for C structures.

However, C++ gives the programmer further features to define types; C++ classes can also have functions, including special member functions and virtual functions. The details of calling member functions across interoperability boundaries are discussed in Chapter 9. In this chapter, I will discuss how managed code can be used to determine the target of a virtual function call (the address of the most derived virtual function) at runtime.

When a native class contains or inherits virtual functions, it will have one or more vtable pointers in the instance data. (The number of vtable pointers depends on the base classes.) Since the (native) C++ compiler is aware of these vtable pointers and the layout of the vtables, it can generate native code that uses the vtable pointer to pick the right element from the vtable. Using the ldind instruction, the C++/CLI compiler can generate managed code that achieves the same. To understand how this is possible, assume a native class Base that defines two virtual functions f1 and f2:

```
class Base
{
public:
  virtual void f1();
  virtual void f2();
};
```

Given a function GetObject that returns a Base*, the virtual function f2 could be called with the following code:

```
Base* pBase = GetObject();
pBase->f2();
```

To determine the address of the (potentially overloaded) virtual function f2, the C++/CLI compiler generates IL code that first pushes the pBase pointer on the stack:

```
ldloc pBase
```

Since the vtable pointer is the first element of the class Base, it can be loaded on the stack with the ldind.i4 instruction (assuming the code targets a 32-bit processor):

```
ldind.i4
```

Since f2 is the second virtual function of Base, the second element in the vtable is needed. To determine the address of this second element, the offset of 4 is added to the vtable pointer on the stack:

```
ldc.i4.4
add
```

Since the address to the correct function pointer in the vtable is now on the stack, the pointer to the most derived implementation of f2 can be determined with the ldind.i4 instruction:

```
ldind.i4
```

For the actual virtual function call, a special IL instruction is used (this will be discussed in Chapter 9).

String Literals

If you compile to managed code, string literals like "abc" and L"abc" can be either native or managed string literals. The compiler determines this depending on the context. In most cases, the context is obvious. For example, if you pass a string literal to printf, it is unambiguous that it should be a native string literal, and if you call Console::WriteLine passing a string literal, it should obviously be a managed string literal. If it is not obvious, the compiler will choose the managed string literal.

When a native string literal is used in managed code, the compiler generates a managed wrapper type that is similar to the wrapper types defined for native classes and structures. In the code shown here, an ANSI code string literal and a Unicode string literal are used:

```
// UsingNativeStringLiterals.cpp
// cl /clr usingNativeStringLiterals.cpp

#include <stdio.h>

int main()
{
  printf("This is an ANSI code string literal. After the colon follows a "
           "Unicode string literal: %S\n",
        L"I am made of wchar_t characters");
}
```

In native code, the two string literals would be of type char const [41] and wchar_t const [22]. To use these types in managed code, the compiler has to generate wrapper types similar to the wrapper types defined for structures. Like wrapper types automatically generated for native classes and structures, these wrapper types are value types containing metadata specifying the length of an instance in bytes. They are defined in a special namespace—<CppImplementaionDetails>—and have the mangled names $ArrayType$$$BYOCJ@$$CBD and $ArrayType$$$BYOBG@$$CB_W.

```
.class private sequential ansi sealed beforefieldinit
'<CppImplementationDetails>'.$ArrayType$$$BYOBG@$$CB_W
      extends [mscorlib]System.ValueType
{
  .size 44
  ... custom attributes elided for clarity here ...
} // end of class '<CppImplementationDetails>'.$ArrayType$$$BYOBG@$$CB_W

.class private sequential ansi sealed beforefieldinit
          '<CppImplementationDetails>'.$ArrayType$$$BYOCJ@$$CBD
      extends [mscorlib]System.ValueType
{
  .size 41
  ... custom attributes elided for clarity here ...
} // end of class '<CppImplementationDetails>'.$ArrayType$$$BYOCJ@$$CBD
```

In native C++, these string literals are internally placed into a data section. To access this data via a value type, the C++/CLI compiler generates metadata for global variables that map to the native string literal data. This is shown in the following ILDASM excerpt:

```
.field static assembly
      valuetype '<CppImplementationDetails>'.$ArrayType$$$BY0BG@$$CB_W
      modopt([mscorlib]System.Runtime.CompilerServices.IsConst)
      '?A0x567a3bdb.unnamed-global-0' at D_00003120

.field static assembly
      valuetype '<CppImplementationDetails>'.$ArrayType$$$BY0CJ@$$CBD
      modopt([mscorlib]System.Runtime.CompilerServices.IsConst)
      '?A0x567a3bdb.unnamed-global-1' at D_0000314C
```

Passing Managed Memory to a Native Function

Native pointers should not refer into the managed heap, because a managed object that a native pointer would refer to could be relocated. So far, I have discussed two concepts for referring into the managed heap. These are tracking handles (and tracking references) that refer to a managed object's header, as well as interior pointers that refer to a part of the managed object's state. The runtime is able to automatically update all tracking handles and interior pointers. However, the runtime is not aware of native pointers referring into the managed heap. Therefore, it cannot update native pointers.

Nevertheless, there can be scenarios in which reading or updating the state of a managed object directly from native code is desired. For example, instead of copying a managed byte array into a native memory block so that native code can access the copied state, it would be more efficient if native code could directly read the managed array's state. For write operations, the situation is similar: instead of modifying a native memory block and copying it byte by byte into a managed array, it would likely be faster to update the managed array directly from native code. Reading or modifying the copied state could also require special attention with respect to concurrent updates from other threads.

.NET has a concept that allows native pointers to temporarily refer to a managed object. To understand this concept, it is useful to take a step back and review interior pointers. An interior pointer allows managed code to iterate through a managed array via pointer arithmetic, as this sample from Chapter 2 shows:

```
void WeakEncrypt(array<unsigned char>^ bytes, unsigned char key)
{
  cli::interior_ptr<unsigned char> pb = &(bytes[0]);
  interior_ptr<unsigned char> pbEnd = pb + bytes->Length;
  while (pb < pbEnd)
  {
    *pb ^= key;
    pb++;
  }
}
```

If you have a native function that expects a pointer to a native array as an argument, an interior pointer is not sufficient. The following prototype shows a native encryption function:

```
void NativeWeakEncrypt(unsigned char* rgb, int cb, unsigned char key);
```

Even though an interior pointer supports pointer arithmetic, it cannot be converted or casted into a native pointer. Trying to call `NativeWeakEncrypt` by passing an interior pointer will cause a compiler error:

```
cli::interior_ptr<Byte> pb = &(bytes[0]);
NativeWeakEncrypt(pb, bytes->Length, key);
  // error: cannot convert from interior_ptr<unsigned char> to unsigned char*
```

`NativeWeakEncrypt` uses the parameter it receives to access memory. If an interior pointer could be passed as a native pointer and the array were relocated during garbage collection, `NativeWeakEncrypt` would touch the wrong memory after the relocation. To avoid this dilemma, objects on the GC heap can be temporarily pinned. While an object is pinned, it cannot be relocated during a garbage collection phase. The following code shows how to pin an object:

```
void CallNativeWeakEncrypt(array<unsigned char>^ bytes, unsigned char key)
{
  cli::pin_ptr<unsigned char> pb = &(bytes[0]);
  NativeWeakEncrypt(static_cast<unsigned char*>(pb), bytes->Length, key);
}
```

Instead of an interior pointer, a *pinned pointer* is used here. Like an interior pointer, a pinned pointer is declared with a template-like syntax. In fact, a pinned pointer is a special kind of interior pointer. It differs from a normal interior pointer because it prevents the referred object from being relocated during garbage collection. To reduce the overhead of pinning, the CLI specifies that pinned pointers can only be defined as local variables. Since local variables are scoped, this implies that a pinned pointer cannot survive a function call. Using `pin_ptr` in any other context (e.g., to define parameters or data members) is illegal.

A pinned pointer affects the whole object it points into. If a pinned pointer refers to any element of a managed array, then the entire array will be unable to be relocated. If pointer arithmetic is misused—for example, to iterate the pointer into the next object's memory—then that object will be pinned instead. To stop the pinning time, you can either set the pinned pointer to `nullptr` or define the pinning pointer in a scope that ends where the pinning phase should end.

Even if you pin an object to pass it to a native function, there is a certain danger. If the native function stores the pointer and uses it after it has returned to the caller, the object will no longer be pinned when the native pointer tries to access it. Therefore, it can be relocated in the meantime. It is even possible that the object's memory has been reclaimed already. The following code shows another obvious misuse of pinned pointers:

```
unsigned char* BadGetNativePointer(array<unsigned char>^ bytes)
{
  pin_ptr<unsigned char> pinptrBytes = &(bytes[0]);
  return pinptrBytes;
}
```

When BadGetNativePointer returns, the byte array will no longer be pinned. However, a native pointer to the byte array will be returned. If this native pointer is used to access the byte array, it will potentially access a different object.

Pinning objects can be a very effective optimization option, but when used in the wrong way, it can also have bad impacts on the GC's performance and memory availability. When garbage collection is done while objects are pinned, parts of the GC heap are likely not compacted. Due to these problems, it is highly recommended to avoid pinning objects if possible. If it's necessary to pin, then pin for the shortest possible time.

You should especially avoid calling a blocking function while pinning an object. In earlier versions of the FCL, System.Net.Socket.BeginReceive suffered from such a problem. Instead of pinning objects while calling a blocking API, you should consider operating on a copied native state instead. In the worst case, this can imply two copy operations, one before the native pointer is passed to a native function, and one after the native function has returned to copy the modified state back. It can also imply further synchronization overhead to prevent another thread from reading the intermediate state that resides in the managed array before the modified state is copied back.

There are different ways to copy data from managed memory to unmanaged memory and back. Copying via memcpy requires a temporary pin_ptr, too—but a short-living one:

```
extern "C"__declspec(dllimport)
void NativeWeakEncrypt(unsigned char* rgb, int cb, unsigned char key);

void CallNativeWeakEncrypt(array<unsigned char>^ bytes, unsigned char key)
{
  if (!bytes)
    throw gcnew ArgumentNullException("bytes");

  int cb = bytes->Length;
  unsigned char* nativeBytes = new unsigned char [cb];
  {
    pin_ptr<unsigned char> pinptrBytes = &(bytes[0]);
    memcpy(nativeBytes, pinptrBytes, cb);
  }
  NativeWeakEncrypt(nativeBytes, cb, key);
  {
    pin_ptr<unsigned char> pinptrBytes = &(bytes[0]);
    memcpy(pinptrBytes, nativeBytes, cb);
  }
  delete[] nativeBytes;
}
```

The static function Copy from the helper class
System::Runtime::InteropServices::Marshal can be a neat helper for copying between managed and native arrays. The following code shows how it can be used:

```
extern "C" __declspec(dllimport)
void NativeWeakEncrypt(unsigned char* rgb, int cb, unsigned char key);

void CallNativeWeakEncrypt(array<unsigned char>^ bytes, unsigned char key)
```

```
{
  if (!bytes)
    throw gcnew ArgumentNullException("bytes");

  int cb = bytes->Length;
  unsigned char* nativeBytes = new unsigned char[cb];

  using System::Runtime::InteropServices::Marshal;
  Marshal::Copy(    bytes, 0,                    // source
                    IntPtr(nativeBytes), cb);    // destination

  NativeWeakEncrypt(nativeBytes, cb, key);

  Marshal::Copy(    IntPtr(nativeBytes),    // source
                    bytes, 0, cb);          // destination

  delete[]nativeBytes;
}
```

Converting Between Managed and Native Strings

C++ programmers often have to deal with a variety of string types. From its C roots, an array of char and wchar_t is often treated as a null-terminated string. The C++ standard library provides the type std::string for convenient string handling. Many other libraries also have string implementations. For example, the MFC and ATL use the type CString. Last but not least, COM has its own string definition, the BSTR. When you write interoperability code, you often have to convert between native strings and managed strings. For example, a native client could call the following managed function:

```
void fManaged(const char* sz);
```

If you want to dump the null-terminated string you got as an argument via Console::WriteLine, you first have to convert it to a System::String. To achieve this, you can use a constructor of System::String that accepts a const char* argument:

```
void fManaged(const char* sz)
{
  Console::WriteLine(gcnew String(sz));
}
```

For pointers to null-terminated wide character strings (wchar_t*), System::String provides an equivalent constructor. For all other native string types, you have to convert to either char* or wchar_t* so that you can use one of the String constructors mentioned. Make sure that you pick the conversion constructor that matches the internal representation of the string.

If you have a string that is not null terminated, two other String constructors should be used:

```
String(char* value, int start, int cChars);
String(wchar_t* value, int start, int cChars);
```

In all these cases, it is the GC's task to care about the resource cleanup when a string is no longer needed by the application.

If converting in the other direction, it is often up to the programmer to clean up a temporary string object. The helper class System::Runtime::InteropServices::Marshal has several static functions that can perform the necessary conversion. These functions are as follows:

```
Marshal::StringToBSTR
Marshal::StringToCoTaskMemAnsi
Marshal::StringToHGlobalAnsi
Marshal::StringToCoTaskMemUni
Marshal::StringToHGlobalUni
```

All these functions create native string objects with the value of the managed string. All the methods are quite self-explanatory—StringToBSTR creates a new COM BSTR instance. StringToCoTaskMemAnsi and StringToHGlobalAnsi allocate memory for the string on the COM heap or the Win32 global heap, and initialize this memory with the ANSI code representation of the managed string's value. StringToCoTaskMemUni and StringToHGlobalUni convert to a native Unicode string that is either allocated on the COM heap or on the Win32 global heap.

In all these cases, the native strings need to be cleaned up explicitly. The helper class Marshal provides the following functions for the cleanup:

```
Marshal::FreeBSTR
Marshal::FreeCoTaskMem
Marshal::FreeHGlobal
```

If you want to convert to a const wchar_t* that is needed only for a short time, you can choose an approach that is more convenient and faster: the header file vcclr.h declares a function called PtrToStringChars:

```
interior_ptr<const wchar_t> PtrToStringChars(const String^ source);
```

Using this function, you can retrieve an interior_ptr<const wchar_t> to the Unicode characters of a managed string. Notice that the return type of PtrToStringChars is interior_ptr<const wchar_t>. The interior pointer refers to state that must not be changed, because managed strings are immutable (as discussed in Chapter 2).

As discussed before, an interior pointer cannot be converted to a native pointer; however, there is a standard conversion from interior_ptr<const wchar_t> to pin_ptr<const wchar_t> and also a standard conversion from pin_ptr<const wchar_t> to const wchar_t*. The following code shows how to use PtrToStringChars:

```
#include <vcclr.h>

void NonBlockingNativeFunction(const wchar_t* wsz);
```

```
void ManagedFunction(String^ str)
{
  pin_ptr<const wchar_t> pinptrStr = PtrToStringChars(str);
  NonBlockingNativeFunction(pinptrStr);
}
```

If you can ensure that the managed string isn't pinned for a long period (especially not for the duration of a blocking function call) and that the managed string's state is not modified, then you should choose this approach over calling any of the Marshal functions mentioned previously. It can save you a memory allocation for the native string's data, a copy operation for the managed string's state, and a memory deallocation to clean up the temporary string.

The next version of Visual Studio (Orcas) will come with some helper templates that care about the conversion and the cleanup of the temporarily created strings. The following code gives you an impression of these helper templates (keep in mind that details may change before Orcas is released):

```
void MarshalingInOrcas()
{
  msclr::interop::marshal_context ctx;
  const char* sz = ctx.marshal_as<const char*, String^> (str);

  // ... use sz while ctx is in scope ...

  // at the end of the scope, the marshal_context destructor
  // deallocates memory used for marshalling
}
```

Mixing the Type Systems When Defining Data Members

The rest of this chapter covers type system interoperability in the context of type definitions. When you define native or managed types, you cannot mix the type system as easily as you can define arguments or local variables in managed functions. For example, a managed type cannot contain native objects. The following code does not compile:

```
#include <string>

ref class ManagedClass
{
 std::string nativeString;  // compiler error C4368: "mixed types are not supported"
 // ...
};
```

Before I cover the options to bypass this restriction, you should understand why this restriction exists. If an instance of a native class could be a sub-object of a managed class, the native instance would be relocated with the containing managed object. The GC is not aware of the native pointers referring to the sub-object. Therefore, none of the native pointers referring to the sub-object would be updated after a relocation of the managed object and its native sub-object.

For example, assume a non-static function is called on the native sub-object. To call this function, the this pointer of the sub-object must be pushed on the stack. When the object is relocated with its containing managed object, the this pointer will not be updated, because the runtime is not aware of any native pointers.

To bypass this restriction, you can add a native pointer as a field of your managed type instead. This implies that you have to create and delete the native object explicitly in your constructor and destructor code, but it allows you to mix the type systems:

```
ref class ManagedClass
{
  std::string* pNativeString;
public:
  ManagedClass(std::string nativeString)
  : pNativeString(new std::string(nativeString))
  {}

  ~ManagedClass()
  {
    delete pNativeString;
  }

  // For classes that wrap a native object, you should also implement a finalizer.
  // This will be covered in Chapter 11.

  // ... other members not relevant here ...
};
```

Now the memory for the native string is allocated on the native heap. Therefore, the string is not relocated when the GC compacts the managed heap.

At first glance, there seems to be another problem. Because pNativeString is of a native type, a programmer could also try to obtain an address of pNativeString:

```
ManagedClass^ mc = gcnew ManagedClass("1234");
std::string** ppNativeString = &mc->pNativeString;
```

When the ManagedClass instance (including the pNativeString field) is relocated by the GC, ppNativeString will no longer refer to pNativeString, but to random other memory. This problem actually does not exist, though, because the expression &mc->pNativeString used in the previous code sample returns an interior_ptr. As mentioned before, there is no conversion from an interior_ptr to a native pointer. Therefore, assigning &mc->pNativeString to ppNativeString, as done in the preceding code sample, is illegal and causes a compiler error.

Referring to Managed Objects in C++ Classes

When you define native classes, you face a similar restriction. To discuss this restriction and how to overcome it, I will implement a native class that can automatically write the content of changed files to the console. The type System::IO::FileSystemWatcher from the FCL assembly System.dll is a helpful tool for this task. As a wrapper of the Win32 API for file system events, it can automatically detect changes in the file system. However, defining a data member of type FileSystemWatcher^ will end up in compiler errors:

```
// ChangedFileDumper.cpp
// compile with "CL /c /clr ChangedFileDumper.cpp"

#using <System.dll>
using System::IO::FileSystemWatcher;

class ChangedFileDumper
{
  FileSystemWatcher^ fsw;    // error C3265: cannot declare a managed 'fsw' in an
                             // unmanaged 'ChangedFileDumper'

  // ...
};
```

Since ChangedFileDumper is a native class, it can be instantiated in any kind of unmanaged memory. This includes the C++ heap, the COM heap, and the stack. In all these cases, the GC would not be aware of the FileSystemWatcher^ data member. Therefore, neither would the GC consider this tracking handle when the GC determines unreferenced objects, nor would this tracking handle data member be updated when the instance is relocated during garbage collection.

On the one hand, it is reasonable that the native class cannot have a field of type FileSystemWatcher^; on the other hand, the class ChangedFileDumper needs to refer to an instance of FileSystemWatcher so that different methods of ChangedFileDumper can access the same FileSystemWatcher instance. Visual C++ comes with a helper template called msclr::gcroot, which is defined in the header file msclr/gcroot.h. This helper allows you to solve this problem:

```
// ChangedFileDumper.cpp
// compile with "CL /c /clr ChangedFileDumper.cpp"

#include <msclr/gcroot.h>  // required for msclr/gcroot.h
using msclr::gcroot;

#using <System.dll>
using System::IO::FileSystemWatcher;

class ChangedFileDumper
{
  gcroot<FileSystemWatcher^> fsw;

  // ...
};
```

The template gcroot has several members that allow you to access the object in a convenient way. It is often possible to treat a variable of type gcroot<FileSystemWatcher^> as if it were of type FileSystemWatcher^. For example, gcroot<FileSystemWatcher^> has a constructor that expects a parameter of type FileSystemWatcher^. This allows you to initialize a gcroot<FileSystemWatcher^> variable with a FileSystemWatcher^ handle. The following code uses this constructor to implement the constructor of the class ChangedFileDumper:

```
ChangedFileDumper::ChangedFileDumper(std::string path)
: fsw(gcnew FileSystemWatcher)
{
  fsw->Path = gcnew String(path.c_str());
}
```

In the body of the ChangedFileDumper, the gcroot<FileSystemWatcher^> data member is used as if it were of type FileSystemWatcher^. Notice that the Path property is a property of FileSystemWatcher, not a property of gcroot. This behavior is possible because the gcroot template overloads the member access operator (operator->) so that it returns the wrapped object.

The gcroot template also implements a conversion operator that can be used to obtain the wrapped tracking handle. This operator can be used to dispose the FileSystemWatcher in the ChangedFileDumper destructor:

```
~ChangedFileDumper()
{
  delete (FileSystemWatcher^)fsw;
}
```

As an alternative, you can also use a template called msclr::auto_gcroot. As you can conclude from its name, this template combines gcroot and auto_handle. On the one hand, it allows a data member of a native type to refer to a managed object. On the other hand, its destructor ensures that the wrapped managed object is disposed. To use msclr::auto_gcroot, you must include the header file msclr/auto_gcroot.h.

Since FileSystemWatcher implements IDisposable, it makes sense to use auto_gcroot instead of gcroot for the ChangedFileDumper class. The following code shows the complete application:

```
// DumpChangedFile.cpp
// build with "cl /clr DumpChangedFile.cpp"

#include <string>
#include <vcclr.h>
#include <msclr/auto_gcroot.h>
using msclr::auto_gcroot;

#using <System.dll>
using namespace System;
using namespace System::IO;

class ChangedFileDumper
{
```

```cpp
  auto_gcroot<FileSystemWatcher^> fsw;

public:
  ChangedFileDumper(std::string path)
  : fsw(gcnew FileSystemWatcher)
  {
    fsw->Path = gcnew String(path.c_str());
  }

  void WaitForChangedFile(int timeout)
  {
    WaitForChangedResult^ res =
        fsw->WaitForChanged(WatcherChangeTypes::Changed, timeout);
    if (!res->TimedOut)
      DumpFile(res->Name);
  }

  void DumpFile(String^ name)
  {
    StreamReader sr(name);
    Console::WriteLine(sr.ReadToEnd());
  }
};

int main()
{
  ChangedFileDumper cfd("c:\\tests");
  cfd.WaitForChangedFile(60000); // wait 1 minute
};
```

Other Uses of gcroot and auto_gcroot

The templates gcroot and auto_gcroot can also be used in two other scenarios. Just as it is
illegal to use tracking handles for data members of native classes, it is also forbidden to define
global variables of a tracking handle type. The same restriction applies to static variables of
managed functions. The following code shows these restrictions:

```cpp
FileSystemWatcher^ fsw; // error: "global variable may not have managed type"

void f()
{
  static FileSystemWatcher^ fsw = gcnew FileSystemWatcher();
        // error: "static variable may not have managed type"

  // ...
}
```

In both cases, gcroot can be used to avoid these compiler errors. However, as I explain
later, it is not always recommended to use gcroot in these cases.

General Hints Regarding gcroot and auto_gcroot

There are a few subtle pitfalls that you should know about when using the gcroot and auto_gcroot templates. As discussed already, in many cases you can use a gcroot or auto_gcroot variable as if it were of the wrapped tracking handle type. However, in a few cases, this is not possible. For example, you cannot invoke a default indexed property via a gcroot or auto_gcroot variable. The following code shows an example:

```
List<int>^ ints = GetIntListFromSomeWhere();
Console::WriteLine(ints[0]);    // legal

gcroot<List<int>^> ints2 = GetIntListFromSomewhere();
Console::WriteLine(ints2[0]);
    // compiler error: gcroot does not support [] operation
```

To solve this problem, you can convert the gcroot variable to the type of the wrapped tracking handle, as shown in the following code:

```
gcroot<List<int>^> ints2 = GetIntListFromSomewhere();
List<int>^ ints3 = ints2;
Console::WriteLine(ints3[0]);  // this option is legal
```

This conversion is possible because gcroot implements an appropriate conversion operator. There is an inconsistency between gcroot and auto_gcroot in that auto_gcroot does not support a conversion to the wrapped tracking handle type. To obtain the wrapped tracking handle from an auto_gcroot variable, you have to call the member function get:

```
auto_gcroot<List<int>^> ints2 = GetIntListFromSomewhere();
List<int>^ ints3 = ints2.get();
Console::WriteLine(ints3[0]);
```

To find out whether a gcroot or an auto_gcroot variable actually refers to a managed object or just contains a nullptr reference, you can use the following expression:

```
if (!ints2)
    ...
```

or its positive variant:

```
if (ints2)
    ...
```

However, it is not possible to achieve the same by writing the following:

```
if (ints2 == nullptr)
    ...
```

Unfortunately, you may face an additional pitfall if you use auto_gcroot. Currently, auto_gcroot has an unintended conversion to String^. This can cause the following undesired behavior:

```
void f1(String^ str) { }
```

```
void f2()
{
  auto_gcroot<FileSystemWatcher^> fsw = gcnew FileSystemWatcher();

  f1(fsw);
    // this line should not compile, because neither an auto_gcroot, nor a
    // FileSystemWatcher should be convertible to a String^, but it does compile
}
```

Reducing the Overhead of gcroot and auto_gcroot

Operations based on gcroot or auto_gcroot variables are slower than operations based on a tracking handle. For a detailed description of the overhead that is caused by each gcroot or auto_gcroot instance, as well as for each usage of operator->, read the following sidebar, entitled "How Is gcroot Implemented?"

To minimize the overhead caused by gcroot and auto_gcroot, there are two optimization strategies as follows:

- Avoid defining gcroot variables whenever possible. There are many situations in which a gcroot or an auto_gcroot variable can actually be avoided. For example, there is usually no need to define a global gcroot variable because you can define a static variable of a managed type instead. Another option may be to reduce the number of gcroot and auto_gcroot variables by combining several tracking handles into a managed collection or a custom managed type. Having one gcroot or auto_gcroot variable that refers to the managed collection or an instance of the custom managed type containing the tracking handles is cheaper than having many gcroot or auto_gcroot variables.

- Avoid access via operator-> if possible. operator-> is convenient but not necessarily efficient. Instead of accessing a managed object via operator-> several times, you can use gcroot's conversion operator or auto_gcroot's get function to obtain the wrapped handle once, and use this wrapped handle to access the managed object.

HOW IS GCROOT IMPLEMENTED?

The gcroot template is a helper that is heavily used in projects extending classic C++ code with .NET features, as well as in projects for managed wrapper libraries. Therefore, is makes sense to take a look at its implementation and its overhead.

Since the purpose of gcroot is to allow fields of a native class to refer to managed objects, it is a template for a native type—not for a managed one. The following code shows the definition of this template in msclr/gcroot.h:

```
template <class T> struct gcroot
{
    typedef System::Runtime::InteropServices::GCHandle GCHandle;

    ... remaining members elided for clarity here ...
};
```

As you can see from the `typedef` in the template definition, a managed type named `GCHandle` is used internally. The constructor of `gcroot` creates a new `GCHandle` by calling the static function `GCHandle::Alloc`. Since `GCHandle` is a managed type, it cannot be used as a data member of the native struct `gcroot`. If I weren't implementing `gcroot` now, I could now use a `gcroot` data member.

To refer to a `GCHandle` in native memory, a native handle can be obtained. This native handle is of type `System::IntPtr`, which is binary compatible with a `void*`. In contrast to a tracking handle or a `GCHandle`, such a native `void*` can be used as a data member of `gcroot`, which is a native type. The following code shows what the constructor of `gcroot` does to get a native handle to the object (this is not precisely the code in `msclr/gcroot.h`, but it does the same thing and is more understandable):

```
template <class T> struct gcroot
{
private:
    void* _handle;
public:
    gcroot(T t) {
        GCHandle gc_handle = GCHandle::Alloc(t);
        System::IntPtr native_handle = GCHandle::ToIntPtr(gc_handle);
        this->_handle = native_handle.ToPointer();
    }
    ... remaining members elided for clarity here ...
};
```

Creating a `GCHandle` allocates memory in an internal data structure, which I will discuss later. To deallocate this memory, the destructor obtains the `GCHandle` object and calls `Free`:

```
~gcroot() {
    GCHandle gch = GCHandle::FromIntPtr(IntPtr(this->_handle));
    gch.Free();
    this->_handle = 0;
}
```

In order to access the managed object that the native handle refers to, you can simply use a `gcroot` variable as if it were a tracking handle. To support this, `gcroot` provides an assignment operator, an implementation of `operator->`, and a conversion operator to the tracking handle:

```
template <class T> struct gcroot
{
    ... remaining members elided for clarity here ...

    gcroot& operator=(T t) {
        GCHandle gch = GCHandle::FromIntPtr(IntPtr(this->_handle));
        gch.Target = t;
        return *this;
    }
    operator T () const {
        GCHandle gch = GCHandle::FromIntPtr(IntPtr(this->_handle));
        return static_cast<T>(gch.Target );
```

```
    }

    T operator->() const {
        GCHandle gch = GCHandle::FromIntPtr(IntPtr(this->_handle));
        return static_cast<T>(gch.Target );
    }
private:
    void* _handle;
};
```

To estimate the costs of a gcroot instance and an access via a gcroot instance, it is helpful to have a certain understanding of the internal implementation of GCHandle. As the gcroot code shows, GCHandle values are created only temporarily, either to get a native handle from a tracking handle or to get a tracking handle from a native handle. Once you have the handle you want, the GCHandle value is no longer necessary. The actual data that maps a native handle to a tracking handle is stored in a dedicated data structure. This data structure is the GCHandleCookieTable, which is internally based on a type with the self-describing name System::Collections::Hashtable. The following illustration shows the relationship between gcroot instances, native handles, tracking handles, managed objects, and the GCHandleCookieTable.

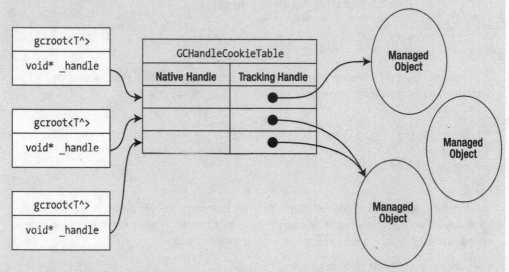

When a new gcroot instance is created, GCHandle::Alloc adds a new entry to the GCHandleCookieTable. GCHandle::Free removes that entry. For every usage of the operator-> and the conversion operator, a GCHandle value has to be created from the native handle. To achieve this, the tool has to consult the GCHandleCookieTable.

Handling Events in Native Classes

In the current version of the file dumper application, the main thread waits until a file is changed or a timeout of 60 seconds is reached. Instead of blocking the main thread, you could use it to allow the user to decide when to stop waiting while another thread deals with file modifications. The FileSystemWatcher's EnableRaisingEvents property provides a simple way to achieve this. The FileSystemWatcher provides five events that can be fired when the EnableRaisingEvents property is set to true. The one that is interesting for the ChangedFileDumper class is the Changed event.

As discussed previously, the gcroot and auto_gcroot templates overload the member access operator (operator->) so that you can easily access members of the wrapped tracking handle. This allows you to easily call member functions on the wrapped object or set the EnableRaisingEvents property to true. However, as soon as you want to register an event via the auto_gcroot variable fsw, you will face an additional problem. The following code will not compile:

```
class ChangedFileDumper
{
  auto_gcroot<FileSystemWatcher^> fsw;

public:
  ChangedFileDumper(std::string path)
  : fsw(gcnew FileSystemWatcher)
  {
    fsw->Path = gcnew String(path.c_str());
    fsw->EnableRaisingEvents = true;
    fsw->Changed +=
        gcnew FileSystemEventHandler(this, & ChangedFileDumper::OnChanged);
    // error C3364: "invalid argument for delegate constructor"
  }

private:
  void OnChanged(Object^ sender, FileSystemEventArgs^ e)
  {
    DumpFile(e->FullPath);
  }

  void DumpFile(String^ name)
  {
    StreamReader sr(name);
    Console::WriteLine(sr.ReadToEnd());
  }
};
```

The event handler must match the requirements of delegate target functions. Unfortunately, ChangedFileDumper::OnChanged (as well as all member functions of native classes) cannot be used as a delegate target. Only global functions and static and non-static methods of managed types can act as delegate targets.

To solve this problem, you could create a managed proxy class that provides a target function. Such a proxy class can be defined inside ChangedFileDumper because native classes can have nested managed classes. To avoid implementing any application logic inside the proxy class, it should simply forward to the real event handler in the native class.

It is not necessary to write all the code for such a proxy class manually, because Visual C++ comes with helper macros in the header file msclr/event.h. Inside a public area of your class, you can define a delegate map. The macros BEGIN_DELEGATE_MAP and END_DELEGATE_MAP create the frame of a delegate map. For every event that should be handled in the native class, one entry should appear in this delegate map. The macro EVENT_DELEGATE_ENTRY produces these entries. To instantiate a delegate for the registration or unregistration of an event, the MAKE_DELEGATE macro is used.

The code shown here implements the same application as before, but now a native class and the macros from msclr/event.h are used:

```cpp
// DumpChangedFiles2.cpp
// cl /clr DumpChangedFiles2.cpp

#include <string>

#include <vcclr.h>
#include <msclr/auto_gcroot.h>
using msclr::auto_gcroot;

#include <msclr/event.h>

#using <System.dll>
using namespace System;
using namespace System::IO;

class ChangedFileDumper
{
  auto_gcroot<FileSystemWatcher^> fsw;

public:
  ChangedFileDumper(std::string path)
  : fsw(gcnew FileSystemWatcher)
  {
    fsw->Path = gcnew String(path.c_str());
    fsw->EnableRaisingEvents = true;
    fsw->Changed += MAKE_DELEGATE(FileSystemEventHandler, OnChanged);
  }

  BEGIN_DELEGATE_MAP(ChangedFileDumper)
    EVENT_DELEGATE_ENTRY(OnChanged, Object^, FileSystemEventArgs^)
```

```
    END_DELEGATE_MAP()

private:
  void OnChanged(Object^ sender, FileSystemEventArgs^ e)
  {
    DumpFile(e->FullPath);
  }

  void DumpFile(String^ name)
  {
    StreamReader sr(name);
    Console::WriteLine(sr.ReadToEnd());
  }
};

int main()
{
  ChangedFileDumper cfd("c:\\tests");
  Console::WriteLine("Press enter to stop the application");
  Console::ReadLine();
}
```

Internals of the Delegate Map

The preceding code shows the simple steps necessary to handle events in native types. If you extend existing code with .NET features, you will likely use the delegate map quite often. To understand how the delegate map is implemented, it is necessary to see what these macros expand to. This is shown in the following code:

```
//////////////////////////////////////////
// Created by "BEGIN_DELEGATE_MAP(ChangedFileDumper)"

ref class delegate_proxy_type;
delegate_proxy_factory< ChangedFileDumper > m_delegate_map_proxy;

ref class delegate_proxy_type
{
    ChangedFileDumper * m_p_native_target;

public:
    delegate_proxy_type(ChangedFileDumper* pNativeTarget) :
    m_p_native_target(pNativeTarget) {}

    void detach() { m_p_native_target = 0; }

//////////////////////////////////////////
// created by "EVENT_DELEGATE_ENTRY(OnCreated, Object^, FileSystemEventArgs^)"
```

```
    void OnCreated(Object^ arg0,FileSystemEventArgs^ arg1)
    {
        if(m_p_native_target == 0)
            throw gcnew System::ArgumentNullException(
                "Delegate call failed: Native sink was not attached or "
                "has already detached from the managed proxy "
                "(m_p_native_target == NULL). Hint: see if native sink "
                "was destructed or not constructed properly");
        m_p_native_target->OnCreated(arg0,arg1);
    }


//////////////////////////////////////////
// created by "END_DELEGATE_MAP"
};
```

As you can see here, the macros for the delegate map define a complete nested ref class named delegate_proxy_type, including method implementations. To forward method calls to the event handlers in the native class, delegate_proxy_type needs a pointer to the native target object. For this reason, the nested proxy class has a data member to store such a pointer and a constructor for the appropriate initialization. The following code shows those parts of the proxy class that manage the pointer to the native target object:

```
ref class delegate_proxy_type
{
    ChangedFileDumper * m_p_native_target;

public:
    delegate_proxy_type(ChangedFileDumper * pNativeTarget)
    :   m_p_native_target(pNativeTarget)
    {}

    void detach()  { m_p_native_target = 0; }
    ...
}
```

delegate_proxy_type also has a detach function to reset the pointer to the native target. This function will be important for later explanations.

The function delegate_proxy_type::OnChanged is used as the delegate target function. This function is added to the proxy class with the EVENT_DELEGATE_ENTRY macro. For every EVENT_DELEGATE_ENTRY in a delegate map, such a target method exists:

```
    void OnChanged(Object^ arg0,FileSystemEventArgs^ arg1)
    {
        if(m_p_native_target == 0)
            throw gcnew System::ArgumentNullException(
                "Delegate call failed: Native sink was not attached or "
                "has already detached from the managed proxy "
                "(m_p_native_target == NULL). Hint: see if native sink "
```

```
                                    "was destructed or not constructed properly");
          m_p_native_target->OnChanged(arg0,arg1);
      }
```

In its implementation, OnChanged checks if a native target pointer has been reset so far, and throws an ArgumentNullException if this is the case. In the case of normal execution, a native target pointer exists, and the call can be forwarded to m_p_native_target->OnChanged.

To register the event handler, an instance of the nested ref class delegate_proxy_type must be created. This is done with the MAKE_DELEGATE macro. In the preceding code, this macro is expanded to the following:

```
gcnew FileSystemEventHandler(
          m_delegate_map_proxy.get_proxy(this),
          &delegate_proxy_type::OnChanged);
```

As you can see here, the target function passed is in fact the OnChanged method of the nested proxy class. Since this is a non-static method, the first argument of the delegate constructor is the object on which OnChanged should be invoked. To pass this argument, the expression m_delegate_map_proxy.get_proxy(this) is used. m_delegate_map_proxy is a data member of ChangedFileDumper. It is introduced to the native class with the macro BEGIN_DELEGATE_MAP:

```
delegate_proxy_factory< ChangedFileDumper >  m_delegate_map_proxy;
```

m_delegate_map_proxy is of type delegate_proxy_factory < ChangedFileDumper >. delegate_proxy_factory is a template for a native class. Since it is used as a data member of ChangedFileDumper, its destructor will be called from the destructor of ChangedFileDumper. The delegate_proxy_factory destructor calls detach on the proxy class. This is done to ensure that the event is not forwarded after the native class has been destroyed.

Summary

Native code can use native types only. Managed code can use managed types as well as native types. Therefore, only native types can be used to define functions that act as interoperability gateways between native code and managed code. To make native types available for managed code, the C++/CLI compiler automatically generates managed wrapper types for native classes, structs, unions, and enums. Managed types cannot be used in native code because native code is not able to deal with instances that can be relocated. However, to temporarily allow native code to access memory on the managed heap, pinned pointers can be used. You also have to be aware of restrictions when you define new types. Fields of managed classes can only be pointers to native classes. If you want a data member of a native type to refer to a managed object, you have to use the gcroot or auto_gcroot helper templates.

While this chapter has discussed how to mix managed and native types, the next chapter will focus on mixing managed and native functions, and on method calls that cross the managed-unmanaged boundary.

■ ■ ■

CHAPTER 9

Managed-Unmanaged Transitions

In Chapter 1, I explained that calling functions across interoperability boundaries can be as easy as calling native functions from native code. Normal method declarations are sufficient for both directions of interoperability. You can simply rely on the C++/CLI compiler to handle all kinds of method calls with any kind of native arguments in the right way. These method calls include the following scenarios:

- Managed code calling global or static functions compiled to native code

- Native code calling global or static functions compiled to managed code

- Managed code calling member functions of C++ classes that are compiled to native code

- Native code calling member functions of C++ classes that are compiled to managed code

- Managed code calling native functions via function pointers

- Native code calling managed functions via function pointers

- Managed code calling native virtual functions

- Native code calling managed virtual functions

Automatic support for all these kinds of method calls across interoperability boundaries has many advantages. If you are new to C++/CLI, this feature is great for a quick start. Even if you are an experienced C++/CLI developer, it can save you a significant amount of time compared to the efforts you have to make in other .NET languages. Enabling your code to pass managed-unmanaged interoperability boundaries without C++/CLI interoperability often requires writing a lot of code manually, which is an error-prone task. Since other languages cannot read C/C++ header files, wrapper functions and wrapper types with the same binary layout as parameter types have to be defined manually. To access the member variables of a native type, you have to define equivalent fields in the managed wrapper type. This is again an error-prone task. Even worse, it can slow down the performance of method calls across managed-unmanaged boundaries.

Despite all the benefits of C++/CLI interoperability, it is still up to you to understand what is being done for you under the hood. This allows you to avoid a few pitfalls, to understand the overhead of method calls passing managed-unmanaged boundaries, and to fine-tune these method calls when it is necessary.

Interoperability, Metadata, and Thunks

Whenever a function is called across a managed-unmanaged boundary, a so-called *thunk* automatically performs a managed-unmanaged transition. To understand both directions of managed-unmanaged transitions, it is important to realize the roles that the software developer, the build tools (compiler and linker), and the CLR play to create a thunk as follows:

- *The developer's role*: Due to the power of C++/CLI interoperability, the developer's task is often the easiest one: ensuring that the target function is declared. This is typically done by including a header file with the function declaration. For fine-tuning, it is also possible to write some extra code dedicated to controlling managed-unmanaged transitions.

- *The build tool's role*: At build time, the compiler and the linker embed metadata containing interoperability information into the generated assembly. To do this, they combine different pieces of information from the code the developer has provided, the headers that the developer included, and the target library.

- *The CLR's role*: The CLR reads the interoperability metadata from the assembly and uses it to generate the thunk when needed.

The metadata generated for calls from native code to managed code is fundamentally different than the metadata for calls from managed code to native code. There are also differences in the way thunks for both directions of interoperability are created. Thunks that enable native callers to call managed functions are created when an assembly is loaded, whereas thunks that can call native code from managed code are dynamically created on demand by the JIT compiler. For this reason, I'll discuss both directions of interoperability separately.

It is important to be aware of these managed-unmanaged transitions because calling a function without such a transition is faster. Avoiding unnecessary managed-unmanaged transitions is an important performance optimization strategy. C++/CLI interoperability gives you many more options for minimizing transitions than other languages. For example, you have a lot of options to refactor your code to effectively reduce the number of calls across interoperability boundaries. Sometimes it is sufficient to move a function implementation from a file that is compiled to native code to a file compiled with /clr to replace many transitions with just one.

However, there are other optimization options, too. To use these optimization options, it is necessary to understand what the compiler and the runtime do in different scenarios of calls across interoperability boundaries.

In order to avoid distracting side information and to concentrate only on important aspects like the generated metadata, I start with simple C functions, not C++ classes. Understanding how C functions are called across interoperability boundaries is helpful for understanding how member functions of C++ classes are called. For the same reasons, I will discuss interoperability via function pointers before I cover virtual function calls across interoperability boundaries.

Calling Managed Functions from Unmanaged Code

Figure 9-1 shows a simple application that is built from two source files: one compiled to native code and one compiled to managed code. In this application, main, which is compiled to native code, calls the managed functions fManaged and fManaged2.

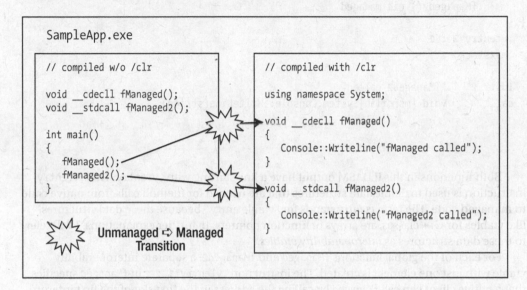

Figure 9-1. *Unmanaged code calling managed code*

It is possible to call fManaged and fManaged2 in main because both functions have a native calling convention. To perform the switch from native code to managed code, fManaged and fManaged2 are called via a thunk.

Interoperability Metadata for Unmanaged-to-Managed Transitions

When a managed function has a native calling convention, the compiler can emit special interoperability metadata. The following listing shows the ILDASM output for fManaged and fManaged2. In this code, you can see an IL instruction that refers to this interoperability metadata:

```
.method assembly static void
        modopt(System.Runtime.CompilerServices.CallConvCdecl)
        fManaged() cil managed
{
  .vtentry 1 : 1
  .maxstack  1

  ldstr      "fManaged called"
  call       void [mscorlib]System.Console::WriteLine(string)
```

```
      ret
}

.method assembly static void
          modopt(System.Runtime.CompilerServices.CallConvStdcall)
          fManaged2() cil managed
{
  .vtentry 2 : 1
  .maxstack 1

  ldstr      "fManaged2 called"
  call       void [mscorlib]System.Console::WriteLine(string)

  ret
}
```

Both functions in this ILDASM output have a line starting with .vtentry. This .vtentry instruction is used to define data structures that are needed for method calls from native code to managed code. The term *vtentry* stands for "vtable entry," because these data structures, like vtables for C++ classes, are arrays of function pointers. In further explanations, I will refer to these data structures as *interoperability vtables*.

For each of the global functions fManaged and fManaged2, a separate interoperability vtable with just one element is created. The instruction .vtentry 1 : 1 in fManaged specifies that a native client can call fManaged by calling the address in the first slot of the first interoperability vtable. For fManaged2, the .vtentry instruction specifies that the first slot of the second vtable should be called.

Interoperability vtables have a fixed location in the assembly, and they are initialized when the assembly (in this case, the sample application) is loaded. All information necessary for the initialization of the interoperability vtables can be found in the assembly manifest. Here is the interesting part of the sample application's assembly manifest:

```
// Image base: 0x00400000
...
.vtfixup [1] int32 retainappdomain at D_00007000 // 06000001
.vtfixup [1] int32 retainappdomain at D_00007004 // 06000002
.vtfixup [1] int32 retainappdomain at D_00007028 // 06000004
.vtfixup [1] int32 retainappdomain at D_0000702C // 06000018
```

From the comment in the first line, you can conclude that the EXE file is loaded at the address 0x00400000. For the first vtable, the metadata provides a mapping from the relative virtual address (RVA) 0x7000 to metadata token 06000001. The runtime can use this information to generate an unmanaged-to-managed thunk for fManaged.

The RVA is relative to the image's base address, 0x00400000. Therefore, the function pointer for the thunk to target function fManaged can be found at the virtual address 0x00407000. To find the thunk to fManaged2, you have to look at the virtual address 0x00407004.

The metadata token identifies the managed target function. As described in Chapter 4, assemblies store metadata in various metadata tables. For functions, there is a special metadata table. In all metadata tables, rows are identified by a 32-bit value called the *metadata token*. Metadata tokens for entries in the metadata table for functions and methods have the pattern 0x06??????.

When an assembly is loaded, the CLR iterates through all .vtfixup entries of the assembly. For each .vtfixup entry, it creates a thunk to the target function dynamically and stores a pointer to that thunk in the interoperability vtable specified by the RVA of the .vtfixup entry.

Default Calling Conventions

In the preceding sample application, a native client can call fManaged and fManaged2 because both functions have a native calling convention: fManaged is a __cdecl function and fManaged2 has the calling convention __stdcall. It is also possible to define managed functions with a managed calling convention called __clrcall.

Functions with the calling convention __clrcall cannot be called by a native client. Therefore, the compiler and the linker produce no interoperability vtable for __clrcall functions. In the ILDASM output for a __clrcall function, you will find no .vtentry instruction, and the manifest will not contain a .vtfixup metadata line for that function.

If you declare or define a function without explicitly specifying a calling convention, the compiler will choose a default calling convention. This default calling convention depends on the compilation model and on other compilation flags.

If you compile to native code (without any of the /clr compiler switches), the default calling convention for global functions like fManaged and for static member functions of native classes is __cdecl. The compiler switches /Gd, /Gr, and /Gz can change the default calling convention.

Table 9-1 shows the different alternatives for calling conventions of managed functions when you compile with /clr.

Table 9-1. *Calling Conventions of Managed Functions*

	__cdecl	__stdcall	__thiscall	__clrcall
All Member Functions of Managed Types	Not allowed	Not allowed	Allowed	Mandatory
Non-Static Managed Member Functions of Unmanaged Types	Allowed	Allowed	Default if function has no args of managed types	Default if function has args of managed types
Static Managed Member Functions of Unmanaged Types	Default if function has no args of managed types	Allowed	Not allowed	Mandatory if function has args of managed types
Global Functions	Default if function has no args of managed types	Allowed	Not allowed	Mandatory if function has args of managed types

Table 9-1 does not mention the __fastcall calling convention, because the current version of the CLR does not support calling __fastcall functions from managed code. You cannot declare or use __fastcall functions if you compile with /clr or any of its alternatives.

To call a __fastcall function from managed code, you have to create a native wrapper function with another calling convention. Fortunately, the Win32 API and many other C-based libraries do not use this calling convention. For C++ classes, this isn't a problem, because __fastcall is not a valid calling convention for member functions.

For the compilation models /clr:pure and /clr:safe, there are further restrictions regarding native calling conventions. If you compile with /clr:pure, you cannot implement managed functions with native calling conventions—only __clrcall functions can be implemented. However, you can still declare functions with the calling conventions __cdecl, __stdcall, and __thiscall when you compile with /clr:pure. (This opens the door to the other direction of interoperability: calling native functions from managed code, which is discussed later in this chapter.)

If you compile with /clr:safe, only __clrcall functions can be defined and called. Calling functions with native calling conventions implies that nonverifiable IL code is generated by the compiler. (There is an exception to this limitation of /clr:safe, but it is only of theoretical value and therefore not covered here.)

Implicit Optimizations of Native-to-Managed Transitions

When a managed function call is done directly, the compiler and the linker are able to perform optimizations automatically. Depending on the usage of the managed function, the compiler can either optimize away calls via thunks, or it can optimize away the .vtfixup metadata that produces these thunks. In the following sections, I'll discuss some scenarios that will help you understand these optimizations.

Native and Managed Callers

Managed functions with native calling conventions can be called in two different ways. Even though the functions fManaged and fManaged2 have a native calling convention, they can be called directly from managed clients. As shown in Figure 9-2, the thunk is only used when a native caller invokes a managed function.

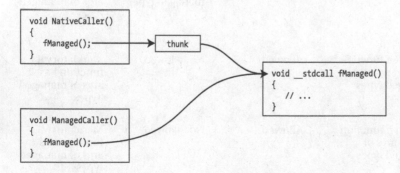

Figure 9-2. *fManaged can have native and managed callers*

Managed Callers Only

The following code shows another special case. Even though the function fManaged has a
native calling convention, it is not called by native functions:

```
// OnlyManagedCallers.cpp
// build with "cl /clr OnlyManagedCallers.cpp"

using namespace System;

void __stdcall fManaged()
{
  Console::WriteLine("fManaged called");
}

int main()
{
  fManaged();
}
```

When the compiler can be sure that a managed function with a native calling convention
is called only from managed code, there is no need for interoperability metadata. Therefore,
in the preceding code, the compiler and the linker do not emit vtfixup metadata for fManaged,
despite the native calling convention. This reduces the assembly load time because fewer
unmanaged-to-managed thunks need to be created and fewer interoperability vtables need
to be initialized when the assembly is loaded.

As mentioned before, it is also possible to explicitly tell the compiler that vtentry and
vtfixup should not be generated. This can be done with a new calling convention named
__clrcall:

```
void __clrcall fManaged()
{
  // ...
}
```

Any attempt to call a managed function with the __clrcall calling convention from
native code will fail. Since the keyword __clrcall is only valid if you compile with /clr[:*],
you cannot even declare a __clrcall function in a file compiled to native code. Trying to call
a __clrcall function within a #pragma unmanaged section will cause self-explanatory compiler
error C3642: "Cannot call a function with __clrcall calling convention from native code."

At first glance, it may seem that the __clrcall calling convention is not necessary,
because the compiler generates vtfixup metadata only if a managed function with a native
calling convention is called by native code. However, if you work with native function pointers
of virtual functions in C++, using this calling convention can be an important performance
benefit. This will be discussed later, in the "Passing Native-Managed Boundaries with Function Pointers" and "Passing Native-Managed Boundaries with Virtual Function Calls" sections.

Calling Native Functions from Managed Code

Just as with native code that calls managed code, interoperability metadata is created when managed functions call native code. This kind of interoperability metadata is called P/Invoke metadata. *P/Invoke* stands for "platform invoke." If you have implemented code to call native functions from other .NET languages, you likely know this term, because in other languages you have to manually write code that produces the P/Invoke metadata.

Unless you have to handle a handful of special cases, C++/CLI generates P/Invoke metadata automatically from C/C++ function declarations. Other .NET languages cannot use C++ types directly; therefore they often have to use the type marshaling features built into the P/Invoke layer. Using the type marshaling provided by the P/Invoke layer is an expensive operation. Since C++/CLI can use C++ types directly (as described in Chapter 8), the P/Invoke metadata generated by the C++/CLI compiler often results in thunks that are considerably faster than P/Invoke metadata manually written for other languages.

Depending on the compilation model and the location of the target function, the content of the generated P/Invoke metadata can vary. For a solid understanding of the P/Invoke layer, its costs, and its optimization options, it is necessary to look at each scenario in turn.

Calling Local Native Functions from Managed Code

The first scenario that I will discuss is a call of a native function that is invoked by a managed function from the same assembly. Figure 9-3 shows this scenario.

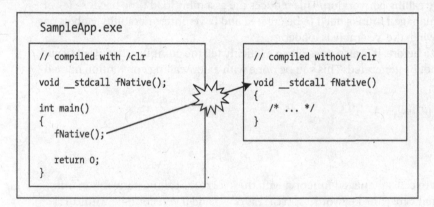

Figure 9-3. *Managed code calling local native code*

To call fNative in main, the compiler emits a CALL instruction as if a managed function were called:

```
.method assembly static int32 main() cil managed
{
  .maxstack  1

  // fNative();
  call fNative()
```

```
// return 0;
ldc.i4.0
ret
}
```

There is a managed function in the metadata of the assembly to allow such a CALL instruction. This managed function is called a P/Invoke function. Even though this metadata appears as a function, it does not contain IL code; it only contains information necessary for building a managed-to-unmanaged thunk. The following code shows the P/Invoke function for fNative:

```
.method public static pinvokeimpl(stdcall) fNative () native unmanaged preservesig
{
  .custom instance void
  [mscorlib]System.Security.SuppressUnmanagedCodeSecurityAttribute::.ctor()
  = ( 01 00 00 00 )

  //  Managed TargetRVA = 0x00001000
}
```

In the first line of this code, you can see that the function is a P/Invoke function because it uses the IL keyword pinvokeimpl. In contrast to functions compiled to IL code, the P/Invoke function also has the flags native and unmanaged, because the target function fNative contains native code that is not generated by the runtime, but by the C++ compiler.

Since the managed caller and the native target function are linked into the one assembly, the RVA of the target function is stored in the P/Invoke metadata, as the comment in the function's body shows. When fNative is called the first time, its P/Invoke metadata is JIT-compiled. The result of this JIT compilation is a managed-to-native thunk.

Notice that the P/Invoke function also contains a special attribute: System::Security::SuppressUnmanagedCodeSecurityAttribute. This attribute is a powerful optimization. Without it, the JIT compiler would generate a thunk that performs security checks before fNative is called. These security checks are only relevant if your code is called from sandboxed assemblies. A thunk that is generated without these security checks performs at least ten times faster than a thunk with these checks.

You can turn off the generation of this attribute for all automatically generated P/Invoke methods of your code with the linker flag /CLRUNMANAGEDCODECHECK. However, due to the performance penalty, I recommend using this option only in special sandboxing scenarios (which are not covered here).

Calling Native Functions Imported from DLLs

P/Invoke metadata is also generated if you call a native function that is imported from a DLL. The following code shows an example of this scenario:

```
// AutoPInvoke.cpp
// compile with "CL /clr AutoPInvoke.cpp"
// or with "CL /clr:pure AutoPInvoke.cpp"

// by including windows.h, the function Beep is declared
#include <windows.h>
```

```
// this line adds the import lib for kernel32.dll to the list of like inputs
#pragma comment(lib, "kernel32.lib")

int main()
{
    Beep(440, 100);
}
```

When you compile the AutoPInvoke sample shown previously with /clr, the resulting P/Invoke metadata is similar to the P/Invoke function for the native function in the same assembly:

```
.method public static pinvokeimpl(lasterr stdcall)
        int32 Beep(
            uint32 modopt([mscorlib]System.Runtime.CompilerServices.IsLong) A_0,
            uint32 modopt([mscorlib]System.Runtime.CompilerServices.IsLong) A_1
        ) native unmanaged preservesig
{
  .custom instance void
        [mscorlib]System.Security.SuppressUnmanagedCodeSecurityAttribute::.ctor()
                = ( 01 00 00 00 )

  //  Managed TargetRVA = 0x0000243A
}
```

Apart from the different method signatures, there is only one difference between the P/Invoke function for Beep and the P/Invoke function for fNative in the sample before. In the metadata for Beep, you can read pinvokeimpl(lasterr stdcall) instead of pinvokeimpl(stdcall). I will address this lasterr flag in the "Optimizing Thunks" section later in this chapter.

Despite the similarities, there is another aspect that needs explanation. The native function Beep is not located in the application, but in a dependent DLL (kernel32.dll). Nevertheless, the P/Invoke metadata refers to an RVA that is relative to the loaded application—not relative to the dependent DLL.

As discussed in Chapter 7, assemblies compiled with /clr and assemblies compiled to native code have load-time dependencies for all imported DLLs (in contrast to assemblies compiled with /clr:pure or /clr:safe). For AutoPInvoke.exe created with /clr, the dumpbin tool shows the following imports:

```
Microsoft (R) COFF/PE Dumper Version 8.00.50727.42
Copyright (C) Microsoft Corporation.  All rights reserved.


Dump of file AutoPInvoke.exe

File Type: EXECUTABLE IMAGE

  Section contains the following imports:
```

```
MSVCR80.dll
        ... further information about MSVCR80.dll skipped for clarity here ...


KERNEL32.dll
            403000 Import Address Table
            4066F8 Import Name Table
                 0 time date stamp
                 0 Index of first forwarder reference

    Import functions table for KERNEL32.dll:
            1F      Beep
            34A     SetUnhandledExceptionFilter
        ... remainder of list of imported functions from kernel32.dll
        skipped for clarity here ...


other imported DLL skipped for clarity here ...
```

When the application is started, a new process is created. The OS loader for processes and
DLLs loads the EXE file and the imported DLLs into the virtual memory. For every DLL that is
loaded, the OS loader iterates through the list of imported functions, determines the virtual
address of each imported function, and writes it into the so-called *import address table*. From
the dumpbin output of AutoPInvoke.exe, you can conclude that the import address table for
kernel32.dll starts at the address 0x403000. After kernel32.dll has been loaded, the import
address table contains all addresses of the imported functions. Since Beep is the first function
in the list of imported functions, the address to Beep is at 0x403000 in the virtual memory. The
address of SetUnhandledExceptionFilter (the second function) can be found at 0x403004, and
so on.

To enable the thunk to call the Beep function, the C++/CLI compiler automatically generates a one-instruction stub function that simply jumps to the function that the first entry
import address table refers to:

```
Address              Code
0040243A             jmp                    dword ptr [__imp__Beep@8 (403000h)]
```

Notice that in the AutoPInvoke sample used here, the P/Invoke metadata for Beep has the
TargetRVA 0000243A. If you add the application's base address, 0x400000, to this TargetRVA, it is
obvious that the thunk refers to this simple stub function.

If you compile this file with /clr:pure, the metadata will no longer contain information
about a TargetRVA. Instead of a local address, the pinvokeimpl specifier contains another piece
of information, as the following ILASM output shows.

```
.method public static pinvokeimpl("KERNEL32.dll" lasterr stdcall)
    int32 Beep(
        uint32 modopt([mscorlib]System.Runtime.CompilerServices.IsLong) A_0,
        uint32 modopt([mscorlib]System.Runtime.CompilerServices.IsLong) A_1
    ) cil managed preservesig
{
```

```
    .custom instance void
        [mscorlib]System.Security.SuppressUnmanagedCodeSecurityAttribute::.ctor()
            = ( 01 00 00 00 )
}
```

Since there is no RVA provided in the P/Invoke metadata used now, the JIT compiler must find another way to determine the address of Beep when it generates the thunk. To generate the thunk now, the JIT compiler has to load the target DLL (unless it has loaded it before). To find the virtual address of the target function, GetProcAddress has to be called. Once this information is available, the thunk can be created. This approach implies that the dependent DLLs are now loaded on demand, not automatically at startup.

Since code compiled with /clr:safe cannot use pointers, native classes, structs, enums, or unions, you cannot include windows.h if you want to compile to verifiable IL code. However, you can implement a P/Invoke function manually. The following code produces exactly the same P/Invoke metadata as the sample compiled with /clr:pure:

```
// ManualPInvoke.cpp
// compile with "CL /clr:safe ManualPInvoke.cpp"

using namespace System::Security;
using namespace System::Runtime::InteropServices;

[SuppressUnmanagedCodeSecurity]
[DllImport("KERNEL32.dll",
          SetLastError=true,
          CallingConvention=CallingConvention::StdCall)]
int Beep(unsigned long, unsigned long);

int main()
{
    Beep(440, 100);
}
```

If you compile with /clr or /clr:pure, you will usually prefer automatically generated P/Invoke functions. However, when I discuss fine-tuning managed-unmanaged transitions and custom P/Invoke marshaling, I will mention a few cases in which you might consider defining manual P/Invoke functions.

Calling C++ Classes Across Managed-Unmanaged Boundaries

Developers new to C++/CLI sometimes confuse managed classes and native classes whose member functions are compiled to managed code. Even when all member functions of a C++ class are compiled to managed code, the resulting class is still a C++ type, not a managed type. However, compiling all member functions of a native class to managed code can imply a native-managed transition if native code calls a member function of the native class. The application shown in Figure 9-4 gives an example:

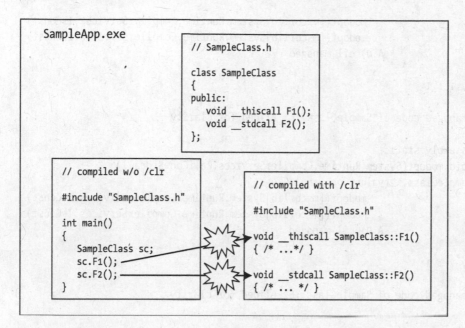

Figure 9-4. *Native classes compiled to managed code can be used by native clients.*

IL metadata is not aware of C++ classes. Therefore, the C++/CLI compiler generates two global functions with the mangled names SampleClass.F1 and SampleClass.F2 for the two member functions of SampleClass. Since F1 and F2 are non-static member functions of SampleClass, they have a hidden this pointer argument of type SampleClass * const. To define this argument of both methods, the C++/CLI compiler generates a managed proxy type, as described in Chapter 8:

```
.class private sequential ansi sealed beforefieldinit SampleClass
      extends [mscorlib]System.ValueType
{
  .pack 0
  .size 1

  // [NativeCppClassAttribute]
  .custom instance void
      [mscorlib]System.Runtime.CompilerServices.NativeCppClassAttribute::.ctor()
      = ( 01 00 00 00 )

  // other attributes elided for clarity here
}
```

In the sample application, both member functions are called from native code. Therefore, the compiler emits .vtentry and .vtfixup metadata for SampleClass.F1 and SampleClass.F2:

```
.method assembly static void
      modopt(System.Runtime.CompilerServices.CallConvThiscall)
      SampleClass.F1(valuetype SampleClass*
```

```
                           modopt([mscorlib]System.Runtime.CompilerServices.IsConst)
                           modopt([mscorlib]System.Runtime.CompilerServices.IsConst)
                    A_0) cil managed
{
  .vtentry 1 : 1

  // ... managed code of SampleClass::F1 elided for clarity
}
.method assembly static
        void modopt(System.Runtime.CompilerServices.CallConvStdcall)
        SampleClass.F2(valuetype SampleClass*
                           modopt([mscorlib]System.Runtime.CompilerServices.IsConst)
                           modopt([mscorlib]System.Runtime.CompilerServices.IsConst)
                    A_0) cil managed
{
  .vtentry 2 : 1

  // ... managed code of SampleClass::F2 elided for clarity
}
```

As with global functions, the compiler generates an interoperability vtable containing an address to the unmanaged-to-managed thunk. When the assembly is loaded, the CLR generates the thunk and stores its address in the interoperability vtable. The native caller can then use the interoperability vtable to invoke the thunk that calls the member functions.

It you switch the compilation models of the source files in the preceding sample, native member functions are called by a managed client. Consequently, the following P/Invoke metadata will be generated in this case:

```
.method public static pinvokeimpl()
        void modopt([mscorlib]System.Runtime.CompilerServices.CallConvThiscall)
        SampleClass.F1(valuetype SampleClass*
                           modopt([mscorlib]System.Runtime.CompilerServices.IsConst)
                           modopt([mscorlib]System.Runtime.CompilerServices.IsConst)
                    A_0) native unmanaged preservesig
{
  .custom instance void
        System.Security.SuppressUnmanagedCodeSecurityAttribute::.ctor()
        = ( 01 00 00 00 )
  //  Managed TargetRVA = 0x00001000
}
```

Passing Native-Managed Boundaries with Function Pointers

Functions pointers can also be used to cross interoperability boundaries in both directions. Figure 9-5 shows a simple application with a managed entry point main that calls a native function fTarget via a function pointer.

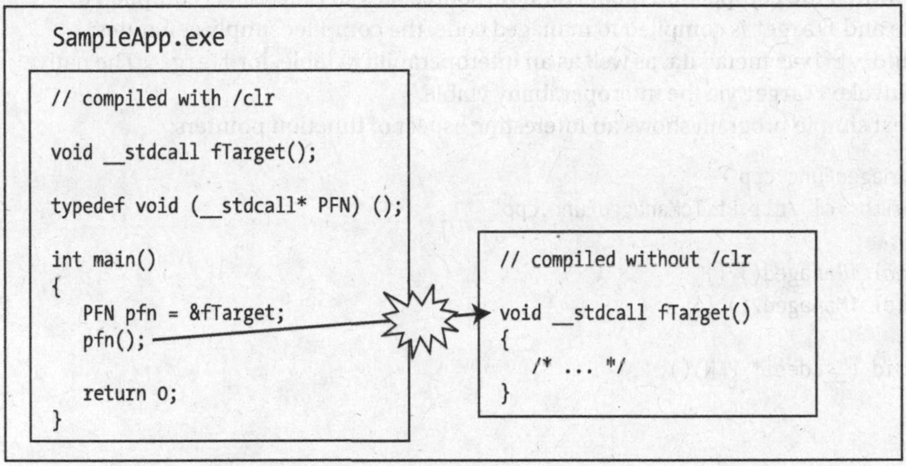

Figure 9-5. *Managed code calling native code via a function pointer*

For the function main, the C++/CLI compiler generates the following IL code:

```
.method assembly static int32
        modopt([mscorlib]System.Runtime.CompilerServices.CallConvCdecl)
        main() cil managed
{
  .maxstack  1
  .locals (method unmanaged stdcall void
          modopt(System.Runtime.CompilerServices.CallConvStdcall) *() pfn)

// PFN pfn = &fManaged;
  ldsfld    int32** __unep@?fTarget@@$$FYGXXZ$PST04000001
  stloc     pfn

// pfn();
  ldloc     pfn
  calli     unmanaged stdcall void
            modopt(System.Runtime.CompilerServices.CallConvStdcall)()

// return 0;
  ldc.i4.0
  ret
}
```

Notice that the compiler has generated a global variable with the mangled name
__unep@?fTarget@@$$FYGXXZ$PST04000001. This variable stores the pointer to the native function fTarget. A CALLI instruction is used to perform the call to fTagret via the function pointer. (CALLI is the abbreviation for "call indirect.") Even through a native function is called from managed code here, no P/Invoke metadata is generated. All metadata necessary to build the thunk is contained in the CALLI instruction's operand. This includes the calling convention and the function arguments.

If you switch the compilation model for both source files so that main is compiled to native code and fTarget is compiled to managed code, the compiler simply generates .vtentry and .vtfixup metadata, as well as an interoperability vtable, for fTarget. The native caller can invoke fTarget via the interoperability vtable.

The next simple program shows an interesting aspect of function pointers:

```
// PtrToManagedFunc.cpp
// build with "cl /clr PtrToManagedFunc.cpp"

void __cdecl fManaged() {}
void __cdecl fManaged2() {}

typedef void (__cdecl* PFN)();

int main()
{
  PFN pfn = &fManaged;
}
```

In this code, neither fManaged nor fManaged2 are called. However, the code in main stores an address to fManaged in a local __cdecl function pointer variable. This variable could be passed to a native function. To allow a native function that receives this pointer to call fManaged, the function pointer does not refer to fManaged, but to the native-to-managed thunk for fManaged. As discussed before, creating this thunk requires .vtentry and .vtfixup metadata and an interoperability vtable. For fManaged2, no interoperability metadata is created, because its address is not used in the program.

If the pointer to the managed function is actually passed to native code, the generated interoperability metadata is necessary to create the required thunk. However, if you only use the function pointer within managed code, the interoperability metadata and the thunk are overhead.

Avoiding this overhead is very simple. Remember, a managed function can be called by native code via a thunk, and by managed code directly (without a thunk). Since managed code can call fManaged without using the thunk, it is also possible to define a __clrcall function pointer that refers to fManaged2. This simple modification avoids the interoperability metadata for fManaged:

```
// ManagedPtrToManagedFunc.cpp
// build with "cl /clr ManagedPtrToManagedFunc.cpp"

void __cdecl fManaged() {}
void __cdecl fManaged2() {}
```

```
typedef void (__clrcall* PFN)();

int main()
{
    PFN pfn = &fManaged;
}
```

Since the variable pfn can now only be used by managed code, there is no need for interoperability metadata or an interoperability vtable.

Using __clrcall instead of a native calling convention can be an important performance optimization because it can avoid the so-called double-thunking problem, which is demonstrated by the sample program in Figure 9-6.

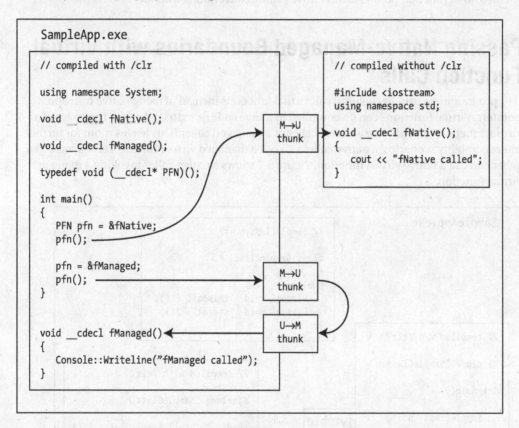

Figure 9-6. *Calling functions with native calling conventions via function pointers*

In this code, the managed function main calls a native function (fNative) as well as a managed function (fManaged) via a function pointer. This function pointer is defined as a __cdecl function pointer.

In main, a local variable pfn of type PFN is defined. First, pfn is initialized with the expression &fNative. Since main is compiled to managed code and the target function is native code, this expression will automatically return a pointer to a managed-to-unmanaged thunk that calls fNative. When the function is invoked via pfn, this thunk does the necessary managed-to-unmanaged transition.

Since the function pointer returned by the expression &fManaged is a function pointer with a native calling convention, it could be passed to native code. Therefore, the expression &fManaged returns a pointer to an unmanaged-to-managed thunk. Since an unmanaged-to-managed thunk can be called directly by unmanaged code, it is an unmanaged function. When managed code wants to call the unmanaged-to-managed thunk via a function pointer, it has to use a managed-to-unmanaged thunk. Instead of calling fManaged from managed code without a transition, fManaged is called via two transitions. This problem is called *double thunking*.

To avoid the double-thunking problem, you should use __clrcall-based function pointers instead of function pointers with native calling conventions whenever this is possible.

Passing Native-Managed Boundaries with Virtual Function Calls

C++ programmers usually prefer to call virtual functions instead of using native function pointers. Virtual functions can be compiled to native code or managed code. The caller of a virtual function can either be a native caller or a managed caller. This leaves room for further interoperability scenarios: a native caller can call a managed virtual function and a managed caller can call a native virtual function. Figure 9-7 shows a native caller invoking a managed virtual function.

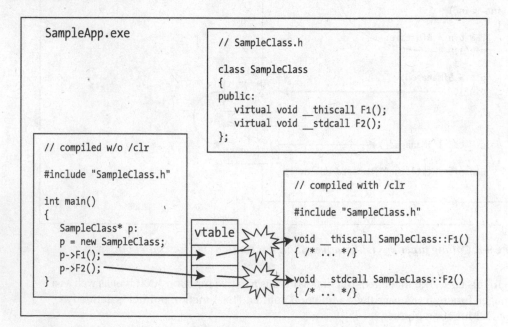

Figure 9-7. *Calling managed virtual functions from native code*

Since the caller of the virtual functions is a native caller, it simply picks a function pointer from a vtable to invoke the virtual function. When a virtual function is compiled to managed code, a pointer to the thunk must end up in the vtable. To create this thunk, the compiler produces .vtentry and .vtfixup metadata for the methods F1 and F2 of SampleClass:

```
.method assembly static void
        modopt([mscorlib]System.Runtime.CompilerServices.CallConvThiscall)
        SampleClass.F1(
                valuetype SampleClass*
                modopt([mscorlib]System.Runtime.CompilerServices.IsConst)
                modopt([mscorlib]System.Runtime.CompilerServices.IsConst) this
        ) cil managed
{
  .vtentry 1 : 1
  // IL code elided for clarity here
}
```

Figure 9-8 shows the opposite direction of managed-unmanaged transitions and virtual function calls. Here, a managed caller (main) invokes a native virtual function (F2).

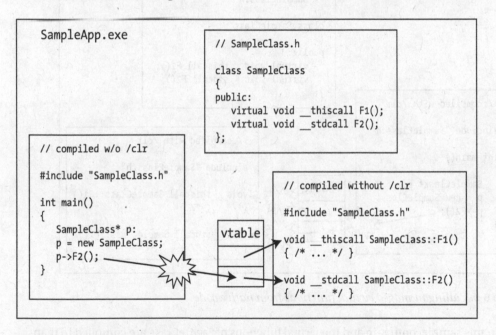

Figure 9-8. *Calling managed virtual functions from native code*

To call the native virtual function F2, the managed caller uses the IL instructions for virtual memory access discussed in Chapter 8 to determine the address to the virtual function pointer from the vtable. Once the virtual function pointer is obtained, the function can be called via the CALLI instruction. For the call p->F2(), the compiler emits the following IL code:

```
ldloc       p        // Push SampleClass pointer on the stack
                     (later used as this argument for call)
```

```
ldloc       p        // Push SampleClass pointer on the stack to get vtable pointer
ldind.i4             // Retrieve vtable pointer
ldc.i4      4        // F2 is second virtual function => offset in vtable is 4
add                  // add this offset to vtable pointer to determine address
                     // at which the virtual function pointer can be found
ldind.i4             // load virtual function pointer from address
// invoke virtual function via its pointer
calli       unmanaged stdcall void
                modopt(System.Runtime.CompilerServices.CallConvStdcall)(native int)
```

Virtual Functions and Double Thunking

The double-thunking problem described in the context of native function pointers can also occur when managed virtual functions are called from managed code. Figure 9-9 shows an example.

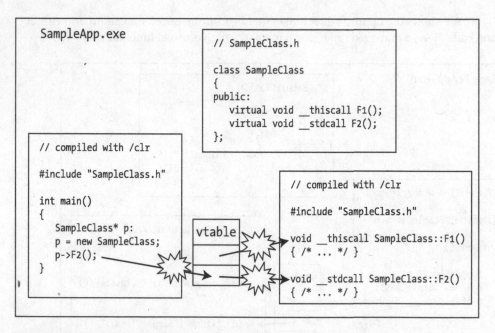

Figure 9-9. *Calling managed virtual functions from native code*

In this sample, both main and the virtual functions of SampleClass are compiled to managed code. Since native callers could also call the virtual functions, the vtable entries in the SampleClass vtable are function pointers to unmanaged-to-managed thunks. When managed code calls such a virtual function, it first picks the corresponding virtual function pointer from the vtable. To call the virtual function via the function pointer, a managed-to-unmanaged thunk is necessary because the vtable entry refers to the unmanaged-to-managed thunk, which is an unmanaged function.

In this scenario, managed code calls the managed function SampleClass::F2 with two transitions, not directly. This is another variant of the double-thunking problem. Since in C++ code, virtual functions are used more often than function pointers, double-thunking occurs more often in this context.

To solve this problem, virtual functions of native classes can be defined with the managed calling convention __clrcall. By using this calling convention, you close the door for native callers—managed callers, on the other hand, do not face the double-thunking problem.

However, you should be aware that you can only avoid double thunking if you use __clrcall when you introduce the virtual function. It is not possible to overwrite a virtual function that has a native calling convention with a __clrcall function. For example, if a native class library defines the virtual function void __thiscall f(), you cannot provide the override void __clrcall f().

Performance of Thunks

So far, I have only mentioned that calls via thunks are slower than method calls that do not cross a managed-unmanaged boundary. To decide whether the overhead of a transition is acceptable or not, you will likely need more precise information. The next sections explain the overhead of the different transitions. I will especially examine transitions based on interoperability vtables, P/Invoke metadata, and the CALLI instruction. Furthermore, I will discuss how to use a special optimization option for P/Invoke metadata and certain internal aspects of managed-unmanaged thunks that can affect the way you write code.

To discuss the overhead of transitions, I have written an application that measures different interoperability scenarios. The code for this application is provided in Appendix B. You can also download it from the Source Code/Download section of the Apress web site (www.apress.com/) so that you can reproduce the performance tests on your machine or adapt them to your own special scenarios.

To determine the performance of thunks for C functions, the application uses a native and a managed global function defined in the application itself (fManagedLocal and fNativeLocal), as well as a native and a managed function imported from an external DLL (fManagedFromDLL and fNativeFromDLL). The application measures how long it takes to call each of these methods directly, as well as via function pointers from native and managed code. For each measurement, 100 million calls are done. Table 9-2 shows the measured results on my machine (Pentium M 780, 2.26 GHz).

Table 9-2. *Performance of Thunks for Global Functions*

Caller	Direct Method Invocations (Not Via Function Pointers)		Indirect Calls (Via Function Pointers)	
	Managed Code	Native Code	Managed Code	Native Code
Callee				
Managed Function from Same Assembly (fManagedLocal)	0.32s M ➤ M	2.12s U ➤ M	Via __stdcall*: 2.30s M ➤ U ➤ M Via __clrcall*: 0.30s M ➤ M	2.07s U ➤ M
Native Function From Same Assembly (fNativeLocal)	0.63s M ➤ U	0.41s U ➤ U	0.63s M ➤ U	0.41s U ➤ U
Managed Function From Imported DLL (fManagedFromDLL)	3.54s M ➤ U ➤ M	2.12s U ➤ M	2.39s M ➤ U ➤ M	2.07s U ➤ M
Native Function from Imported DLL (fNativeFromDLL)	1.97s M ➤ U	0.41s U ➤ U	0.63s M ➤ U	0.41s U ➤ U

In addition to C functions, the application measures calls to virtual and nonvirtual functions of C++ classes defined in the application itself, as well as in an external DLL. The results are shown in Table 9-3. Again, all functions are called from managed code as well as from native code.

Table 9-3. *Performance of Thunks for Member Functions of Native Classes*

Caller	Nonvirtual function calls		Virtual function calls	
	Managed Code	Native Code	Managed Code	Native Code
Callee				
Native Class from Same Assembly with Managed Member Functions	0.27s M ➤ M	2.25s U ➤ M	__thiscall virtual function: 2.39s M ➤ U ➤ M __clrcall virtual function: 0.40s M ➤ M	2.25s U ➤ M
Native Class from Same Assembly with Native Member Functions	0.74s M ➤ U	0.48s U ➤ U	0.72s M ➤ U	0.54s U ➤ U
Native Class from Imported DLL with Managed Member Functions	3.80s M ➤ U ➤ M	2.30s U ➤ M	2.39s M ➤ U ➤ M	2.25s U ➤ M
Native Class from Imported DLL with Native Member Functions	2.12s M ➤ U	0.49s U ➤ U	0.72s M ➤ U	0.55s U ➤ U

As you can see in both tables, calls across managed-unmanaged boundaries produced by C++/CLI can be more than 500 percent slower than calls without transitions. However, unless you have a large number of transitions, this overhead can likely be ignored. The difference in overhead between the 10 million calls to fManagedLocal from native callers (~2.12s) and the 10 million calls from managed callers (~0.32s) is about 1.8 seconds.

In addition to the measured time, both tables also show the transitions that occur in the different scenarios. For example, for the direct call to fManagedLocal from managed code, the text "M ➤ M" shows that a call from managed code to managed code has occurred. Cells with the text "U ➤ M" indicate an unmanaged-to-managed transition. Likewise, "M ➤ U" stands for a managed-to-unmanaged transition.

For the indirect call to fManagedLocal from managed code, the text M ➤ U ➤ M indicates a transition from managed code to unmanaged code and back to managed code. This is the double-thunking scenario discussed earlier. In addition to the double-thunking case, Table 9-2 also shows the cost for an indirect method call with a __clrcall function pointer, which can prevent double thunking, as discussed earlier. As you can see, double thunking can easily increase the costs for method calls by more than 600 percent. Table 9-3 shows similar results for the double-thunking problem related to virtual function calls.

Optimizing Thunks

For unmanaged-to-managed transitions, there is no potential for improving the performance of the generated thunks. There are no hidden keywords or attributes that can be used for optimizations of transitions in this direction. An unmanaged-to-managed thunk has to perform certain expensive operations. For example, it is possible that a managed function is called by a thread that has not yet executed managed code. The unmanaged-to-managed thunk must be prepared for that case so that a native thread will be automatically promoted to a managed thread before the managed function is called. In case of a mixed-code DLL, it is also possible that the managed part of the assembly has not been initialized. In this case, the thunk has to ensure the managed initialization.

You cannot optimize the performance of unmanaged-to-managed thunks. Your only optimization option is to reduce the number of unmanaged-to-managed transitions. As mentioned earlier, this can either be done by refactoring code so that multiple transitions are replaced by one, or by using the __clrcall calling convention to prevent double thunking.

In contrast to unmanaged-to-managed thunks, the performance of managed-to-unmanaged thunks can be significantly optimized. As the output of the test application shows, 10 million calls to the imported function fNativeFromDLL take about 1.97 seconds, whereas the same number of calls to the function fNativeLocal, which is in the same assembly as the caller, execute in approximately 0.63 seconds.

It is possible to optimize the thunk for fNativeFromDLL so that it performs equally fast. To give you a solid understanding of thunk optimizations, I'll explain how thunks are invoked and how they work. Thunks generated for P/Invoke functions can be grouped into three performance categories as follows:

- *Inlined thunks*: As you can conclude from the name, the native code of an inlined thunk is inlined into the caller's code. This saves the costs of calling a thunk function explicitly, and it allows the JIT compiler and the processor to further optimize code execution. Therefore, inlined thunks are the fastest ones.

- *Non-inlined thunks*: The CLR can also generate a thunk as a separate function that has to be called with an explicit function call (usually a native CALL instruction). Calling a function via a non-inlined thunk is usually between 100 percent and 300 percent slower than calling the same function via an inlined thunk.

- *Generic thunks*: The P/Invoke layer offers some special type marshaling features that map arguments from the managed to the native type system before the target method is called, and vice versa when the call returns. P/Invoke functions automatically generated by C++/CLI never use these features; however, you can implement custom P/Invoke metadata that produces a generic thunk. Like non-inlined thunks, calling generic thunks requires an explicit function call. To perform parameter marshaling, a generic thunk calls a generic helper function that consumes further metadata from the P/Invoke function, which is obviously slower than leaving the stack untouched when invoking the target function. Generic thunks are by far the slowest thunks.

GetLastError-Caching

Since these thunks are created from interoperability metadata, it makes sense to compare the P/Invoke functions that the compiler generates for fNativeFromDLL and fNativeLocal:

```
.method public static pinvokeimpl(lasterr stdcall)
        void modopt([mscorlib]System.Runtime.CompilerServices.CallConvStdcall)
                fNativeFromDLL() native unmanaged preservesig
{ /* further metadata elided for clarity */}


.method public static pinvokeimpl(stdcall)
        void modopt([mscorlib]System.Runtime.CompilerServices.CallConvStdcall)
                fNativeLocal() native unmanaged preservesig
{ /* further metadata elided for clarity */}
```

The metadata for fNativeFromDLL contains the pinvokeimpl specifier pinvokeimpl (lasterr stdcall), whereas the pinvokeimpl specifier for fNative contains only the keyword stdcall. The keyword lasterr instructs the JIT compiler to generate a managed-to-unmanaged thunk that performs the so-called GetLastError-caching.

To understand the motivation for GetLastError-caching, it is necessary to take a look at the error handling strategy of most Win32 API functions. Unless a function returns an HRESULT value, functions from the Win32 API express that they have not executed successfully by returning either the BOOL value FALSE or a HANDLE of an illegal value (typically either NULL or the macro INVALID_HANDLE_VALUE, which has the value -1).

To get further information about the error, an error code can be retrieved by calling GetLastError. If this function had been called via a normal managed-to-unmanaged thunk, you could easily get an error value that is not set by the function you expected, but by a totally different function. Executing managed code often causes further calls to Win32 API functions internally. For example, assume that the IL instruction call is executed to invoke a method. It is easily possible that this will cause further calls to LoadLibraryEx, because the method that should be invoked has to be JIT-compiled first, and quite often, the JIT compiler has to load an additional assembly. Also, IL instructions like newobj, newarr, and box can obviously cause the managed heap to allocate further memory via calls to VirtualAlloc and related APIs. These internal method calls can obviously overwrite the GetLastError value. To face this problem, the CLR allows managed-to-unmanaged thunks to perform GetLastError-caching.

Thunks that perform GetLastError-caching read the GetLastError value after calling the target function and store it in CLR-specific thread local storage (TLS). When managed code calls GetLastError to retrieve the error code, the cached error code is used instead of the real error code returned by GetLastError!

To achieve this, the JIT compiler treats P/Invoke metadata for the GetLastError function of kernel32.dll specially. The thunk that is generated for P/Invoke metadata for GetLastError calls FalseGetLastError from mscowks.dll instead of kernel32.dll's GetLastError function. This function returns the cached error value from the CLR-specific TLS.

There are two reasons why thunks that update the cached GetLastError value are more expensive than thunks without GetLastError-caching. Obviously, determining the last error value and storing it in TLS takes time. Furthermore, thunks with GetLastError-caching are never inlined, whereas thunks that do not perform GetLastError-caching are usually inlined. (The CLR 2.0 does not inline P/Invoke thunks for functions that return either float or double, even if they do not support GetLastError-caching. However, that special case shall be ignored here.)

By default, P/Invoke metadata that is automatically created for functions imported from DLLs have the lasterror flag to ensure that GetLastError works for all Win32 API calls. For native local functions, C++/CLI interoperability automatically generates P/Invoke metadata without the lasterror flag because SetLastError and GetLastError are usually not the preferred error reporting mechanisms for non-Win32 APIs.

Since the thunk for fNativeFromDLL performs GetLastError-caching, it is not inlined, in contrast to the thunk for fNativeLocal. This explains the difference in the execution performance of the two thunks. However, you can use the linker command-line option /CLRSUPPORTLASTERROR:NO to instruct the linker to generate P/Invoke metadata without the lasterror flag. I strictly advise against using this option because of the large number of Win32 functions that report error codes via the GetLastError value.

If a native function that never touches the GetLastError value is called very often from managed code, and you want to optimize the performance of its thunk, you can define custom P/Invoke metadata instead. The following code shows an example:

```
[System::Security::SuppressUnmanagedCodeSecurity]
[System::Runtime::InteropServices::DllImport(
        "TestLib.dll",
        EntryPoint="fNativeFromDLL",
        ExactSpelling="true",
        SetLastError=false)]
void fNativeFromDLL_NoGLE();
```

While you'll have to write some extra code, this approach will help you avoid the trouble of getting incorrect Win32 error values for all other imported functions, while still benefiting from a fast inlined thunk without the overhead of GetLastError-caching. Notice that the custom P/Invoke function is called fNativeFromDLL_NoGLE instead of just fNativeFromDLL. This prevents naming conflicts with the native function. The information about the entry point's name is provided via the EntryPoint and the ExactSpelling properties of the DllImportAttribute.

To avoid these naming conflicts, I recommend defining the P/Invoke function in a namespace or managed class, as shown here:

```
namespace NativeFuncs
{
    [System::Security::SuppressUnmanagedCodeSecurity]
    [System::Runtime::InteropServices::DllImport(
        "kernel32.dll",
        SetLastError=false)]
        void fNativeFromDll(DWORD frequency, DWORD duration);
};
```

Writing a custom P/Invoke function in C++/CLI is often much easier than writing an equivalent function in other languages. Since native types can seamlessly be used in C++/CLI, you can simply copy the native function declaration and replace some native declaration aspects with equivalent managed aspects. As an example, have a look at the declaration of Beep in winbase.h:

```
WINBASEAPI
BOOL
WINAPI
Beep(
    __in DWORD dwFreq,
    __in DWORD dwDuration
  );
```

In this code, the macro WINBASEAPI evaluates to __declspec(dllimport). The managed equivalent of __declspec(dllimport) is the DllImportAttribute. Therefore, you must remove the WINBASEAPI macro and apply the DllImportAttribute instead. The WINAPI macro evaluates to __stdcall. It is used to specify the calling convention of Beep. Instead of using this native calling convention, your P/Invoke function must apply the DllImportAttribute as shown here:

```
namespace Win32Native
{
    using namespace System::Runtime::InteropServices;

    [System::Security::SuppressUnmanagedCodeSecurity]
    [DllImport("kernel32.dll",
            SetLastError=false,
            CallingConvention = CallingConvention::StdCall)]
    void Beep(DWORD frequency, DWORD duration);
};
```

The default setting for the CallingConvention property of the DllImportAttribute is CallingConvention::WinApi. This setting is used to specify that the default calling convention of the platform's system APIs should be chosen. For the Win32 API, this is __stdcall. Since Beep is a function of the system API, it is also possible to keep this default setting instead of specifying CallingConvention = CallingConvention::StdCall.

Be Aware of Implicit GetLastError-Caching Optimizations

There are two scenarios that can result in wrong GetLastError values due to the GetLastError-caching optimizations that are done by C++/CLI and the CLR. Both scenarios are unlikely, but according to Murphy's Law, "unlikely" means that they will surely occur at some time. Therefore, you should be aware of them.

The first scenario is related to the optimizations done for native functions that are not imported from a DLL, but reside in the same project. As mentioned before, for these native local functions, C++/CLI automatically generates P/Invoke metadata without the lasterror flag, because it is very uncommon to use the GetLastError value to communicate error codes within a project. However, the MSDN documentation on GetLastError allows you to use SetLastError and GetLastError for your own functions. Therefore, this optimization can theoretically cause wrong GetLastError values. As an example, the output of the following application depends on the compilation model:

```
// GLECachingTrouble1.cpp
// build with "CL /clr GLECachingTrouble1.cpp"
// or with    "CL GLECachingTrouble1.cpp"

#include <windows.h>
#include <stdio.h>

void managedFunc()
{
  SetLastError(0x42);
}


// remember that you usually should not use #pragma [un]managed.
// It is used here only to avoid discussing two different source files.
#pragma managed(push, off)

void nativeFunc()
{
  SetLastError(0x12345678);
}

#pragma managed(pop)

int main()
{
  managedFunc();
  nativeFunc();

  // if app is built with /clr, the next line writes "0x42" instead of "0x12345678"!
  printf("0x%X", GetLastError());
}
```

This simple program first calls the managed function managedFunc, which internally calls SetLastError. Since SetLastError is an imported function, it is called by a thunk that supports GetLastError-caching. This means that after the call to SetLastError, the current error value (0x42) is cached by the thunk.

After that, managedFunc returns to main and main calls nativeFunc. Notice that nativeFunc is a native function is the same assembly as main. If you compile the application to native code, nativeFunc will set the GetLastError code to 0x12345678. If you compile with /clr, nativeFunc will be called via a thunk. Since nativeFunc is a function from the same project, the P/Invoke metadata generated for it does not have the lasterr modifier, and therefore its thunk does not support GetLastError-caching. Because of that, the cached error value is not modified when nativeFunc returns. The call to GetLastError inside of the printf method is redirected to mscorwks!FalseGetLastError, which returns the cached error value. As a result, the error value 0x42, which was set in managedFunc, is returned by the GetLastError call in main, even though nativeFunc has called SetLastError to modify this value to 0x12345678.

If you compile this application without /clr, the value 0x12345678 will be written to the console instead of 0x42.

The second potential for trouble with wrong GetLastError values is related to indirect function calls. As discussed before, when a function pointer is used to call a native function from managed code, the IL instruction CALLI is emitted by the compiler, and the JIT compiler generates the thunk. As with thunks for native local functions, thunks generated from CALLI instructions are inlined and do not perform GetLastError-caching. On the one hand, this results in fast thunks. On the other hand, this can also result in lost GetLastError values.

Like the application shown before, the following application produces different outputs depending on the compilation model used:

```
// GLECachingTrouble2.cpp
// build with "CL /clr GLECachingTrouble2.cpp"
// or with     "CL GLECachingTrouble2.cpp"

#include <windows.h>
#include <stdio.h>

int main()
{
  // since Beep is called with an illegal frequency here, it will fail
  if (!Beep(12345678, 100))
    // the GetLastError code is 0x57: ERROR_INVALID_PARAMETER
    printf("Direct call caused error code 0x%X\n", GetLastError());

  // set the lasterror value to a value other than before
  SetLastError(0);

  // now let's call Beep via a function pointer
  typedef BOOL (WINAPI* PFNBEEP)(DWORD, DWORD);
  PFNBEEP pfn = &Beep;
  if (!pfn(12345678, 100))
```

```
    // when this application is built with /clr, GetLastError will be 0,
    // otherwise it will be 0x57!
    printf("Indirect call caused error code 0x%X\n", GetLastError());
}
```

When this application is built with /clr, the output will be as follows:

```
Direct call caused error code 0x57
Indirect call caused error code 0x0
```

If you face this problem in your code, you must move the indirect function call and the call to GetLastError to native code. This will ensure that neither the native function nor the GetLastError function will be called via a thunk, and the correct GetLastError value will be returned.

Generic Thunks and P/Invoke Type Marshaling

So far, I have discussed P/Invoke metadata and thunks only from a performance point of view. If you call managed functions in a context that is not performance critical, you probably prefer convenience over performance. C++/CLI interoperability already provides a lot of convenience—you only need normal function declarations to call a managed function from native code. However, depending on the argument types of the target method, it is still possible that you have to write some code yourself to marshal managed types to native argument types manually.

In the following code sample, the managed class System:Environment is used to get the name of the user that executes the current thread. To pass the content of the managed string returned by Environment::UserName to a function like MessageBoxA, which expects a native null-terminated ANSI code string, the managed string must be marshaled first. Therefore, Marshal::StringToCoTaskMemAnsi is called. To clean up the native string returned by Marshal::StringToCoTaskMemAnsi, the helper function Marshal::FreeCoTaskMem is used:

```
// ManualMarshaling.cpp
// build with "CL /clr ManualMarshaling.cpp"

#include <windows.h>
#pragma comment(lib, "user32.lib")

using namespace System;
using namespace System::Runtime::InteropServices;

int main()
{
  String^ strUserName = Environment::UserName;
  IntPtr iptrUserName = Marshal::StringToCoTaskMemAnsi(strUserName);
  const char* szUserName = static_cast<const char*>(iptrUserName.ToPointer());
  MessageBoxA(NULL, szUserName, "Current User", 0);
  Marshal::FreeCoTaskMem(iptrUserName);
}
```

Instead of writing explicit code to marshal managed string arguments to native strings passed to the target function, you can write a custom P/Invoke function that benefits from P/Invoke type marshaling:

```cpp
// PInvokeMarshaling.cpp"
// build with "CL /clr PInvokeMarshaling.cpp"

#include <windows.h>

using namespace System;
using namespace System::Runtime::InteropServices;

namespace PInvoke
{
    [DllImport("user32.dll",
            CharSet=CharSet::Ansi,             // marshal String^ to LPCSTR
            EntryPoint = "MessageBoxA",
            ExactSpelling = true)]
    UINT MessageBoxA(HWND, String^, String^, UINT);
}

int main()
{
    String^ strUserName = Environment::UserName;
    PInvoke::MessageBoxA(NULL, strUserName, "Current User", 0);
}
```

Summary

Managed-unmanaged transitions are based on metadata and thunks. The compiler produces the necessary metadata and the CLR produces the thunks. For each native function that is called from managed code, P/Invoke metadata is automatically generated. Whenever a managed function is called from native code, the compiler generates an interoperability vtable. If an address of a managed function is stored in a function pointer with a native calling convention, native code can use this function pointer to call the managed function. Therefore, an interoperability vtable is produced for such a managed function, too. Since virtual functions are called internally via function pointers, interoperability vtables are produced for virtual functions, too.

There are two major strategies for optimizing managed-unmanaged transitions. You can either reduce the number of transitions or you can optimize the performance of the generated thunks. To reduce the number of transitions as well as the amount of generated interop metadata, the __clrcall calling convention can be used. By defining custom P/Invoke functions or using a few linker switches, you can optimize the performance of the generated thunks.

Managed-unmanaged transitions often require a deep understanding of the interoperability features provided by the CLR, as well as the C++/CLI language features that allow you to use these features. Many developers appreciate it when managed-unmanaged transitions are hidden behind a simpler façade. The next chapter describes how to hide managed-unmanaged transitions in managed libraries that wrap native APIs.

■ ■ ■

CHAPTER 10

Wrapping Native Libraries

The last two chapters covered details about C++/CLI interoperability. These features are not only useful for extending existing projects with features from managed libraries (which was discussed in Chapter 7), but they can also be useful if you want to give a native library a managed face so that it can be used by other .NET languages.

There are many different scenarios for wrapping native libraries. You can wrap a library whose sources you control, you can wrap part of the Win32 API that is not yet covered by the FCL, and you can even wrap a third-party library. The library you wrap can be implemented as a static library or a DLL. Furthermore, the wrapped library can be a C or a C++ library. This chapter gives you practical advice, general recommendations for all scenarios mentioned, and guidance for a couple of concrete problems.

Up-Front Considerations

Before you start writing code, you should consider different alternatives for wrapping a native library and the consequences that each alternative implies for you as well as the users of your library.

Should You Implement Wrapper Types in a Separate DLL or Integrate Them into the Native Library Project?

As discussed in Chapter 7, you can extend Visual C++ projects with files compiled to managed code. At first, it may seem like an interesting option to integrate the managed wrapper types into the wrapped library, because this means that there will be one less DLL or one less static library that you have to take care of. If you integrate managed wrappers into a DLL, this also means that there is one less DLL that needs to be loaded by the client. Loading fewer DLLs reduces the load time, the required virtual memory, and the likelihood that a dependent DLL has to be rebased, because it cannot be loaded at its natural base address.

However, integrating wrapper types into the wrapped library is seldom useful. To understand the reasons, it is necessary to look at static library projects and DLL projects separately.

Even though it sounds strange, extending a static library project with managed types is possible. However, using managed types from a static library can easily cause type identity problems. In Chapter 4, I discussed that the identity of managed types is scoped by the assembly in which they are defined. The CLR is able to distinguish two types in two different assemblies even if they have the same name. If two different projects use the same managed type from a static library, the type will be linked into both assemblies. Since a managed type's identity is based on the assembly identity, the two types will have different identities even if they originate from the same static library.

For native DLL projects, it is not recommended to integrate managed wrapper types into the DLL, because this would implicitly create a load-time dependency to the CLR 2.0. As a consequence, users of your library would then be required to ensure that version 2.0 of the CLR is installed on the target machine and that the target application does not load an earlier CLR version, even if only native code of the library is executed.

Which Features of the Native Library Should Be Exposed?

As usual in software development, it is useful to precisely define the developer's task before starting to write code. I am aware that the sentence you just read might sound as if I copied it from a second-rate book about software design from the early '90s, but for wrapping native libraries, defining the tasks carefully is of special importance.

If you have to wrap a native library, the task seems obvious—there is an already existing native library, and a managed API has to be implemented to bring the features of the native library to the managed world.

For most wrapping projects, this generic task description is insufficient by far. Without a more precise view of the task, you will likely write one managed wrapper class for each native type of a C++ library. If the native library consists of more than one central abstraction, wrapping one-to-one is often a bad idea, because this often results in complications that don't benefit your concrete problem, as well as a significant amount of unused code.

To find a better task description, you should take a step back and do some thinking to understand the concrete problem. To find a description that is more specific than the preceding one, you should especially ask yourself two questions:

- What subset of the native API is really needed by managed code?

- What are the use cases for which the native API is needed by managed clients?

Once you know the answers to these questions, you are often able to simplify your task by cutting any features that are not needed and by defining new abstractions that wrap based on use cases. For example, assume the following native API:

```
namespace NativeLib
{
  class CryptoAlgorithm
  {
  public:
    virtual void Encrypt(/* ... arguments can be ignored so far ... */) = 0;
    virtual void Decrypt(/* ... arguments can be ignored so far ... */) = 0;
  };

  class SampleCipher : public CryptoAlgorithm
  {
```

```
    /* ... implementation can be ignored so far ... */
};

class AnotherCipherAlgorithm : public CryptoAlgorithm
{
    /* ... implementation can be ignored so far ... */
};
}
```

This API allows a programmer to do the following:

- Instantiate and use `SampleCipher`

- Instantiate and use `AnotherCipherAlgorithm`

- Derive a class from `CryptoAlgorithm`, `SampleCipher`, or `AnotherCipherAlgorithm`, and override `Encrypt` or `Decrypt`

Supporting these three features in a managed wrapper is way more complicated than it may seem at first. The support for inheritance of wrapper classes especially adds a lot of complexity. As I will discuss later in the chapter, supporting virtual functions requires extra proxy classes, which is a runtime overhead as well as an implementation overhead.

However, chances are good that a wrapper library is only needed to use one or both algorithms. Wrapping this API without supporting inheritance simplifies the task. With this simplification, there is no need to create a wrapper type for the abstract class `CryptoAlgorithm`. Also, it is not necessary to treat the virtual functions `Encrypt` and `Decrypt` specially. To make clear that you don't want to support inheritance, it is sufficient to declare the wrapper classes for `SampleCipher` and `AnotherCipherAlgorithm` as sealed classes.

Language Interoperability

One of the major goals of .NET is language interoperability. If you wrap a native library, language interoperability is of special importance because the clients of the wrapper library are likely developers using C# or other .NET languages. As defined in Chapter 1, the Common Language Infrastructure (CLI) is the base specification of .NET. An important aspect of this specification is the Common Type System (CTS). Even though all .NET languages share the same type system, not all .NET languages support all features of that type system.

To provide a clear definition of language interoperability, the CLI contains the Common Language Specification (CLS). The CLS is a contract between developers writing .NET languages and developers writing language-interoperable class libraries. The CLS specifies what CTS features a .NET language should support at least. To ensure that a library can be used by all .NET languages that conform to the CLS, the set of CLS features is the upper limit for all parts of a class library that are visible outside of an assembly. These are all public types and all members of public types that have public, public protected, or protected visibility.

The `CLSCompliantAttribute` can be used to express that a type or type member is CLS-compliant. By default, types that are not marked with this attribute are considered to be non-CLS-compliant. By applying this attribute at the assembly level, you can specify that all types in the assembly should be considered CLS-compliant by default. The following code shows how to apply this attribute to assemblies and types:

```
using namespace System;

[assembly: CLSCompliant(true)];
  // public types are CLS-compliant unless otherwise stated

namespace ManagedWrapper
{
  public ref class SampleCipher sealed
  {
    // ...
  };

  [CLSCompliant(false)]  // this class is explicitly marked as not CLS-compliant
  public ref class AnotherCipherAlgorithm sealed
  {
    // ...
  };
}
```

According to CLS rule 11, all types used in a signature of an externally visible member (method, property, field, or event) should be CLS-compliant. To apply the [CLSCompliant] attribute correctly, you must know whether the types you use as method parameters and such are CLS-compliant or not. To determine the CLS compliance of a type, you must inspect the attributes of the assembly that contains the type definition, as well the attributes applied to the type itself.

The FCL uses the CLSCompliant attribute, too. As shown in the code sample, mscorlib and most other assemblies from the FCL apply the [CLSCompliant(true)] attribute at the assembly level and mark types that are not CLS-compliant with [CLSCompliant(false)].

You should be aware that mscorlib marks the following commonly used primitive types as *non*-CLS-compliant: System::SByte, System::UInt16, System::UInt32, and System::UInt64. You must not use these types (or the equivalent C++ type names char, unsigned short, unsigned int, unsigned long, and unsigned long long) in signatures of type members that are considered CLS-compliant.

When a type is considered CLS-compliant, its members are also considered CLS-compliant, unless they are explicitly marked as non-CLS-compliant, as shown in the following sample:

```
using namespace System;

[assembly: CLSCompliant(true)];
  // public types are CLS-compliant unless otherwise stated

namespace ManagedWrapper
{
  public ref class SampleCipher sealed
```

```
    // SampleCipher is CLS-compliant because of assembly level attribute
{
public:
  void M1(int);

  // M2 is marked as not CLS-compliant, because it has an argument of
  // a not CLS-compliant type
  [CLSCompliant(false)]
  void M2(unsigned int);
};
}
```

Unfortunately, the C++/CLI compiler does not emit warnings when a type or a function is marked as CLS-compliant even if it does not conform to one or more of the CLS rules. To decide whether you should mark a type or type member as CLS-compliant, you should know the following important CLS rules:

- Names of types and type members must be distinguishable by case-insensitive languages (CLS rule 4).

- Global static fields and methods are not CLS-compliant (CLS rule 36).

- Custom attributes should only contain fields of type System::Type, System::String, System::Char, System::Boolean, System::Int[16|32|64], System::Single, and System::Double (CLS rule 34).

- Managed exceptions should be of type System::Exception or of a type derived from System::Exception (CLS rule 40).

- Property accessors must either be all virtual or all nonvirtual (CLS rule 26).

- Boxed value types are not CLS-compliant (CLS rule 3). As an example, the following method is not CLS-compliant: void f(int^ boxedInt);.

- Unmanaged pointer types are not CLS-compliant (CLS rule 17). This rule also implies C++ references. As discussed in Chapter 8, native classes, structures, and unions are accessed via native pointers, too. This implies that these native types are not CLS compliant, either.

Wrapping C++ Classes

Even though the C++ type system and .NET's CTS have certain similarities, wrapping C++ classes to managed classes often results in bad surprises. Obviously, if C++ features that do not have equivalent managed features are used, wrapping can be difficult. As an example, consider a class library that uses multiple inheritance intensively. Even if the class library uses only C++ constructs that have similar counterparts in the native world, mapping is not always obvious. Let's have a look at some different issues in turn.

As discussed in Chapter 8, it is not possible to define a managed wrapper class with a field of type NativeLib::SampleCipher. Since only pointers to native classes are allowed as field types, NativeLib::SampleCipher* must be used instead. In the constructor of the wrapper class, the instance must be created, and the destructor is necessary to delete the wrapped object.

```
namespace ManagedWrapper
{
  public ref class SampleCipher sealed
  {
    NativeLib::SampleCipher* pWrappedObject;

  public:
    SampleCipher(/* arguments ignored so far */)
    {
      pWrappedObject = new NativeLib::SampleCipher(/* arguments ignored so far */);
    }

    ~SampleCipher()
    {
      delete pWrappedObject;
    }

    /* ... */
  };
}
```

In addition to the destructor, it would also be useful to implement a finalizer, which is explained in Chapter 11.

Mapping Native Types to CLS-Compliant Types

Once you have created the wrapper class, you have to add members that allow a .NET client to invoke the member functions on the wrapped object. To ensure language interoperability, the members of your wrapper class must have only CLS-compliant types in their signature. If a function from the native API has an unsigned integer type, it is often sufficient to use a signed type of the same size instead. Finding equivalent types for native pointers and native references is not always that easy. In a few cases, you can use System::IntPtr instead of native pointers. This allows managed code to receive a native pointer and treat it as a handle that can be passed as an argument of a later function call. This case is simple because System::IntPtr has the same binary layout as a native pointer. In all other cases, a manual conversion of one or more parameters is necessary. Even though this can be time-consuming, there is no way to avoid this extra cost. Let's have a look at different wrappings that you may face.

For arguments of C++ reference types and pointer arguments with pass-by-reference semantics, it is recommended to define tracking reference arguments in the managed wrapper function. As an example, consider the following native function:

```
void f(int& i);
```

For this function, a reasonable wrapper could be the following:

```
void fWrapper(int% i)
{
  int j = i;
  f(j);
  i = j;
}
```

A native int reference must be passed to call the native function. Since there is no conversion from a tracking reference to a native reference, the argument must be marshaled manually. Since there is a standard conversion from int to int&, a local variable of type int is used as a buffer for the by-reference argument. Before the native function is called, this buffer is initialized with the value passed as the argument i. When the native function returns to the wrapper, the value referred by the argument i is updated with the changes made to the buffer j.

As you can see in this sample, in addition to the costs of managed-unmanaged transitions, wrapper libraries often need extra processor cycles for type marshaling. For more complex types (discussed later), this overhead can be significantly higher.

You should also be aware that some other .NET languages, including C#, distinguish by-reference arguments and out-only arguments. For a by-reference argument, an initialized variable must be passed, and the called function can modify this value or leave the value untouched. For an out-only argument, an uninitialized variable can be passed, and the called function must modify or initialize its value.

By default, a tracking reference is considered to have by-reference semantics. If you want to define an argument with out-only semantics, you have to use the OutAttribute from the namespace System::Runtime::InteropServices, as shown here:

```
void fWrapper([Out] int% i);
```

Argument types of native functions often have the const modifier, as shown in the following sample:

```
void f(int& i1, const int& i2);
```

As discussed in Chapter 8, the const modifier is translated to an optional signature modifier. Managed callers that do not understand the const signature modifier can still call an fWrapper function, defined as follows:

```
void fWrapper(int% i1, const int% i2);
```

When the native argument is a pointer to an array, tracking reference arguments are not sufficient. To discuss this case, let's assume that the native SampleCipher class has a constructor that expects arguments to pass the encryption key:

```
namespace NativeLib
{
  class SampleCipher : public CryptoAlgorithm
  {
  public:
    SampleCipher(const unsigned char* pKey, int nKeySizeInBytes);
    /* ... implementation can be ignored so far ... */
  };
}
```

Mapping `const unsigned char*` to `const unsigned char%` would not be sufficient here, because the encryption key passed to the constructor of the native type contains more than one byte. The following code shows a better approach:

```
namespace ManagedWrapper
{
  public ref class SampleCipher
  {
    NativeLib::SampleCipher* pWrappedObject;
  public:
    SampleCipher(array<Byte>^ key);

    /* ... */
  };
}
```

In this constructor, both native arguments (`pKey` and `nKeySizeInBytes`) are mapped to a single argument of a managed array type. This is possible because the size of a managed array can be determined at runtime.

The implementation of this constructor depends on the implementation of the native `SampleCipher` class. If the constructor of the native class internally copies the key that is passed via the argument `pKey`, you can use a pinned pointer to pass the key:

```
SampleCipher::SampleCipher(array<Byte>^ key)
{
  if (!key)
    throw gcnew ArgumentNullException("key");

  pin_ptr<unsigned char> pp = &key[0];
  pWrappedObject = new NativeLib::SampleCipher(pp, key->Length);
}
```

However, a pinned pointer cannot be used if the native `SampleCipher` class is implemented as follows:

```
namespace NativeLib
{
  class SampleCipher : public CryptoAlgorithm
  {
    const unsigned char* pKey;
    const int nKeySizeInBytes;
  public:
    SampleCipher(const unsigned char* pKey, int nKeySizeInBytes)
    : pKey(pKey), nKeySizeInBytes(nKeySizeInBytes)
    {}

    /* ... rest of the class can be ignored here ... */
  };
}
```

This constructor expects the client to ensure that the memory for the key is not deallocated and the pointer to the key remains valid until the SampleCipher instance is destroyed. The constructor of the wrapper class does not meet both requirements. Since no tracking handle to the managed array is stored in the managed wrapper class, the GC could clean up the managed array before the native class is destroyed. Even if a tracking handle to the managed array ensures that the memory is not reclaimed, the array could be relocated during garbage collection. In this case, the native pointer would no longer refer to the managed array. To ensure that the key's memory is not reclaimed and that the key's data is not relocated during garbage collection, it should be copied on the native heap. This requires changes in the constructor as well as the destructor of the managed wrapper class. The following code shows how the constructor and the destructor could be implemented:

```
public ref class SampleCipher
{
  unsigned char* pKey;
  NativeLib::SampleCipher* pWrappedObject;
public:
  SampleCipher(array<Byte>^ key)
  : pKey(0),
    pWrappedObject(0)
  {
    if (!key)
      throw gcnew ArgumentNullException("key");

    pKey = new unsigned char[key->Length];
    if (!pKey)
      throw gcnew OutOfMemoryException("Allocation on C++ free store failed");

    try
    {
      Marshal::Copy(key, 0, IntPtr(pKey), key->Length);

      pWrappedObject = new NativeLib::SampleCipher(pKey, key->Length);
      if (!pWrappedObject)
        throw gcnew OutOfMemoryException("Allocation on C++ free store failed");
    }
    catch (Object^)
    {
      delete[] pKey;
      throw;
    }
  }

  ~SampleCipher()
  {
    try
    {
      delete pWrappedObject;
```

```
      }
      finally
      {
        // delete pKey even if destructor of pWrappedObject threw an exception
        delete[] pKey;
      }
    }

    /* rest of the class will be discussed later */
};
```

Apart from some esoteric problems discussed in Chapter 11, the code shown here provides exception-safe resource allocation and deallocation. In case of a failure during the construction of a ManagedWrapper::SampleCipher instance, all intermediately allocated resources are deallocated. The destructor is implemented so that the native array for the key is deleted even if the destructor of the wrapped object throws an exception.

This code also shows a characteristic overhead of many managed wrappers. On top of the overhead for calling the wrapped managed functions from native code, there is often an extra overhead that is caused by mappings between native and managed types.

Mapping C++ Exceptions to Managed Exceptions

In addition to exception-safe resource management, managed wrapper libraries must also care about mapping C++ exceptions thrown by the native library to managed exceptions. For example, let's assume that the SampleCipher algorithm supports only 128-bit and 256-bit key sizes. The constructor of NativeLib::SampleCipher could throw a NativeLib::CipherException when a key of the wrong size is passed. As discussed in Chapter 9, C++ exceptions are mapped to System::Runtime::InteropServices::SEHExceptions, which are not useful for the user of a wrapper library. Therefore it is necessary to catch native exceptions and rethrow managed exceptions with equivalent information.

To map exceptions in constructors, the function-try block can be used as shown in the following code. As discussed in Chapter 6, this allows you to catch exceptions thrown during member initialization as well as exceptions thrown in the constructor's body.

```
SampleCipher::SampleCipher(array<Byte>^ key)
try
: pKey(0),
  pWrappedObject(0)
{
..// same implementation as before
}
catch(NativeLib::CipherException& ex)
{
  throw gcnew CipherException(gcnew String(ex.what()));
}
```

Even though no exceptions are expected from the member initialization list in the preceding code, it uses a function-try block. This ensures that exceptions are caught when you extend the member initialization by adding a member variable to the class or by deriving SampleCipher from another class.

Mapping Arguments of Managed Array Types to Native Types

Now that the constructor is implemented, let's continue with the Encrypt and Decrypt functions. So far I have deferred describing the signature of these functions—but here they are:

```
class CryptoAlgorithm
{
public:
  virtual void Encrypt( const unsigned char* pData, int nDataLength,
                        unsigned char* pBuffer, int nBufferLength,
                        int& nNumEncryptedBytes) = 0;
  virtual void Decrypt( const unsigned char* pData, int nDataLength,
                        unsigned char* pBuffer, int nBufferLength,
                        int& nNumEncryptedBytes) = 0;
};
```

Data that must be encrypted or decrypted is passed via the pData and nDataLength arguments. Before you call Encrypt or Decrypt, you must allocate a buffer. The pBuffer argument must be a pointer to that buffer and the length of the buffer must be passed via the nBufferLength argument. The length of the output data is returned via the nNumEncryptedBytes argument.

To map Encrypt and Decrypt, you can define the following method in ManagedWrapper::SampleCipher:

```
namespace ManagedWrapper
{
public ref class SampleCipher sealed
{
  // ...
  void Encrypt( array<Byte>^ data, array<Byte>^ buffer, int% nNumOutBytes)
  {
    if (!data)
      throw gcnew ArgumentException("data");
    if (!buffer)
      throw gcnew ArgumentException("buffer");

    pin_ptr<unsigned char> ppData = &data[0];
    pin_ptr<unsigned char> ppBuffer = &buffer[0];
    int temp = nNumOutBytes;
    pWrappedObject->Encrypt(ppData, data->Length, ppBuffer, buffer->Length, temp);
    nNumOutBytes = temp;
  }
}
```

In this implementation, I assume that NativeLib::SampleCipher::Encrypt is a non-blocking operation and that it returns in reasonable time. If you cannot make this assumption, you should avoid pinning the managed objects while calling the native Encrypt function. You can achieve this by copying the managed array to native data before you pass the array to Encrypt, and by copying the native encrypted data into the buffer managed array. On the one hand, this is an extra overhead for type marshaling, but on the other hand, it can prevent long pinning times.

Mapping Other Non-Primitive Arguments

So far, all the argument types I have mapped have been either primitive types, or pointers or references to primitive types. If you have to map functions with arguments whose types are C++ classes, or pointer or references to C++ classes, additional work is often necessary. Depending on the concrete case, there are different options. To discuss these options in a concrete context, let's have a look at another native class that should be wrapped:

```
class EncryptingSender
{
  CryptoAlgorithm& cryptoAlg;

public:
  EncryptingSender(CryptoAlgorithm& cryptoAlg)
  : cryptoAlg(cryptoAlg)
  {}

  void SendData(const unsigned char* pData, int nDataLength)
  {
    unsigned char* pEncryptedData = new unsigned char[nDataLength];
    int nEncryptedDataLength = 0;

    // virtual function call
    cryptoAlg.Encrypt(pData, nDataLength,
                      pEncryptedData, nDataLength, nEncryptedDataLength);

    SendEncryptedData(pEncryptedData, nEncryptedDataLength);
  }

private:
  void SendEncryptedData(const unsigned char* pEncryptedData, int nDataLength)
  { /* sending the actual data is not relevant for the discussion here */ }
};
```

As you may guess from the name of this class, its purpose is to send encrypted data. The actual destination, as well as the protocol used to send the data, can be ignored here. To perform the encryption, classes derived from CryptoAlgorithm (like SampleCipher) can be used. You can specify the encryption algorithm via the constructor argument of type CryptoAlgorithm&. The CryptoAlgorithm instance passed as a constructor argument is used in the SendData function to call the virtual function Encrypt. The following native code shows how you can use EncryptingSender:

```
using namespace NativeLib;
unsigned char key[] = {0, 1, 2, 3, 4, 5, 6, 7, 8, 9, 10, 11, 12, 13, 14, 15};
SampleCipher sc(key, 16);
EncryptingSender sender(sc);

unsigned char pData[] = { '1', '2', '3' };
sender.SendData(pData, 3);
```

To wrap NativeLib::EncryptingSender, you can define a ManagedWrapper::Encrypt➡ ingSender ref class. Like the wrapper class for SampleCipher, this wrapper class needs a pointer field that refers to the wrapped object. Instantiating the wrapped EncryptingSender object requires a NativeLib::CryptoAlgorithm object. If SampleCipher is the only encryption algorithm you want to support, you can define a constructor that expects an argument of type array<unsigned char>^ for the encryption key. Like the constructor of ManagedWrapper::SampleCipher, the constructor of the EncryptingSender wrapper class could use this array to instantiate a native NativeLib::SampleCipher. A reference to this object could then be passed to the constructor of NativeLib::EncryptingSender:

```
public ref class EncryptingSender
{
  NativeLib::SampleCipher* pSampleCipher;
  NativeLib::EncryptingSender* pEncryptingSender;

public:
  EncryptingSender(array<Byte>^ key)
  try
  : pSampleCipher(0),
    pEncryptingSender(0)
  {
    if (!key)
      throw gcnew ArgumentNullException("key");

    pin_ptr<unsigned char> ppKey = &key[0];
    pSampleCipher = new NativeLib::SampleCipher(ppKey, key->Length);
    if (!pSampleCipher)
      throw gcnew OutOfMemoryException("Allocation on C++ free store failed");
    try
    {
      pEncryptingSender = new NativeLib::EncryptingSender(*pSampleCipher);
      if (!pEncryptingSender)
        throw gcnew OutOfMemoryException("Allocation on C++ free store failed");
    }
    catch (Object^)
    {
      delete pSampleCipher;
      throw;
```

```
      }
    }
    catch(NativeLib::CipherException& ex)
    {
      throw gcnew CipherException(gcnew String(ex.what()));
    }

    // .. exception safe cleanup and other functions skipped for clarity
};
```

Using this approach, you don't have to map the parameter of type CryptoAlgorithm& to a managed type. However, this approach is sometimes insufficient. For example, you may want to allow a programmer to pass an existing SampleCipher object instead of creating a new one. To achieve this, the constructor of ManagedWrapper::EncryptingSender would have an argument of type SampleCipher^. To instantiate NativeLib::EncryptingSender inside the constructor, it is necessary to determine the NativeLib::SampleCipher object wrapped by a ManagedWrapper::SampleCipher. Determining the wrapped object from a ManagedWrapper::SampleCipher instance requires a new method:

```
public ref class SampleCipher sealed
{
  unsigned char* pKey;
  NativeLib::SampleCipher* pWrappedObject;

internal:
  [CLSCompliant(false)]
  NativeLib::SampleCipher& GetWrappedObject()
  {
    return *pWrappedObject;
  }

... rest of SampleCipher as before ...
};
```

The following code shows how this constructor could be implemented:

```
public ref class EncryptingSender
{
  NativeLib::EncryptingSender* pEncryptingSender;

public:
  EncryptingSender(SampleCipher^ cipher)
  {
    if (!cipher)
      throw gcnew ArgumentException("cipher");

    pEncryptingSender =
        new NativeLib::EncryptingSender(cipher->GetWrappedObject());
    if (!pEncryptingSender)
```

```
      throw gcnew OutOfMemoryException("Allocation on C++ free store failed");
   }

   // ... rest of EncryptingSender as before ...
};
```

The implementation so far allows only a ManagedWrapper::SampleCipher to be passed. If you want to use EncryptingSender with any CryptoAlgorithm wrapper, you have to change your design so that different wrapper classes can implement GetWrappedObject in a polymorphic way. This can be achieved with a managed interface:

```
public interface class INativeCryptoAlgorithm
{
   [CLSCompliant(false)]
   NativeLib::CryptoAlgorithm& GetWrappedObject();
};
```

To implement this interface, the wrapper for SampleCipher must be changed as follows:

```
public ref class SampleCipher sealed : INativeCryptoAlgorithm
{
   // ...

internal:
   [CLSCompliant(false)]
   virtual NativeLib::CryptoAlgorithm& GetWrappedObject()
               = INativeCryptoAlgorithm::GetWrappedObject
   {
      return *pWrappedObject;
   }
};
```

I have implemented this method as an internal method because a client of the wrapper library should not be able to call methods directly on the wrapped object. If you explicitly want to allow a client to get access to the wrapped object, you should use System::IntPtr to pass a pointer to it, because System::IntPtr is a CLS-compliant type.

The constructor of ManagedWrapper::EncryptingSender now has an argument of type INativeCryptoAlgorithm^. Using this argument, GetWrappedObject can be called to determine the NativeLib::CryptoAlgorithm object that is needed to create the wrapped EncryptingSender instance:

```
EncryptingSender::EncryptingSender(INativeCryptoAlgorithm^ cipher)
{
   if (!cipher)
      throw gcnew ArgumentException("cipher");

   pEncryptingSender =
      new NativeLib::EncryptingSender(cipher->GetWrappedObject());
   if (!pEncryptingSender)
      throw gcnew OutOfMemoryException("Allocation on C++ free store failed");
}
```

Supporting Inheritance and Virtual Functions

If you wrap other cipher algorithms so that they support INativeCryptoAlgorithm, they can be passed to the constructor of ManagedWrapper::EncryptingSender, too. However, so far a managed client cannot implement a custom cipher algorithm that is passed to EncryptingSender. This requires more work because a managed class cannot simply override virtual functions of a native class. To achieve this, the implementation of the managed wrapper classes must be changed again.

This time, you need an abstract managed class that wraps NativeLib::CryptoAlgorithm. In addition to the GetWrappedObject method, this wrapper class must provide abstract functions:

```
public ref class CryptoAlgorithm abstract
{
public protected:
  virtual void Encrypt( array<Byte>^ data,
                        array<Byte>^ buffer, int% nNumOutBytes) abstract;
  virtual void Decrypt( array<Byte>^ data,
                        array<Byte>^ buffer, int% nNumOutBytes) abstract; -

  // rest of this class will be discussed later
};
```

To implement a custom crypto algorithm, you must derive a managed class from ManagedWrapper::CryptoAlgorithm and override the virtual methods Encrypt and Decrypt. However, these two abstract methods are not sufficient to allow a client to override NativeLib::CryptoAlgorithm's virtual functions Encrypt and Decrypt. Virtual methods of a native class like NativeLib::CryptoAlgorithm can only be overridden by a derived native class. Therefore, you have to create a native class that derives from NativeLib::CryptoAlgorithm and overrides the virtual functions:

```
class CryptoAlgorithmProxy : public NativeLib::CryptoAlgorithm
{
public:
  virtual void Encrypt( const unsigned char* pData, int nNumInBytes,
                        unsigned char* pBuffer, int  nBufferLen,
                        int& nNumOutBytes);
  virtual void Decrypt( const unsigned char* pData, int nNumInBytes,
                        unsigned char* pBuffer, int nBufferLen,
                        int& nNumOutBytes);

  // rest of this class discussed later.
};
```

I call this class CryptoAlgorithmProxy because it acts as a proxy for the managed wrapper class that provides the actual implementation of Encrypt and Decrypt. Its virtual functions must be implemented so that the equivalent virtual functions of ManagedWrapper::CryptoAlgorithm are called. For these functions to be called, CryptoAlgorithmProxy needs a tracking handle to the target ManagedWrapper::CryptoAlgorithm class. Such a tracking handle can be passed as a constructor argument. To store the tracking handle, the gcroot template is needed. (Since CryptoAlgorithmProxy is a native class, it cannot contain member variables of tracking handle types.)

```
class CryptoAlgorithmProxy : public NativeLib::CryptoAlgorithm
{
  gcroot<CryptoAlgorithm^> target;

public:
  CryptoAlgorithmProxy(CryptoAlgorithm^ target)
  : target(target)
  {}

  // Encrypt and Decrypt are discussed later
};
```

Instead of wrapping the abstract native class CryptoAlgorithm, the managed wrapper class acts as a wrapper for the concrete derived class CryptoAlgorithmProxy. The following code shows how this is done:

```
public ref class CryptoAlgorithm abstract
: INativeCryptoAlgorithm
{
  CryptoAlgorithmProxy* pWrappedObject;
public:
  CryptoAlgorithm()
  {
    pWrappedObject = new CryptoAlgorithmProxy(this);
    if (!pWrappedObject)
      throw gcnew OutOfMemoryException("Allocation on C++ free store failed");
  }
  ~CryptoAlgorithm()
  {
    delete pWrappedObject;
  }
internal:
  [CLSCompliant(false)]
  virtual NativeLib::CryptoAlgorithm& GetWrappedObject()
      = INativeCryptoAlgorithm::GetWrappedObject
  {
    return *pWrappedObject;
  }

public protected:
  virtual void Encrypt( array<Byte>^ data,
                        array<Byte>^ buffer, int% nNumEncryptedBytes) abstract;
  virtual void Decrypt( array<Byte>^ data,
                        array<Byte>^ buffer, int% nNumEncryptedBytes) abstract;
};
```

As mentioned before, the `CryptoAlgorithmProxy` class has to implement the virtual functions so that it forwards virtual function calls to equivalent functions of `ManagedWrapper::CryptoAlgorithm`. The following code shows how `CryptoAlgorithmProxy::Encrypt` forwards the method call to `ManagedWrapper::CryptoAlgorithm::Encrypt`:

```
void CryptoAlgorithmProxy::Encrypt( const unsigned char* pData, int nDataLength,
                    unsigned char* pBuffer, int nBufferLength,
                    int& nNumOutBytes)
{
  array<unsigned char>^ data = gcnew array<unsigned char>(nDataLength);
  Marshal::Copy(IntPtr(const_cast<unsigned char*>(pData)), data, 0, nDataLength);
  array<unsigned char>^ buffer = gcnew array<unsigned char>(nBufferLength);
  target->Encrypt(data, buffer, nNumOutBytes);
  Marshal::Copy(buffer, 0,  IntPtr(pBuffer), nBufferLength);
}
```

General Recommendations

In addition to the concrete steps I have discussed, you should keep the following general recommendations for implementing managed wrappers in mind.

Simplify Wrappers Right from the Start

As the preceding sections have shown, wrapping class hierarchies can be a work-intensive task. While it is sometimes necessary to wrap C++ classes so that you can override their virtual functions in managed classes, it is seldom useful to wrap all classes this way. Determining when a feature is really needed is key to simplifying your task.

You should also avoid reinventing the wheel. Before you wrap a library, make sure that the FCL does not already provide a class with the required features. The FCL often has more features than it seems. For example, the base class library already has a bunch of encryption algorithms. You can find them in the namespace `System::Security::Cryptography`. If the encryption algorithm you need is already implemented by the FCL, it is not necessary to wrap it again. If there is no implementation of the algorithm you want to wrap in the FCL, but the application is not strictly bound to the algorithm provided by the native API, it is typically preferable to use one of the standard algorithms provided by the FCL.

Be Aware of the .NET Mentality

In addition to keeping an eye on the CLS rules, you should try to define your types so that they are inline with .NET philosophy. You should especially use the various options for defining types and type members discussed in Chapter 5. Here are some examples:

- Map C++ classes and virtual functions to .NET components and events whenever appropriate.

- Use properties instead of explicit `Get` and `Set` functions.

- Use collection classes to handle one-to-n relationships.

- Use a managed enum type to map related #defines.

In addition to the features of the type system, you should also consider the features of the FCL. Given that the FCL implements security algorithms, you should consider making your algorithm exchangeable by algorithms from the FCL. In this case, you would accept the design provided by the FCL and inherit the abstract base class SymmetricAlgorithm and the interface ICryptoTransform from the namespace System::Security::Cryptography.

Adapting the design of the FCL typically simplifies the wrapper library from a user's perspective. The amount of work required by this approach depends on the design of the native API and the design of the FCL types you want to support. Whether this additional work is acceptable must be decided for each case individually. For this scenario, assume that the security algorithm is only used for one special case, and thus is not worth integrating into the FCL.

If the library you map manages tabular data, you should also take a look at the types System::Data::DataTable and System::Data::DataSet from the ADO.NET part of the FCL. Even though these types are not within the scope of this book, I mention them here as they can be helpful in wrapping scenarios, too.

Wrapping tabular data in a DataTable or DataSet can simplify the life of your library's users, because these data containers are used for various purposes in .NET programming. Instances of both types can be serialized to XML or a binary format, they can be passed across .NET Remoting or even Web Services boundaries, and they are often used as data sources in Windows Forms, Windows Presentation Foundation (WPF), and ADO.NET applications. Both types also support change tracking via so-called diffgrams, and database-like views and filters.

Summary

Developing good wrappers around native libraries requires a combination of different qualities and capabilities. First of all, it requires good design capabilities. Wrapping a library one-to-one is seldom a good approach. Filtering out the features that are not relevant for the users of the wrapper can simplify the task enormously. Giving the remaining features a managed face requires knowledge about the CLS, as well as about existing features of the FCL and patterns commonly used in .NET.

As this chapter has shown, there are different options to wrap C++ classes. Depending on the features your wrapper class has to provide to a managed client, this implementation can be more or less complex. If all you need to do is instantiate and call a native class from .NET, then your major task is to map the member functions of the native class to CLS-compliant member functions of the managed class. If you have to consider inheritance hierarchies of native types as well, a wrapper can be significantly more complex.

Wrapping a native library implies wrapping native resources (e.g., the native memory needed to create the wrapped objects). In Chapter 11, I discuss how to implement wrapper libraries so that the native resources are cleaned up in a reliable way.

CHAPTER 11

■ ■ ■

Reliable Resource Management

Most libraries that wrap a native API also wrap native resources. In .NET terminology, a *native resource* can be defined as a native pointer or a handle that is obtained from a native operation and that requires another native operation for cleanup. As discussed in Chapter 10, a managed wrapper for a C++ class needs a field that points to the wrapped object. In this case, this field is a managed resource, because for resource cleanup, the native object must be deleted via this field. If you wrap a C-based library like the Win32 API, you usually have to define fields of handle types (e.g., handles for named pipes or for database connections) in your managed wrapper class. Since allocated handles require cleanup, too, they are also native resources. Ensuring that native resources are cleaned up in a reliable way is a task that is much more complicated than it seems at first.

In this chapter, I will implement multiple versions of a managed library that wraps a simple native API. Since the Win32 and many other APIs are still C-based libraries, I will wrap a simple C API instead of a C++-based class library this time. The native API that is used for this purpose is shown in the following code. The code is commented so that you can easily compile it and follow the different steps.

```
// XYZLib.cpp
// build with "CL /LD /clr XYZLib.cpp"
//            + "MT /outputresource:XYZLib.dll;#2 /manifest: XYZLib.dll.manifest"

#include <windows.h>
#pragma comment(lib, "kernel32.lib")

#include <iostream>
using namespace std;

typedef void* HXYZ;

struct XYZConnectionState
{
  /* data needed to manage an XYZConnection */
};

extern "C" __declspec(dllexport) HXYZ XYZConnect()
{
  XYZConnectionState* pState = new XYZConnectionState();
```

```
  // initialize pState for connection

  cout << "processing XYZConnect" << endl;
  return (HXYZ)pState;
}

extern "C" __declspec(dllexport) double XYZGetData(HXYZ hxyz)
{
  cout << "processing XYZGetData" << endl;
  cout << "  ...pretending some work..." << endl;
  Sleep(1000);
  XYZConnectionState* pState = (XYZConnectionState*)hxyz;
  cout << "finished processing XYZGetData" << endl;
  return 42.0;
}

extern "C" __declspec(dllexport) void XYZDisconnect(HXYZ hxyz)
{
  cout << "processing XYZDisconnect" << endl;
}
```

This API will allow you to get data from a fictive XYZ server. To connect to the server, a user can call XYZConnect, which returns a handle that represents the established connection. To retrieve data, you can call XYZGetData passing the connection handle. To close the connection, you must call the function XYZDisconnect.

This library follows a pattern that is often used in C-based libraries. A structure is defined to maintain the implementation's private state. When a resource is allocated, an instance of this structure is created on the native heap; this instance identifies a connection. However, instead of returning a typed pointer to this connection state to the client, XYZConnectionState returns a void *. This allows the library developer to keep the XYZConnectionState structure private.

A client can use a header file like the one following to call these functions:

```
// XYZ.h

typedef void* HXYZ;

extern "C" __declspec(dllimport)
HXYZ XYZConnect();

extern "C" __declspec(dllimport)
double XYZGetData(HXYZ hxyz);

extern "C" __declspec(dllimport)
void XYZDisconnect(HXYZ hxyz);
```

If you ignore some reliability issues for now, a native application could use these functions in the following way:

```cpp
// NativeClient.cpp
// build with "CL /EHa NativeClient.cpp"

#include <iostream>
using namespace std;

#include "XYZ.h"
#pragma comment (lib, "XYZLib.lib")

int main()
{
  HXYZ hxyz = XYZConnect();
  double data = ::XYZGetData(hxyz);
  cout << "Data: " << data << endl;
  XYZDisconnect(hxyz);
}
```

Wrapping Native Resources

It would be easy to compile the same application with /clr, but to support using this API in a .NET-like way in C++/CLI or any other .NET language, it is necessary to wrap it in a managed class library. Since this API contains only one abstraction, it can be wrapped in a single managed class. Here is a first approach for such a managed wrapper:

```cpp
// ManagedWrapper1.cpp
// build with "CL /LD /clr ManagedWrapper1.cpp"

#include "XYZ.h"
#pragma comment(lib, "XYZLib.lib")

public ref class XYZConnection
{
  HXYZ hxyz;
public:
  XYZConnection()
  : hxyz(::XYZConnect())
  {}

  double GetData()
  {
    return ::XYZGetData(this->hxyz);
  }
};
```

To provide a cleanup option, a destructor should be implemented, too:

```
XYZConnection::~XYZConnection()
{
  if (hxyz)
  {
    ::XYZDisconnect(hxyz);
    hxyz = 0;
  }
}
```

As discussed in Chapter 6, it is legal to call Dispose more than once on a single object. The destructor shown here is able to handle multiple Dispose calls; however, this destructor does not support simultaneous Dispose calls by different threads. If two threads call Dispose simultaneously, XYZDisconnect will likely be called twice for a single handle. If the native library you wrap supports simultaneous calls by different threads, then it is straightforward to support multithreaded access in the managed wrapper class as well. To allow different threads to simultaneously call an instance of your wrapper class, you must also be prepared for multiple simultaneous Dispose calls. To handle simultaneous Dispose calls, you can modify your destructor as follows:

```
XYZConnection::~XYZConnection()
{
    HXYZ hxyzOld;
    {
      pin_ptr<HXYZ> pHXYZ = &hxyz;
      hxyzOld = InterlockedExchangePointer(pHXYZ, NULL);
    }
    if (hxyzOld)
      ::XYZDisconnect(hxyzOld);
}
```

In this destructor, the Win32 function InterlockedExchangePointer is used to ensure that simultaneous Dispose calls from different threads do not cause double cleanup. InterlockedExchangePointer expects a native void** as the first argument. To pass an address of the hxyz field, a pin_ptr is necessary. (Instead of using InterlockedExchangePointer, you can use the managed alternative System::Threading::Interlocked::Exchange. However, in this case, you would have to change the type of the field hxyz from the native handle type HXYZ to the managed type System::IntPtr. This would imply type conversions whenever the native handle is needed.)

Since most native libraries are not thread safe, further destructor samples in this chapter will not be thread safe either.

A managed client for XYZConnection can be implemented as shown here:

```
// ManagedClient1.cpp
// compile with "CL /clr ManagedClient1.cpp"

#using "ManagedWrapper1.dll"
```

```
int main()
{
  XYZConnection cn;
  System::Console::WriteLine(cn.GetData());
}
```

Limits of IDisposable::Dispose

Even though IDisposable is widely accepted in the .NET world, there are some limits that have
to be mentioned. An obvious limit is that you can easily forget to call Dispose. C++/CLI and
the managed libraries shipped with Visual C++ provide various features for disposing objects.
You can either dispose an object manually via delete, or you can use local variables or fields
with the implicitly dereferenced syntax so that an object is disposed automatically. You can
also use auto_handle and auto_gcroot for automatic disposal of objects. Other .NET languages
do not have features with comparable power. For example, C# supports automatic cleanup for
local variables only (via the using construct)—there is no C# support for automatically disposing fields. Manually implementing destruction logic in an exception-safe way can be
error-prone work.

There are also scenarios in which programmers can't decide whether IDisposable should
be called or not. Assume you have a Windows Forms control and you want to assign a new
font object to the control's Font property. Should the Font object that you overwrite be disposed? Chances are high that you simply can't say—maybe another control still needs that
font, maybe not. Instead of disposing a font that is potentially still needed, it is preferable to
leave the font undisposed even though this causes a temporary resource leak. Typically,
resource leaks caused by undisposed .NET objects are only temporary leaks, because .NET
comes with an additional last-chance option—which is discussed in the next section.

Garbage Collection and Last-Chance Cleanup

To handle leaking native resources, the GC supports a last-chance cleanup function. Before
the GC actually reclaims an object's memory, it can call a special function on the object to
inform it about its upcoming end. This function is called a *finalizer*. Technically spoken, a
finalizer is an override of the virtual function System::Object::Finalize, but a C++/CLI programmer uses a special language construct to implement finalization logic. In addition to a
destructor function ~T, a type can also have a finalization function !T. This is shown in the
following code:

```
public ref class SampleClass
{
  ... other members ...

  ~SampleClass()
  {
    ... this destructor is called via IDisposable::Dispose for normal cleanup ...
  }
```

```
  !SampleClass()
  {
    ... this function is called by GC for last-chance cleanup ...
  }


  ...
};
```

Finalizers are integrated into the Dispose pattern described in Chapter 6. The following pseudocode shows what the compiler generates for a class that contains a destructor (~T) and a finalization function (!T):

```
// pseudocode
public ref class SampleClass : IDisposable
{
public:
  virtual void Dispose() sealed          // implements IDisposable::Dispose
  {
    Dispose(true);

    GC::SuppressFinalize(this);
  }

protected:
  virtual void Finalize() override       // implements the finalizer
  {
    Dispose(false);
  }

  virtual void Dispose(bool disposing)
  {
    if (disposing)
      ~SampleClass (); // call destructor
    else
      !SampleClass();  // call the finalization function
  }

private:
  ~SampleClass ()
  {
    /* destructor code provided by the programmer*/
  }

  !SampleClass ()
  {
    /* finalization function provided by the programmer*/
  }

  // other members not relevant here
}
```

Notice that the compiler generates a `Dispose` function that calls
`System::GC::SuppressFinalize`. This helper function is provided by the FCL to ensure that
the finalizer is not called for an object. The `Dispose` implementation passes the `this` handle
to `SuppressFinalize` so that the object just disposed is not finalized. Calling `Dispose` and a
finalizer on the same object would likely end up in double cleanup, and would also
negatively impact performance.

As you can see in the preceding sample code, the compiler overrides
`System::Object::Finalize`. Instead of calling the finalization function
(`SampleClass::!SampleClass`) directly, the override of `Finalize` calls the virtual function
`Dispose(bool)`. However, in contrast to the `IDisposable::Dispose` implementation, the
finalizer passes `false` as the argument. `Dispose(bool)` is implemented so that it calls the
destructor (`SampleClass::~SampleClass`) if `true` is passed, and the finalization function
(`SampleClass::!SampleClass`) if the argument is `false`. This design enables derived classes to
implement custom destructors and finalization functions that extend the cleanup logic of the
base class.

What Should a Finalizer Clean Up?

There is an important difference between the cleanup work done during normal object
destruction and during finalization. When an object is finalized, it should clean up *only* native
resources. During finalization, you are *not* allowed to call another finalizable .NET object,
because the called object could be finalized already. The order of finalization calls is undeter-
mined. (There is one exception to this rule, which I will discuss later in this chapter.)

The wrapper class shown in the following code has two fields: a native handle (`hxyz`) and a
tracking reference to a finalizable object (`memberObj`). Notice that the destructor cleans up the
managed resource and the native resource (it deletes `memberObj` and calls `XYZDisconnect`). In
contrast to the destructor, the finalization function cleans up only the native resource.

```
public ref class XYZConnection
{
  HXYZ hxyz;
  AFinalizableObject^ memberObj;
public:
  XYZConnection()
  : hxyz(::XYZConnect())
  { ... }

  ~XYZConnection()
  {
    try
    {
      // cleanup managed resources: dispose member variables here
      delete memberObj;
      memberObj = nullptr;
    }
    finally
    {
      // cleanup native resources even if member variables could not be disposed
```

```
      if (hxyz)
      {
        ::XYZDisconnect(hxyz);
        hxyz = 0;
      }
    }
  }

  !XYZConnection()
  {
    // do not call any finalizable objects here,
    // they are probably finalized already!

    if (hxyz)
    ::XYZDisconnect(hxyz);
  }

  ...
};
```

Apart from some really rare exceptions, you should implement finalization logic only in classes that wrap native resources. A class that implements finalization logic should always implement a destructor for normal cleanup, too. Often the destructor is implemented by simply forwarding the call to the finalization function.

When implementing finalization logic, do not make assumptions about the thread that performs the finalization. The current CLR implementation uses a special thread that is dedicated to calling the finalizers. However, the CLI does not specify how finalization should be implemented with respect to threads. In future versions, there may be more than one finalizer thread to ensure that finalization does not end up in a bottleneck.

Finalization Issue 1: Timing

Even though the XYZConnection implementation suggested so far looks straightforward, it contains a severe bug: there is a race condition between the finalizer thread and the threads using the managed wrapper. It can cause a call to the finalizer even though the native handle is still needed. Do not even consider implementing a finalizer unless you understand how to avoid this bug.

To understand the finalization timing problem, it is necessary to have a certain understanding of the garbage collection process and some of its optimization strategies. Key to understanding garbage collection is the distinction between objects and referencing variables. In this context, referencing variables can be tracking handles (T^), tracking references (T%), variables of reference types that use the implicitly dereferenced syntax (T), interior pointers, and pinned pointers. To simplify the following explanations, I will summarize all these kinds of referencing variables as *references*. The GC is aware of all references and also of all objects on the managed heap. Since auto_handle variables, gcroot variables, and auto_gcroot variables internally manage tracking handles, the runtime is indirectly aware of those, too.

To determine the objects that are no longer used, the GC distinguishes between root references and non-root references. A *root reference* is a reference that can directly be used by managed code.

A reference defined as a non-static field can only be accessed via an instance of that type. Therefore, it is a non-root reference. A reference defined as a static field of a managed type is a root reference because managed code can access it directly (via the static type's name—not via another object). In addition to static and non-static fields, managed code also allows you to place references on the stack (e.g., via parameters or local variables). For a basic understanding of the GC process, it is sufficient to assume that references on the stack are root references, too. However, I will soon refine this statement.

Objects that are neither directly nor indirectly reachable via any of the current root references are no longer needed by the application. If a root reference refers to an object on the managed heap, the object is still reachable for the application's code. If a reachable object refers to other objects, these objects are reachable, too. Determining the reachable objects is a recursive process because every object that is detected to be reachable can cause other objects to be reachable, too. The root references are the roots of a tree of reachable objects— hence the name *root* references. Such a tree of objects is often called object *graph*.

When Is a Reference on the Stack a Root Reference?

As mentioned before, it is a simplification to assume that references stored on the stack are always root references. It depends on the current point of execution whether a reference on the stack is considered a root reference or not.

At first, it sounds straightforward that all references on the stack are roots, because each function can use the references in its stack frame. In fact, garbage collection would work correctly if all stack variables were considered to be root references until the method returns. However, the garbage collector is more optimized than that. Not all variables on the stack are used until the function returns. As an example, the following code shows a function that uses several local variables. In the comments, you can see when each of the references is used for the last time.

```cpp
using namespace System;

int main()
{
  Uri^ uri = gcnew Uri("http://www.heege.net/blog/default.aspx");

  String^ scheme = uri->Scheme;
  String^ host = uri->Host;
  String^ localpath = uri->LocalPath;
  // variable "localpath" is not used afterwards

  int port = uri->Port;
  // variable "uri" is not used afterwards

  Console::WriteLine("Scheme: {0}", scheme);
  // variable "scheme" is not used afterwards

  Console::WriteLine("Host: {0}", host);
  // variable "host" is not used afterwards
}
```

During JIT compilation, the compiler automatically generates data that specifies at what native instruction in the JIT-compiled code a local variable is used for the last time. During garbage collection, the CLR can use this data to determine if a reference on the stack is still a root reference or not.

This precise definition of a root reference is an important optimization of the GC. A single root reference can be expensive, because it can be the root of a large graph of objects. The longer the memory of the objects of such a large graph is not reclaimed, the more garbage collections are necessary.

On the other hand, this optimization can have side effects that must be discussed here. One of these problems is related to debugging of managed code; another problem caused by this optimization is the finalization timing problem. Since the debug-related problem is simpler and helpful for illustrating the finalization timing problem, I'll discuss that one first.

During a debug session, the programmer expects to see the state of local variables and parameters as well as the state of objects referenced by local variables and parameters in debug windows, like the Locals window or the Watch window of Visual Studio. The GC is not able to consider references used in these debug windows as root references. When the reference on the stack is no longer used in the debugged code, a referenced object can be garbage-collected. Therefore, it can destroy an object that the programmer wants to inspect in a debug window.

This problem can be avoided with the System::Diagnostics::Debuggable attribute, which can be applied at the assembly level. This attribute ensures that stack variables are considered to be root references until the function returns. By default, this attribute is not used, but if you link your code with the /ASSEMBLYDEBUG linker option, this attribute will be emitted. In Visual Studio solutions, this linker flag is automatically used for debug builds, but it is not used for release builds.

Reproducing the Finalization Timing Problem

At the end of the day, the debug-related problem just described is neither critical nor difficult to solve. The finalization timing problem, however, is a more serious one. To demonstrate this problem in a reproducible way, assume the wrapper class shown here:

```
// ManagedWrapper2.cpp
// build with "CL /LD /clr ManagedWrapper2.cpp"

#include "XYZ.h"
#pragma comment(lib, "XYZLib.lib")

#include <windows.h>

public ref class XYZConnection
{
  HXYZ hxyz;

public:
  XYZConnection()
  : hxyz(::XYZConnect())
  {}
```

```
  double GetData()
  {
    return ::XYZGetData(this->hxyz);  // XYZGetData needs 1 second to execute
  }

  ~XYZConnection()
  {
    if (hxyz)
    {
      ::XYZDisconnect(hxyz);
      hxyz = 0;
    }
  }

  !XYZConnection()
  {
    System::Console::WriteLine("In finalizer now!");

    if (hxyz)
      ::XYZDisconnect(hxyz);
  }
};
```

A client application that causes the finalization timing problem is shown here. This program creates a thread that sleeps for 1/2 second and causes a garbage collection after that. While the thread is sleeping, an instance of the XYZConnection wrapper is created and GetData is called.

```
// ManagedClient2.cpp
// compile with "CL /clr ManagedClient2.cpp"

#using "ManagedWrapper2.dll"

using namespace System;
using namespace System::Threading;

void ThreadMain()
{
  // pretend some work here
  Thread::Sleep(500);
  // assume the next operation causes a garbage collection by accident
  GC::Collect();
}

int main()
{
  // to demonstrate the timing problem, start another thread that
```

```
    // causes GC after half a second
    Thread t(gcnew ThreadStart(&ThreadMain));
    t.Start();

    XYZConnection^ cn = gcnew XYZConnection();

    // call cn->GetData() before the second is over
    // (remember that XYZGetData runs ~ 1 second)
    double data = cn->GetData();
    System::Console::WriteLine("returned data: {0}", data);

    // ensure that the thread has finished before you dispose it
    t.Join();
}
```

Notice that in this application, a programmer does not dispose the XYZConnection object. This means that the finalizer is responsible for cleaning up the native resource. The problem with this application is that the finalizer is called too early. The output of the program is shown here:

```
processing XYZConnect
processing XYZGetData
   ...pretending some work...
In finalizer now!
processing XYZDisconnect
finished processing XYZGetData
returned data: 42
```

As this output shows, the finalizer calls the native cleanup function XYZDisconnect *while* the native worker function XYZGetData is using the handle. In this scenario, the finalizer is called too early.

This timing problem occurs because of the optimization that the JIT compiler does for root references on the stack. In main, the GetData method of the wrapper class is called:

```
double data = cn->GetData();
```

To call this function, the cn variable is passed as the this tracking handle argument of the function call. After the argument is passed, the cn variable is no longer used. Therefore, cn is no longer a root reference. Now, the only root reference to the XYZConnection object is the this parameter of the GetData function:

```
double GetData()
{
  return ::XYZGetData(this->hxyz);
}
```

In GetData, this last root reference is used to retrieve the native handle. After that, it is no longer used. Therefore, the this parameter is no longer a root reference when XYZGetData is called. When a garbage collection occurs while XYZGetData executes, the object will be finalized too early. The sample program enforces this problem scenario by causing a garbage collection from the second thread before XYZGetData returns. To achieve this, XYZGetData sleeps 1 second before it returns, whereas the second thread waits only 1/2 second before it calls GC::Collect.

Preventing Objects from Being Finalized During P/Invoke Calls

If you build the class library with the linker flag /ASSEMBLYDEBUG, it is ensured that all referencing variables of a function's stack frame will be considered root references until the function returns. While this would solve the problem, it would also turn off this powerful optimization.

As a more fine-grained alternative, you can make sure that the this pointer remains a root reference until the native function call returns. To achieve that, the function could be implemented as follows:

```
double GetData()
{
  double retVal = ::XYZGetData((HXYZ)this->hxyz);

  DoNothing(this);

  return retVal;
}
```

Since DoNothing is called after the P/Invoke function with the this tracking handle as an argument, the this argument of GetData will remain a root reference until the P/Invoke function returns. The helper function DoNothing could be implemented as follows:

```
[System::Runtime::CompilerServices::MethodImpl(
       System::Runtime::CompilerServices::MethodImplOptions::NoInlining)]
void DoNothing(System::Object^ obj)
{
}
```

The MethodImplAttribute used here ensures that the JIT compiler does not inline the empty function—otherwise the resulting IL code would remain the same as before and the function call would have no effect.

Fortunately, it is not necessary to implement that function manually, because it exists already. It is called GC::KeepAlive. The following GetData implementation shows how to use this function:

```
double GetData()
{
  double retVal = ::XYZGetData((HXYZ)this->hxyz);

  GC::KeepAlive(this);

  return retVal;
}
```

The finalization timing problem can also occur while the destructor calls XYZDisconnect. Therefore, the destructor should be modified, too.

```
~XYZConnection()
{
  if (hxyz)
  {
    ::XYZDisconnect(hxyz);
    hxyz = 0;
  }

  GC::KeepAlive(this);
}
```

Finalization Issue 2: Graph Promotion

Another issue with finalization is called the *graph promotion problem*. To understand this problem, you'll have to refine your view of the garbage collection process. As discussed so far, the GC has to iterate through all root references to determine the deletable objects. The objects that are not reachable via a root reference are no longer needed by the application. However, these objects may need to be finalized. All objects that implement a finalizer and have not suppressed finalization end up in a special queue—called the finalization-reachable queue. The finalization thread is responsible for calling the finalizer for all entries in this queue.

Memory for each object that requires finalization must not be reclaimed until the object's finalizer has been called. Furthermore, objects that need to be finalized may have references to other objects. The finalizer could use these references, too. This means the references in the finalization-reachable queue must be treated like root references. The whole graph of objects that are rooted by a finalizable object is reachable until the finalizer has finished. Even if the finalizer does not call these objects, their memory cannot be reclaimed until the finalizer has finished and a later garbage collection detects that these objects are not reachable any longer. This fact is known as the graph promotion problem.

To avoid graph promotion in finalizable objects, it is recommended to isolate the finalization logic into a separate class. The only field of such a class should be the one that refers to the native resource. In the sample used here, this would be the HXYZ handle. The following code shows such a handle wrapper class:

```
// ManagedWrapper3.cpp
// build with "CL /LD /clr ManagedWrapper3.cpp"
//    + "MT /outputresource:ManagedWrapper3.dll;#2 " (continued in next line)
//        "/manifest: ManagedWrapper3.dll.manifest"

#include "XYZ.h"
#pragma comment(lib, "XYZLib.lib")

#include <windows.h>
```

```
using namespace System;

ref class XYZHandle
{
  HXYZ hxyz;
public:
  property HXYZ Handle
  {
    HXYZ get()
    {
      return this->hxyz;
    }
    void set (HXYZ handle)
    {
      if (this->hxyz)
        throw gcnew System::InvalidOperationException();
      this->hxyz = handle;
    }
  }
  ~XYZHandle()
  {
    if (hxyz)
    {
      ::XYZDisconnect(hxyz);
      hxyz = 0;
    }

    GC::KeepAlive(this);
  }
  !XYZHandle()
  {
    if (this->hxyz)
      ::XYZDisconnect(this->hxyz);
    this->hxyz = 0;
  }
};
... definition of XYZ Connection provided soon ...
```

The handle wrapper class provides a `Handle` property to assign and retrieve the wrapped handle, a destructor for normal cleanup, and a finalizer for last-chance cleanup. Since the finalizer of the handle wrapper ensures the handle's last-chance cleanup, the `XYZConnection` class no longer needs a finalizer. The following code shows how the `XYZConnection` using the `XYZHandle` class can be implemented:

```
// managedWrapper3.cpp
... definition of XYZHandle shown earlier ...
public ref class XYZConnection
{
```

```
XYZHandle xyzHandle;
    // implicitly dereferenced variable => destruction code generated

... other objects referenced here do not suffer from graph promotion ...

public:
  XYZConnection()
  {
    xyzHandle.Handle = ::XYZConnect();
  }

  double GetData()
  {
    HXYZ h = this->xyzHandle.Handle;
    if (h == 0)
      throw gcnew ObjectDisposedException("XYZConnection");

    double retVal = ::XYZGetData(h);
    GC::KeepAlive(this);
    return retVal;
  }
};
```

Prioritizing Finalization

As mentioned earlier, it is illegal to call a finalizable object in a finalizer, because it is possible that the finalizable object has been finalized already. You must not make assumptions about the order in which objects are finalized—with one exception.

In the namespace System::Runtime::ConstrainedExecution, there is a special base class called CriticalFinalizerObject. Finalizers of classes that are derived from CriticalFinalizerObject are guaranteed to be called *after* all finalizers of classes that are not derived from that base class. This leaves room for a small refinement of the finalization restriction. In non-critical finalizers it is still illegal to call other objects with non-critical finalizers, but it is *legal* to call instances of types that derive from CriticalFinalizerObject.

The class System::IO::FileStream uses this refinement. To wrap the native file handle, FileStream uses a handle wrapper class that is derived from CriticalFinalizerObject. In the critical finalizer of this handle wrapper class, the file handle is closed. In FileStream's non-critical finalizer, cached data is flushed to the wrapped file. To flush the cached data, the file handle is needed. To pass the file handle, the finalizer of FileStream uses the handle wrapper class. Since the handle wrapper class has a critical finalizer, the FileStream finalizer is allowed to use the handle wrapper class, and the file handle will be closed *after* FileStream's non-critical finalizer has flushed the cached data.

Finalization Issue 3: Asynchronous Exceptions

For many use cases, the cleanup logic discussed so far is sufficient. As I will explain in the next sections, there is still a small potential for resource leaks, but unless your application has really high reliability and availability requirements, these cases can be ignored. Especially if you can afford to shut down and restart your application in the case of a resource leak and the resource you wrap is automatically cleaned up at process shutdown, you can ignore the following discussion. However, if the wrapper library you implement is used in a server application with high availability and reliability requirements, shutting down a process and restarting the application is not an option.

There are some scenarios in which the wrapper class and the handle class implemented so far are not able to perform last-chance cleanup for native resources. These cleanup issues are caused by asynchronous exceptions. Most exceptions programmers face in .NET development are synchronous exceptions. Synchronous exceptions are caused by the operations that a thread executes and by methods that are called in a thread. As an example, the IL operation `castclass`, which is emitted for `safe_cast` operations, can throw a `System::InvalidCastException`, and a call to `System::Console::WriteLine` can throw a `System::FormatException`. Synchronous exceptions are typically mentioned in a function's documentation. In contrast to that, asynchronous exceptions can be thrown at any instruction. Exceptions that can be thrown asynchronously include the following:

- `System::StackOverflowException`

- `System::OutOfMemoryException`

- `System::ExecutionEngineException`

For many applications, the best way to react to these exceptions is to shut down the process and restart the application. A process shutdown typically cleans up the native resources, so there is often no need to treat these exceptions specially. In fact, the default behavior of the CLR is to shut down the process after such an exception.

However, there are some server products for which a process shutdown is not an option. This is especially true for SQL Server 2005, because restarting a database server is an extremely expensive operation. SQL Server 2005 allows the implementation of stored procedures in managed code. Instead of shutting down the process because of an asynchronous exception, the SQL Server process is able to treat critical situations like a stack overflow so that the process is able to survive; only the thread with the overflowed stack and other threads that execute code for the same database have to be terminated. In the future, there will likely be more server products with similar behavior.

For server products that can survive critical situations like stack overflows, resource handling must be done with even more care, because asynchronous exceptions can cause resource leaks. The constructor of the wrapper class `XYZConnection` can cause a resource leak due to an asynchronous exception:

```
XYZConnection()
{
  xyzHandle.Handle = ::XYZConnect();
}
```

When an asynchronous exception is thrown after the call to the native XYZConnect function but before the returned handle is assigned to the Handle property, a resource is correctly allocated, but the handle is not stored in the wrapper object. Therefore, the finalizer of the wrapper class cannot use this handle for cleanup.

A similar problem can occur in the destructor:

```
~XYZHandle()
{
  if (hxyz)
  {
    ::XYZDisconnect(hxyz);
    hxyz = 0;
  }

  GC::KeepAlive(this);
}
```

When an asynchronous exception is thrown after the call to XYZDisconnect but before 0 is assigned to hxyz, a further Dispose call could cause double cleanup. If you use the thread-safe variant based on InterlockedExchangePointer, you will likely end up with a resource leak instead of double cleanup.

To avoid asynchronous exceptions in these critical phases, the CLR version 2.0 provides a set of very special features. Each of these features targets different kinds of asynchronous exceptions, which are discussed in the following sections.

ThreadAbortException

A typical asynchronous exception is System::Threading::ThreadAbortException, which is thrown to abort a thread. The most obvious way a thread can be aborted is the Thread.Abort API.

Version 2.0 of the CLR guarantees that a ThreadAbortException is *not* thrown inside a catch or a finally block. This feature prevents error handling and cleanup code from being rudely interrupted. If you want to ensure that a ThreadAbortException cannot be thrown between the native call that allocates a native resource and the storage of the native handle in the wrapper class, you can modify your code so that both operations are executed inside a finally block. The following code solves the problem:

```
XYZConnection()
{
  try {}
  finally
  {
    xyzHandle.Handle = ::XYZConnect();
  }
}
```

In a very similar way, the shutdown logic can be implemented:

```
~XYZHandle()
{
  try {}
  finally
  {
    if (hxyz)
    {
      ::XYZDisconnect(hxyz);
      hxyz = 0;
    }
  }

  GC::KeepAlive(this);
}
```

One may criticize that this code misuses a well-known language construct, but using `try...finally` in this scenario is part of an officially recommended pattern for reliable resource cleanup. The following explanations complete the discussion of this pattern by discussing the other asynchronous exceptions mentioned previously.

StackOverflowException

The second asynchronous exception that is important for reliable resource management is `System::StackOverflowException`. The managed stack in the CLR is heavily based on the native stack. Elements pushed on the managed stack exist either on the native stack or in processor registers. A `System::StackOverflowException` occurs as a result of a native stack overflow exception, which is a Win32 SEH exception with the exception code `EXCEPTION_STACK_OVERFLOW (=0xC00000FD)`.

A stack overflow exception can be very difficult to handle properly because the lack of stack space does not leave many options for reacting. Calling a function implies pushing all parameters and the return address on the stack that has just run out of space. After a stack overflow, such an operation will likely fail.

In the resource allocation code shown following, a stack overflow could in fact occur after the native function is called, but before the property setter for the handle property finishes its work:

```
XYZConnection()
{
  try {}
  finally
  {
    xyzHandle.Handle = ::XYZConnect();
  }
}
```

Instead of providing some smart features to handle a StackOverflowException, version 2.0 of the CLR comes with a feature that tries to forecast the lack of stack space so that a StackOverflowException is thrown *before* you actually start executing critical code. To achieve this, the code can be modified like this:

```
XYZConnection()
{
  using System::Runtime::CompilerServices::RuntimeHelpers;
  RuntimeHelpers::PrepareConstrainedRegions();
  try {}
  finally
  {
    xyzHandle.Handle = ::XYZConnect();
  }
}
```

The same approach can also be used for the cleanup code inside the XYZHandle class:

```
~XYZHandle()
{
  using System::Runtime::CompilerServices::RuntimeHelpers;
  RuntimeHelpers::PrepareConstrainedRegions();
  try {}
  finally
  {
    if (hxyz)
    {
      ::XYZDisconnect(hxyz);
      hxyz = 0;
    }
  }

  GC::KeepAlive(this);
}
```

The pattern used here is called a *constrained execution region* (CER). A CER is a piece of code implemented in a finally block that follows a try block that is prefixed with a call to PrepareConstrainedRegions.

From the namespace name System::Runtime::CompilerServices, you can assume that the intention of the CLR developers was that .NET languages should hide this construct behind nicer language features. Future versions of the C++/CLI compiler will hopefully allow you to write the following code instead:

```
// not supported by Visual C++ 2005, but hopefully in a later version
__declspec(constrained) XYZConnection()
{
  xyzHandle.Handle = ::XYZConnect();
}
```

In the current version of C++/CLI, as well as C#, the explicit call to `PrepareConstrainedRegions` and the `try...finally` block are necessary to reduce the likelihood of a stack overflow during a critical phase. However, `PrepareConstrainedRegions` definitely has its limits. Since the managed stack is implemented based on the native stack, a stack overflow that occurs while the native function `XYZConnect` is executed ends up in a managed `StackOverflowException`. `PrepareConstrainedRegions` is not able to determine the stack space required by the call to the native `XYZConnect` function. To take a native function into account, `PrepareConstrainedRegions` can only guess a value.

OutOfMemoryException

Another asynchronous exception that needs attention is `System::OutOfMemoryException`. At first, it seems that an `OutOfMemroyException` is not an asynchronous exception at all, because according to the official MSDN documentation, an `OutOfMemoryException` can be thrown by the IL instructions `newobj`, `newarr`, and `box`.

It is obvious that a `gcnew` operation (which is translated to the IL instructions `newobj` or `newarr`) can result in an `OutOfMemoryException`. Boxing can also cause an `OutOfMemoryException` because each time a value is boxed, a new object is instantiated on the GC heap. In all these cases, an `OutOfMemoryException` is not thrown asynchronously, but as a result of the normal execution flow.

However, according to the MSDN article "Keep Your Code Running with the Reliability Features of the .NET Framework," by Stephen Toub (`http://msdn.microsoft.com/msdnmag/issues/05/10/Reliability`), an `OutOfMemoryException` can be thrown in asynchronous scenarios, too. Toub writes, "An `OutOfMemoryException` is thrown during an attempt to procure more memory for a process when there is not enough contiguous memory available to satisfy the demand . . . Calling a method that references a type for the first time will result in the relevant assembly being delay-loaded into memory, thus requiring allocations. Executing a previously unexecuted method requires that method to be just-in-time (JIT) compiled, requiring memory allocations to store the generated code and associated runtime data structures."

According to Brian Grunkemeyer, on the BCL Team Blog (`http://blogs.msdn.com/bclteam/archive/2005/06/14/429181.aspx`), "CERs are eagerly prepared, meaning that when we see one, we will eagerly JIT any code found in its statically-discoverable call graph." This means that an `OutOfMemoryException` caused by JIT compilation may be thrown *before* the CER is entered. The reason why I use the careful phrasing "may be thrown" here is that only the statically discoverable call graph can be JIT-compiled when a CER is prepared. Virtual methods called within a CER are not part of the statically discoverable call graph. When a managed function calls a native function that does a callback into managed code, the managed callback function isn't part of the statically discoverable call graph either.

If you are aware of such a callback from native code, you can use the helper function `RuntimeHelpers::PrepareMethod`. To prepare a virtual function that you want to call during a CER so that the most derived override is JIT-compiled before the CER starts, you can use `PrepareMethod` as well. Analogous to `PrepareMethod`, there is also a `PrepareDelegate` function that you must use to ensure that the target of a delegate is JIT-compiled before the CER starts.

Even if you use `PrepareMethod`, `PrepareDelegate`, and `PrepareConstrainedRegions`, allocation of memory on the managed heap can still cause an `OutOfMemoryException`. There is not that much that the runtime can do to prevent an `OutOfMemoryException` from being thrown.

It is the programmer's responsibility to prevent memory allocations in CERs. Several operations are explicitly forbidden in CERs. These operations include the following:

- Usage of gcnew, because it results in newobj and newarr IL instructions.

- Boxing.

- Acquiring a CLR-specific object-based thread lock via Monitor.Enter or msclr::lock. Entering such a lock can result in a new lock structure being allocated.

- CAS checks.

- Calling .NET objects via special proxy objects called transparent proxies.

In the current release of the CLR and the C++/CLI language, these constraints are nothing more than guidelines. Neither the runtime nor the compilers check whether a method is actually implemented according to the CER restrictions or not.

ExecutionEngineException

Finally, an exception of type System::ExecutionEngineException can be thrown asynchronously. MSDN documents this exception as follows: "Execution engine errors are fatal errors that should never occur. Such errors occur mainly when the execution engine has been corrupted or data is missing. The system can throw this exception at any time" (see http://msdn.microsoft.com/library/default.asp?url=/library/en-us/cpref/html/frlrfsystemexecutionengineexceptionclasstopic.asp).

It is also worth mentioning this exception because it shows the natural limits of .NET's reliability features. Sophisticated server products such as SQL Server 2005 can provide a certain degree of self-healing capability. For example, when the execution of a managed stored procedure causes a stack overflow, the server process itself and all managed stored procedures from other databases remain intact. Only the part of the application that caused the trouble has to be shut down.

These self-healing capabilities are based on the CLR. When the CLR itself is in a bad state, you have definitely reached the limits of all these capabilities. As a result, you simply have to accept the fact that an ExecutionEngineException could be thrown. There is no sensible way to treat it. However, there is a sensible way to avoid it. Most cases of an ExecutionEngineException are not caused by the CLR itself, but by native code that illegally modifies either the internal state of the runtime or of memory on the managed heap. To avoid these illegal operations, restrict yourself to executing unsafe code in server products like SQL Server 2005 only when you really need to.

SafeHandle

There is a helper class called SafeHandle that allows you to benefit from all the reliability features discussed so far. SafeHandle is an abstract class that can be used to write a wrapper class. The following code shows how you can modify the XYZHandle class from the previous examples:

```
// ManagedWrapper4.cpp
// build with "CL /LD /clr ManagedWrapper4.cpp"
```

```
//    + "MT /outputresource:ManagedWrapper4.dll;#2 " (continued in next line)
//          "/manifest: ManagedWrapper4.dll.manifest"

#include "XYZ.h"
#pragma comment(lib, "XYZLib.lib")

using namespace System;
using namespace System::Runtime::InteropServices;
using namespace System::Runtime::CompilerServices;
using namespace System::Runtime::ConstrainedExecution;

private ref class XYZHandle : SafeHandle
{
public:
  XYZHandle() : SafeHandle(IntPtr::Zero, true)
  {}

  property virtual bool IsInvalid
  {
    bool get() override
    {
      return SafeHandle::handle == IntPtr::Zero;
    }
  }

  // this function is an override that is called within a CER
  [ReliabilityContract(Consistency::WillNotCorruptState, Cer::Success)]
  virtual bool ReleaseHandle() override
  {
    ::XYZDisconnect(SafeHandle::handle.ToPointer());
    return true;
  }
};

... definition of class XYZConnection is discussed soon ...
```

Like the DllImportAttribute, the SafeHandle class is defined in the namespace System::Runtime::InteropServices. It is not by accident that both types are defined in this namespace—the features of SafeHandle are enabled by custom P/Invoke marshaling. This means that you have to write P/Invoke functions yourself instead of relying on the C++/CLI compiler and the linker to actually create these functions for you. This is an extra piece of work, but since C++/CLI is able to use native types in managed code, it is much less work in C++/CLI than in other .NET languages. You can write this P/Invoke function simply by modifying normal C and C++ function declarations. P/Invoke functions for XYZConnect and XYZGetData are necessary for writing the XYZConnection class:

```
extern "C" __declspec(dllimport)
HXYZ XYZConnect();
```

```
extern "C" __declspec(dllimport)
double XYZGetData(HXYZ hxyz);
```

The extern "C" linkage modifier is neither allowed nor necessary in P/Invoke functions. In C++, it is used to ensure that global functions can be called from C code. When generating a managed-to-unmanaged thunk from a P/Invoke function, the JIT compiler automatically looks for functions without mangled names in the target DLL.

You can replace the __declspec(dllimport) specification by applying the DllImportAttribute with the name of the target DLL to the P/Invoke function.

```
[DllImport("XYZLib.dll")]
... function declaration goes here ...
```

Key to enabling the features of SafeHandle is the replacement of the native handle type with XYZHandle^—a tracking handle to the SafeHandle-derived handle class. To avoid naming conflicts with the global functions from the native API, the P/Invoke functions are defined as private static member functions of the native class:

```
public ref class XYZConnection
{
  [DllImport("XYZLib.dll")]
  static XYZHandle^ XYZConnect();

  [DllImport("XYZLib.dll")]
  static double XYZGetData(XYZHandle^ xyzHandle);

  ... rest of class definition ...
};
```

The two P/Invoke functions defined here provide custom marshaling. XYZConnect returns an XYZHandle^. The managed-to-unmanaged thunk for this function performs several steps:

1. It creates a new instance of XYZHandle. This instance will later be passed as the return value to the managed caller.

2. It starts a CER.

3. In this CER, it calls the native function.

4. In this CER, it assigns the returned handle to the XYZHandle object created in step 1.

5. It finishes the CER.

The managed-to-unmanaged thunk for the function XYZGetData does not need to start a CER, because it does not assign a native handle to an XYZHandle object. Instead, it simply marshals the XYZHandle^ argument to a native HXYZ type.

The following code shows the complete class definition. Notice that the constructor initializes the xyzHandle field by calling the P/Invoke function XYZConnect.

```
// ManagedWrapper4.cpp

... definition of XYZHandle shown earlier ...
```

```cpp
public ref class XYZConnection
{
  [DllImport("XYZLib.dll")]
  static XYZHandle^ XYZConnect();

  [DllImport("XYZLib.dll")]
  static double XYZGetData(XYZHandle^ xyzHandle);

  XYZHandle^ xyzHandle;

public:
  XYZConnection()
  {
    xyzHandle = XYZConnection::XYZConnect();
  }
  ~XYZConnection()
  {
    delete xyzHandle;
  }
  double GetData()
  {
    if (this->xyzHandle->IsInvalid)
      throw gcnew ObjectDisposedException("XYZConnection");

    return XYZConnection::XYZGetData(this->xyzHandle);
  }
};
```

There is an important limit of SafeHandle that you must be aware of. The P/Invoke layer marshals SafeHandle-derived types to a native handle of the native pointer size—32-bit on a 32-bit CLR and 64-bit on a 64-bit CLR. If the wrapped native API works with handles that have a different size, SafeHandle must not be used. As an example, the Event Tracing for Windows API uses 64-bit handles, even in the Win32 API. For more information on this API, consult the documentation of the RegisterTraceGuids function.

If your wrapper library explicitly allows callers with restricted CAS permissions (which is not covered in this book), I highly recommend using SafeHandle, because it avoids a special exploit: the handle-recycling attack. For more information on handle-recycling attacks, see http://blogs.msdn.com/bclteam/archive/2006/06/23/644343.aspx and www.freepatentsonline.com/20060004805.html.

Summary

For managed objects, object destruction and memory reclamation are decoupled. This supports reliable code in two ways. First, accessing managed objects that are already destroyed cannot corrupt the state of some other random object; instead, it often ends up in a well-defined reaction—the ObjectDisposedException. The second benefit is that the runtime can call the finalizer to perform last-chance cleanup before memory of an undestructed object is reclaimed. This is helpful to ensure reliable cleanup of non-memory resources, but it can also be the source of pitfalls like the finalization timing race condition or the graph promotion problem. Furthermore, normal finalizers are often not reliable enough for long-running servers like SQL Server 2005. To further increase reliability, the CLR version 2.0 introduces CERs, which ensure that regions of constrained code cannot be interrupted by an asynchronous exception. One way to avoid these pitfalls and to benefit from CERs is the use of the SafeHandle base class.

CHAPTER 12

■ ■ ■

Assembly Startup and Runtime Initialization

Most C++/CLI use cases discussed in this book are based on mixed-code assemblies. This chapter will give you a solid understanding of what is going on behind the scenes when a mixed-code assembly is started. Not only is the knowledge you'll get from this chapter helpful for understanding how C++/CLI works, but it can also be important for troubleshooting C++/CLI-related problems.

For mixed-code assemblies, the startup and shutdown process changes because two runtimes must be considered: the CLR and the CRT. Because there are fundamental differences between the startup of mixed-code applications and DLLs, each case is discussed separately.

Application Startup

To understand how a C++ application is started and executed, it is necessary to inspect different kinds of entry points. The first entry point that is executed is the PE entry point. This entry point is invoked by the operating system's loader for DLLs and EXE files. The OS loader finds the address of this entry point in the PE header of the EXE file. The PE entry point is a function with the following signature:

```
int __stdcall PEEntryPoint();
```

Depending on the kind of application, different functions are used. For a managed EXE file, the linker uses an entry point provided by the CLR. When the linker produces a native application, this entry point is provided by the CRT. Table 12-1 shows the different PE entry points that are chosen in different scenarios.

Table 12-1. *PE Entry Points*

Condition	Entry Point	Library Containing Entry Point
Only native inputs, `main` defined	`_mainCRTStartup`	`msvcrt[d].lib`
Only native inputs, `wmain` defined	`_wmainCRTStartup`	`msvcrt[d].lib`
Only native inputs, `WinMain(,,,)` defined	`_WinMainCRTStartup`	`msvcrt[d].lib`
Only native inputs, `wWinMain(,,,)` defined	`_wWinMainCRTStartup`	`msvcrt[d].lib`
Only native inputs, linker switch `/ENTRY` used	Native function specified via `/ENTRY`	
At least one input compiled with `/clr[:*]`	`_CorExeMain`	`mscoree.lib` (`mscoree.dll`)

As you can see in Table 12-1, a function named `_CorExeMain` is always used when there is at least one managed input to the linker. As discussed in Chapter 1, a .NET assembly is created in this case. `_CorExeMain` is implemented in `mscoree.dll`, a DLL that acts as the starting point for the CLR. Several other .NET languages, including C# and VB .NET, also use `_CorExeMain` as the entry point of a managed application. `_CorExeMain` performs several steps as follows:

- It loads and starts the CLR.

- It prepares the EXE assembly to execute managed code. For `/clr` or `/clr:pure` assemblies, this implies the initialization of the CRT.

- It executes the assembly's entry point.

- It shuts down the CRT and the CLR.

CLR Startup

Before `_CorExeMain` starts the runtime, it searches for an application configuration file. Certain settings in this file can influence which version of the CLR is used and how the CLR is initialized. In the configuration file shown here, you can see the different configuration options:

```
<!-- yourapp.exe.config -->
<configuration>
  <startup>
   <supportedRuntime version="v2.0.50727"/>
   <!-- if your app works with a later version of the CLR, add an entry here -->
  </startup>

  <runtime>

  <gcServer enabled="false"/>
    <!-- set this to true to optimize GC for throughput instead of
         responsiveness -->
```

```
    <legacyNullReferenceExceptionPolicy enabled="false"/>
      <!-- set to "true" if you want the Win32 exception 0xC0000005 to be
           mapped to System::NullReferenceException (like in 1.1).-->
      <!-- set to "false" if you want 0xC0000005 to be mapped to
           System::AccessViolationException (default in 2.0) -->

    <legacyImpersonationPolicy enabled="false"/>
      <!-- set this to true if WindowsIdentity should not flow across
           asynchronous points -->

    <legacyV1CASPolicy enabled="false"/>
      <!-- set to true to avoid support for unrestricted identity permissions -->

  </runtime>
</configuration>
```

C++/CLI applications can only execute with CLR version 2.0 or higher. Therefore, configuring a supported or a required runtime version will make sense when the next version of the CLR is released. Other configurations can influence how the GC works and whether the CLR provides backward compatibility with older CLR versions. The .NET Framework SDK documentation contains a reference of the configuration file schema, including descriptions of the elements used in this sample configuration file. For now, it is sufficient to know that an application configuration file can configure the chosen runtime version and certain aspects of CLR's behavior.

Loading the Application Assembly

Before the Windows process loader can call the entry point _CorExeMain, it performs the native process startup. This includes creating a process and its virtual memory, mapping the EXE file into that virtual memory, and loading dependent DLLs. The native process startup is sufficient to call native code in the EXE file, but it is not sufficient for the execution of managed code. To use the EXE file's managed code, the CLR has to be initialized and it has to load the EXE file as an assembly. This does not mean that the EXE file is mapped twice into the virtual memory, but it means that the CLR is aware of the EXE file's metadata and its managed code. Loading an assembly implies another step that is of interest for C++/CLI developers. A special function called the *module constructor* is called when the EXE assembly is loaded. Assemblies can implement such a module constructor to provide custom load-time initialization. Managed applications created with /clr or /clr:pure use this module constructor to initialize the CRT and to perform initializations of managed code.

CRT Initialization in /clr[:pure] Assemblies

The CRT has been extended so that it can also be used from managed code. This is essential for extending existing applications with managed code. For mixed-code as well as native applications, the CRT provides many more features and services than many programmers think of. Here are some of them as follows:

- The CRT implements the heap (`malloc`/`free`).

- The CRT implements the C++ free store (`new`/`delete`). This is usually done in terms of the heap.

- The CRT supports throwing and catching C++ exceptions.

- The CRT ensures initialization of global variables by calling the appropriate constructors when code is loaded.

- The CRT ensures uninitialization of global variables by calling the appropriate destructors when code is unloaded.

- The CRT implements the actual native entry point.

- For an EXE file, the entry point parses the command line and calls `main` passing the command-line arguments.

The CRT has been extended to support all these features in scenarios in which managed and unmanaged code is executed. In `/clr[:pure]` assemblies, the CRT is initialized differently than it is in native applications and DLLs. If you use ILDASM to inspect a typical Hello World application compiled with `/clr`, you will see that the assembly contains a lot of variables, types, and functions that do not come from your source file. Figure 12-1 shows an ILDASM window for a mixed-code assembly. All this extra stuff exists only to initialize and uninitialize the CRT and to perform managed startup.

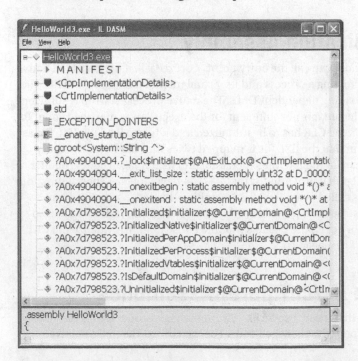

Figure 12-1. *Managed startup logic*

Linking the CRT in Mixed-Code Assemblies

As discussed in Chapter 7, only the DLL variant of the CRT can be used to produce mixed-code assemblies. In the following sections, I will explain how the compiler and the linker work together to integrate the CRT into an assembly.

Depending on the compilation model and CRT variant (multithreaded DLL /MD or multithreaded debug DLL /MDd), the compiler automatically ensures that certain linker options are effective. To achieve this, the compiler uses *linker directives*. Linker directives can be used to store linker switches in an object file or a static library. In addition to the linker switches passed via the command line, the linker directives contained in the linker inputs are automatically used. Table 12-2 shows the linker directives added for different compiler settings and compilation models, as well as the resulting load-time dependencies to CRT DLLs.

Table 12-2. *Implicit Linker Directives*

Compiler Options	Resulting Linker Flags	Load-Time Dependencies to CRT DLLs
/MD (without /clr[:*])	/DEFAULTLIB:"MSVCRT" /DEFAULTLIB:"OLDNAMES"	msvcr80.dll
/MDd (without /clr[:*])	/DEFAULTLIB:"MSVCRTD" /DEFAULTLIB:"OLDNAMES"	msvcr80d.dll
/clr:safe	No linker directive	No dependency to a CRT DLL
/clr /MD	/DEFAULTLIB:"MSCOREE" /DEFAULTLIB:"MSVCRT" /DEFAULTLIB:"OLDNAMES" /DEFAULTLIB:"MSVCMRT" /INCLUDE:?.cctor@@$$FYMXXZ	msvcr80.dll msvcm80.dll
/clr /MDd	/DEFAULTLIB:"MSCOREE" /DEFAULTLIB:"MSVCRTD" /DEFAULTLIB:"OLDNAMES" /DEFAULTLIB:"MSVCMRTD" /INCLUDE:?.cctor@@$$FYMXXZ	msvcr80d.dll msvcm80.dll
/clr:pure /MD	/DEFAULTLIB:"MSCOREE" /DEFAULTLIB:"OLDNAMES" /DEFAULTLIB:"MSVCURT" /INCLUDE:?.cctor@@$$FYMXXZ	No load-time dependency to msvcr80.dll or msvcm80.dll, but both DLLs are dynamically loaded at runtime
/clr:pure /MDd	/DEFAULTLIB:"MSCOREE" /DEFAULTLIB:"OLDNAMES" /DEFAULTLIB:"MSVCURTD" /INCLUDE:?.cctor@@$$FYMXXZ	No load-time dependency to msvcr80.dll or msvcm80.dll, but both DLLs are dynamically loaded at runtime
/clr[:pure] and /Zl	/INCLUDE:?.cctor@@$$FYMXXZ	No dependency to a CRT DLL
/Zl (without /clr[:*])	No linker directive	No dependency to a CRT DLL

In Table 12-2, you can see that the linker flags /DEFAULTLIB and /INCLUDE are used to integrate the CRT into linker's output. The linker flag /DEFAULTLIB can be used to define default input libraries. When the linker resolves references to functions and variables, it first searches in its linker inputs (the object files and static libraries specified via the command line). When a reference cannot be resolved, the linker searches the reference in the default libraries (specified via /DEFAULTLIB). This means that you can override a function from a default library by providing the same function in your own code.

The linker option /INCLUDE can be used to ensure that a function is linked into the output file even if it is not explicitly called from another function.

In the first two rows of Table 12-2, you can see that the static library msvcrt[d].lib is used as a default input library if you compile to native code. This static library contains the PE entry point shown in Table 12-1, and it also acts as the import library for the CRT DLL (msvcr80[d].dll). This explains why msvcr80[d].dll is a dependency of the generated DLL or EXE file.

The third row of Table 12-2 shows that if you compile with /clr:safe, no implicit default library is used. Therefore, there is also no dependency to a CRT DLL. Since the CRT contains native code, which is by definition not verifiable, assemblies built with /clr:safe do not depend on the CRT.

Table 12-2 also shows that several default libraries are used if you compile with /clr. Since you can use the CRT if you compile with /clr, msvcrt[d].lib is one of these dependencies. As in the native compilation model, this ensures that msvcr80[d].dll is loaded as a dependent DLL at application startup. However, if the linker produces a managed EXE file, msvcr80[d].dll is not used to provide the PE entry point. As shown in Table 12-1, the PE entry point for a managed EXE file is _CorExeMain from mscoree.dll. To resolve _CorExeMain, mscoree.lib (the import library for mscoree.dll) is used as another default library. Also notice that a function with the mangled name ?.cctor@@$$FYMXXZ is linked into the assembly. This function is the module constructor I mentioned earlier. It plays an important role in the initialization of mixed-code assemblies and will be discussed in the next section. To resolve the module constructor function, a static library called msvcmrt[d].lib is used as a further default library. Just as msvcrt[d].lib is an import library for msvcr80[d].dll, msvcmrt[d].lib is an import library for msvcm80[d].lib, which implements parts of the CRT that are used by mixed-code assemblies. Therefore, assemblies built with /clr also depend on msvcm8[d].dll.

Since assemblies built with /clr:pure have only one load-time dependency (mscoree.dll), there is a special default library to integrate the CRT. Table 12-2 shows that this library is msvcurt[d].lib.

Finally, there is an option to customize the CRT integration or to build /clr or /clr:pure assemblies that do not depend on the CRT at all. This can be done with the compiler option /Zl (uppercase Z followed by lowercase L). This will be discussed later in the chapter, in the sidebar entitled "Building EXE Assemblies That Do Not Depend on the CRT."

The Module Constructor

The undecorated function signature for the module constructor is the following:

```
void __clrcall .cctor();
```

The name .cctor is a special name that is also used for type initializers (static constructors of managed types). Just as a type initializer is automatically called by the CLR to initialize a type, the module constructor is automatically called to initialize a module. The module constructor is the first managed function of a module that is called. Since most assemblies have exactly one module, the module constructor can be seen as an assembly initializer.

As discussed before, when a managed EXE file is started, the PE entry point (mscoree!_CorExeMain) first loads the and starts the CLR. After that, it prepares the loaded EXE file for managed execution. Once this has happened, the EXE's module constructor is called. In the module constructor, the CRT is initialized. This initialization occurs in the following order:

- Vtables are initialized.

- The command line is parsed.

- Global data (global variables and static variables of native types) is initialized.

    - Constructors for global data that is defined in source files compiled to native code are called first.

    - Constructors for global data that is defined in source files compiled to managed code are initialized second.

It is important to be aware that global data defined in native object files is initialized *before* global data defined in managed object files. Switching the compilation model of a file can change the construction order of global variables.

The Managed Entry Point

In addition to the PE entry point, which is always mscoree!_CorExeMain, an EXE assembly has a managed entry point. In contrast to the PE entry point, the managed entry point is a managed function. After the module constructor has initialized the assembly, the managed entry point is executed. Technically, the managed entry point is a managed function with the IL metadata .entrypoint, as shown in the following sample:

```
// HelloWorld.il
// compileWith "ILASM HelloWorld.il"
.assembly HelloWorld {}
.assembly extern mscorlib {}

.method static void AppEntryPoint() cil managed
{
  .entrypoint
  .maxstack 1
  ldstr "Hello World"
  call void [mscorlib]System.Console::WriteLine(string)
  ret
}
```

Like PE entry points for native EXE files, managed entry points for managed EXE files are automatically chosen by the linker depending on the existence of logical entry point functions provided by the programmer. Table 12-3 shows the managed entry points.

Table 12-3. *Managed Entry Points*

Condition	Managed Entry Point
main(array<String^>^) defined	int __clrcall _mainCRTStartupStrArray()
main() defined with other signature	int __clrcall _mainCRTStartup()
wmain defined	int __clrcall _wmainCRTStartup()
WinMain(,,,) defined	int __clrcall _WinMainCRTStartup()
wWinMain(,,,) defined	int __clrcall _wWinMainCRTStartup()
Linker switch /ENTRY used	Managed function specified via /ENTRY

Several of the functions listed here have the same name as PE entry points listed in Table 12-1; but in contrast to the PE entry points, the functions mentioned here are managed functions with the __clrcall calling convention. Like PE entry points of native files, these managed entry points invoke the logical entry point [w]main or [w]WinMain—the function that C++ programmers usually consider to be the application's entry point.

Table 12-3 also shows that the linker directive /ENTRY can be used to choose a different managed entry point. This can be helpful if you want to create an assembly with /clr or /clr:pure that does not depend on the CRT. Read the accompanying sidebar for more information on that topic.

BUILDING EXE ASSEMBLIES THAT DO NOT DEPEND ON THE CRT

Table 12-2 shows that the compiler ensures CRT initialization by telling the linker to include the module constructor and by specifying default libraries. If you don't want to link with the CRT, you should compile with /Zl (uppercase *Z* followed by lowercase *L*). In Visual Studio projects, you can set this option via the project properties. Simply set the "Configuration Properties ➤ C/C++ ➤ Advanced ➤ Omit default library names" property to True. As Table 12-2 shows, the compiler still includes a module constructor in this case. Since no default library provides an implementation of the module constructor, you have to implement it manually. The following code shows how this is possible:

```
// ModuleCtor.cpp
// compile with "cl /c /clr ModuleCtor.cpp"

#pragma warning(disable:4483)

void __clrcall __identifier(".cctor")()
{
}
```

To implement the module constructor, the sample code uses the __identifier construct. The C++/CLI standard supports the __identifier construct to create special identifiers. Using this, you can define identifiers that would usually conflict with keyword names. The code shown here defines a variable u of a type named union:

```
__identifier(union) u;
```

This feature is intended to support language interoperability. Other .NET programmers might define a type named union, because this would not conflict with a keyword of their .NET language of choice. Using __identifier, a C++/CLI programmer can still use such a type.

To define a function named .cctor, a special variant of the C++/CLI __identifier construct is used. In this variant, the identifier is provided as a string literal: __identifier(".cctor"). By default, this variant of __identifier is not allowed, and causes compiler error C4483: "Syntax error: expected C++ keyword." According to the C++/CLI standard, "The string-literal form is reserved for use by C++/CLI implementations." Integrating the CRT is part of the C++/CLI implementation. To enable the string literal form, a #pragma warning directive can be used. This is a little bit odd, because in this case, #pragma warning does not turn off a compiler warning, but a compiler error.

EXE files compiled without the CRT also need to define a custom managed entry point. This can be done with the linker option /ENTRY. The following code shows a CRT-independent managed EXE:

```cpp
// NoCRT.cpp
// compile with "cl /clr /Zl NoCRT.cpp"

// needed to call GetStdHandle and WriteConsoleW
// to write something to the console via a native API
#include <windows.h>
#pragma comment(lib, "kernel32.lib")

// module constructor
#pragma warning(disable: 4483)
void __clrcall __identifier(".cctor")()
{
}

// entry points
#pragma comment(lib, "mscoree.lib")
  // this pragma ensures that the PE entry point _CorExeMain can be linked
#pragma comment(linker, "/ENTRY:main")
  // this pragma sets the managed entry point to the function main

int __clrcall main()
{
  // we can't use printf or std::cout here,
  // so we use the Win32 alternative
  wchar_t text[] = L"Hello ";
  HANDLE hConOut = ::GetStdHandle(STD_OUTPUT_HANDLE);
  DWORD cchWritten = 0;
  ::WriteConsoleW(hConOut,
                  text,
                  sizeof(text)/sizeof(*text)-1,
                  &cchWritten,
                  NULL);

  System::Console::WriteLine(" world");
}
```

Notice that in this sample, I use Win32 API functions instead of printf or cout from the CRT.

DLL Startup

Often, the majority of the executed code is not written in the application itself, but in various DLLs that the application loads. There are significant differences between application startup and DLL startup. When a mixed-code EXE file is loaded to start an application, the CLR is automatically initialized. In mixed-code DLLs, this can be different. Mixed-code DLLs can be used to delay-load the CLR. This means that the CLR is initialized only when managed code is executed. In addition to that, DLL startup code is executed with special restrictions that must be considered when writing mixed-code DLLs. To understand how this delay-loading feature works, and to avoid some critical initialization pitfalls, it is necessary to discuss the startup of DLLs, too.

DLLs can also have a PE entry point. The signature for a DLL entry point is somewhat more complex:

```
BOOL __stdcall PEEntryPoint_DLL(
     HINSTANCE hinstDLL,
     DWORD fdwReason,
     LPVOID lpvReserved
);
```

Unlike an application's entry point, a DLL entry point is called more than once. It is called once when the DLL is loaded into a process and once when it is unloaded. Furthermore, it can be called twice for each thread created after the DLL is loaded: once when the thread is starting up and once when it is shutting down.

Many developers know this signature from a function named DllMain, but precisely spoken, DllMain is usually not the PE entry point of a DLL. For native DLLs, the entry point is usually a function named _DllMainCRTStartup. It is the task of this function to initialize the CRT at startup and to perform the CRT deinitialization when the DLL is unloaded. The programmer can implement a function named DllMain to do custom initialization and uninitialization. When _DllMainCRTStartup has initialized the CRT, it forwards the call to DllMain. When _DllMainCRTStartup is called due to a DLL unloading, it first calls DllMain, and then it performs the uninitialization of the CRT.

For mixed-code DLLs, there is an additional layer. When the linker produces a DLL assembly, a function named _CorDllMain is used as the PE entry point. This function enables the delay-loading of the CLR. Instead of initializing the CLR directly, it patches all thunks for managed functions that can be handed out to the native world. In Chapter 9, I explained that the compiler and linker generate .vtfixup metadata and an interoperability vtable for every managed function that can be called from native code. Each of the interoperability vtables is patched during mixed-code DLL startup. This patch introduces some code that loads the CLR if it has not been loaded already and that performs the initialization of the managed parts of an assembly if this has not been done before.

The following sample code shows a DLL that can delay-load the CLR:

```
// Lib1.cpp
// compile with "CL /clr /LD Lib1.cpp"

extern "C"  __declspec(dllexport)
void __stdcall fManaged()
{
  System::Console::WriteLine("fManaged called");
}
```

In this code, a managed function is exported by a DLL. Since the managed function has a native calling convention, the client can be a native application. When Lib1.dll is loaded, _CorDllMain patches the DLL's entry point for fManaged.

In the next example, delay-loading the CLR can occur because a managed method is called inside the DLL's code. Assume you have a DLL with one native exported function.

```
// Lib2NativeParts.cpp
// compile with "cl /c /MD Lib2NativeParts.cpp"

#include <stdio.h>

void __stdcall fManaged(); // implemented in

lib2ManagedParts.cpp
void __stdcall fNative();  // implemented in this file

extern "C" __declspec(dllexport)
void __stdcall f(bool b)
{
  if (b)
    fManaged();
  else
    fNative();
}

void __stdcall fNative()
{
  printf("fNative called\n");
}
```

This code exports a native function void __stdcall f(bool b). Since the compiler flag /clr is not used here, all code in Lib2NativeParts.cpp is compiled to native code. Depending on the argument passed, f internally calls fManaged or fNative. Both functions can be called because they both have the native calling convention __stdcall. In this sample, fManaged is defined in a separate file Lib2ManagedParts.cpp:

```
// Lib2ManagedParts.cpp
// compile with "cl /clr /LD lib2ManagedParts.cpp " (continued in next line)
//               "/link /out:Lib2.dll lib2NativeParts.obj"

void __stdcall fManaged()
{
  System::Console::WriteLine("fManaged called\n");
}
```

As you can see from the comment at the beginning of the file, Lib2NativeParts.obj and Lib2ManagedParts.obj are linked into a DLL named Lib2.dll. When a native client calls the exported function f, there is no need to start the CLR, because f is a native function. When the argument true is passed, f internally calls fManaged. To perform this method call, an unmanaged-to-managed transition has to be made. As discussed in Chapter 9, this transition is done via the interoperability vtable. Due to the patches done in _CorDllMain, the CLR can be delay-loaded before this transition occurs.

There is yet another important scenario for delay-loading the CLR. This scenario is based on virtual functions. Assume you have a native abstract base class that acts as an interface between a DLL and its client.

```
// Interface.h
// This file is included in the client and the server

struct Interface
{
  virtual void f() = 0;
};
```

The following code declares a class that implements this interface:

```
// InterfaceImpl.h

#include "Interface.h"

class InterfaceImpl : public Interface
{
public:
  virtual void f(); // overrides Interface::f
};
```

The next file implements the method f as a managed function:

```
// InterfaceImpl.cpp
// compile with "CL /c /clr InterfaceImpl.cpp"

#include "InterfaceImpl.h"

void InterfaceImpl::f()
{
  System::Console::WriteLine("InterfaceImpl::f called");
}
```

To export such an implementation to a client, a DLL can export a native function returning an interface pointer:

```
// Lib3.cpp
// compile with "CL /LD /MD Lib3.cpp /link InterfaceImpl.obj"

#include "InterfaceImpl.h"

// Interface impl as a global variable
InterfaceImpl impl;
```

```
// exported method returns address to global variable
extern "C" __declspec(dllexport)
Interface* GetInterface()
{
  return &impl;
}
```

Last but not least, let's have a look at a native client for this library:

```
// Lib3Client.cpp
// compile with "CL /MD Lib3Client.cpp"

#include "Interface.h"

#pragma comment (lib, "Lib3.lib")

extern "C" __declspec(dllimport)
Interface* GetInterface();

int main()
{
  Interface* pItf = GetInterface();
  pItf->f();
}
```

In this sample, the CLR is not initialized when main calls GetInterface. Returning the interface pointer does not require the runtime to be initialized, either. Only when the interface method is called the first time is the CLR initialized. This scenario is important because calling virtual method calls across DLL boundaries is the fundamental method invocation mechanism of COM interfaces. This means that you can delay-load the CLR even if you implement COM objects.

CRT Initialization in /clr DLLs

So far I have discussed only the initialization of the CLR. When DLLs are used, the CRT is at least as important. In contrast to the CLR, the CRT cannot be delay-loaded, because native code may depend on it. For example, in the preceding code, there is a global variable used to hold the interface implementation in Lib3.cpp:

```
// Interface impl as a global variable
InterfaceImpl impl;
```

An address to this variable is returned by the exported function GetInterface, which is a native function. Without the CRT initialization, this variable would be uninitialized.

In native DLLs, the CRT initialization is performed by the DLL's entry point. Mixed-code DLLs have to use _CorDllMain as their PE entry point to enable delay-loading of the CRT. To initialize the CRT, there is an additional entry point. This entry point is a native function that is called by _CorDllMain. In the following explanations, I will call this entry point the mixed-code DLL's native entry point.

The mixed-code DLL's native entry point is managed in the CLR header of an assembly. The following command line can be used to show the CLR header of the mixed-code Lib3.dll:

```
dumpbin /clrheader Lib3.dll
```

If you execute this command, you will see the following output:

```
Microsoft (R) COFF/PE Dumper Version 8.00.50727.762
Copyright (C) Microsoft Corporation.  All rights reserved.

Dump of file Lib3.dll

File Type: DLL

  clr Header:

            48 cb
          2.05 runtime version
          31D0 [    3480] RVA [size] of MetaData Directory
            10 flags
          13EC entry point (100013EC)
             0 [       0] RVA [size] of Resources Directory
             0 [       0] RVA [size] of StrongNameSignature Directory
             0 [       0] RVA [size] of CodeManagerTable Directory
          6650 [      18] RVA [size] of VTableFixups Directory
             0 [       0] RVA [size] of ExportAddressTableJumps Directory
             0 [       0] RVA [size] of ManagedNativeHeader Directory
```

The mixed-code DLL's native entry point that the linker has chosen for Lib3.dll is __DllMainCRTStartup. As discussed in the context of native DLLs, this is the function that is responsible for initializing and uninitializing the CRT. Due to this function call, the global variable in Lib3.cpp is initialized. Furthermore, __DllMainCRTStartup forwards calls to DllMain, which can be used by programmers to extend the native initialization and uninitialization. The next section discusses restrictions for DllMain in mixed-code assemblies.

Custom Startup Logic and Load-Time Deadlocks

DllMain in native as well as mixed-code DLLs must be implemented with special care. If you do not follow certain rules, a deadlock can occur while a DLL is being loaded. DllMain is called either directly or indirectly via the DLL's PE entry point. Before calling the PE entry point of a DLL, the operating system's image loader acquires a special critical section with the famous name *loader lock*. This loader lock can affect the PE entry point itself as well as all functions that are directly or indirectly called by the PE entry point. In native DLL scenarios, these are typically __DllMainCRTStartup, DllMain, and all functions called by DllMain. For mixed-code

DLLs, this is also _CorDllMain. The functions _CorDllMain and _DllMainCRTStartup have been implemented with the loader lock in mind. For DllMain, it is your responsibility to avoid deadlocks. The Win32 API documentation does not define precisely what is allowed and what isn't. The following are two restrictions described in the official documentation:

- "Because DLL notifications are serialized, entry-point functions should not attempt to communicate with other threads or processes. Deadlocks may occur as a result."

- "The entry point function should perform only simple initialization or termination tasks. It must not call the LoadLibrary or LoadLibraryEx function (or a function that calls these functions), because this may create dependency loops in the DLL load order."

The documentation mentions only a few operations explicitly that can safely be called within your code as follows:

- "The entry-point function can call functions in Kernel32.dll that do not load other DLLs. For example, DllMain can create synchronization objects such as critical sections and mutexes, and use TLS."

If you implement a mixed-code DLL, the two restrictions quoted previously imply another very important restriction: It is illegal to execute managed code in DllMain or a function called directly or indirectly by DllMain. Executing managed code can easily load other assemblies, which would cause a call to LoadLibraryEx. Furthermore, managed execution can silently create dependencies to other threads. This can occur especially during garbage collection. These dependencies can cause deadlocks. In the C++ Managed Extensions language from Visual Studio .NET 2002 and 2003, this potential deadlock was known as the "mixed DLL loading problem." Visual Studio 2005 and .NET 2.0 provide much more help to detect, prevent, and solve this problem.

To understand how this additional support works, let's have a look at some code that demonstrates how you should *not* implement DllMain:

```
// Lib4.cpp
// compile with "cl /clr /LD lib4.cpp"

#include <windows.h>

BOOL APIENTRY DllMain(HINSTANCE, DWORD, LPVOID)
{
  System::Console::WriteLine("DllMain called");
}

extern "C" __declspec(dllexport) void f()
{
  System::Console::WriteLine("f called");
}
```

Since `Lib4.cpp` is compiled with `/clr`, `DllMain` would be compiled to managed code. The compiler is smart enough to give you a warning here:

```
warning C4747: Calling managed '_DllMain@12': Managed code may not be run under
loader lock, including the DLL entrypoint and calls reached from the DLL entrypoint
```

For now, let's ignore this warning and create a client for this application:

```cpp
// Lib4Client.cpp
// compile with "CL /MD Lib4Client.cpp"

#pragma comment (lib, "Lib4.lib")
extern "C" __declspec(dllimport) void f();

int main()
{
  f();
}
```

When `Lib4Client.exe` is started from the command line, `Lib4.dll` is loaded and initialized. During this initialization, `_CorDllMain` calls `__DllMainCRTStartup`. When `__DllMainCRTStartup` tries to call `DllMain`, the CRT implementation detects that managed code would be executed next. To prevent the execution of managed code, the dialog box shown in Figure 12-2 pops up, and the application is terminated.

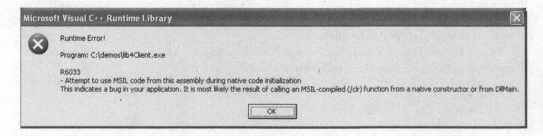

Figure 12-2. *Don't call managed code in DllMain.*

In contrast to the deadlock, the display of this error message is reproducible. As soon as managed code is about to be executed either directly or indirectly in `DllMain`, a dialog box like this one appears and the application terminates with error level 255. Should you execute managed code in your DLL initialization or uninitialization code, it is very likely that you will detect this early in the development phase due to this dialog box. Therefore, this dialog can be seen as a helpful tool to avoid the mixed DLL loading problem.

If you run `Lib4Client.exe` in a debugger like WinDBG or the Visual Studio .NET debugger, you will likely see different behavior. Unless you have changed the default configuration, the execution of the debugger will stop as if it has entered a breakpoint, and the output window will show you the following text:

```
<mda:msg xmlns:mda="http://schemas.microsoft.com/CLR/2004/10/mda">
  <!--
      DLL 'C:\Data\Books\AppliedCPPCLI\sources\chapter9\lib5.dll' is attempting
      managed execution inside OS Loader lock. Do not attempt to run managed code
      inside a DllMain or image initialization function since doing so can cause
      the application to hang.
  -->
  <mda:loaderLockMsg break="true"/>
</mda:msg>
```

The breakpoint and the output are caused by a *managed debugging assistant (MDA)*. MDAs are assertion-like constructs in the CLR and the base class library. There are various ways to turn MDAs on or off. Figure 12-3 shows how you can configure MDAs in Visual Studio 2005 via the menu item Debug ➤ Exceptions.

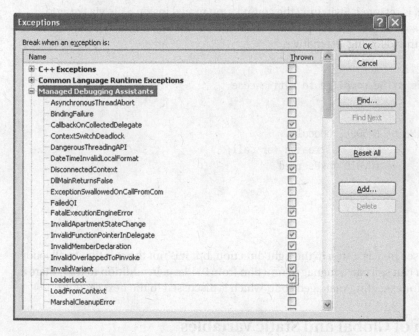

Figure 12-3. *Configuring the loader lock MDA in Visual Studio .NET*

To provide further protection, the Visual C++ project wizards for DLLs generate the following code:

```
#ifdef _MANAGED
#pragma managed(push, off)
#endif

BOOL APIENTRY DllMain( HMODULE hModule,
                       DWORD  ul_reason_for_call,
                       LPVOID lpReserved
                     )
{
    ...
}

#ifdef _MANAGED
#pragma managed(pop)
#endif
```

When the file containing this code is compiled with /clr, the compilation model is temporarily switched to native compilation to compile DllMain. After that, the current compilation model is restored. Switching the compilation model inside a file via #pragma [un]managed is the source of some evil pitfalls (which will be discussed shortly). To reduce the problems, I prefer the following alternative:

```
#if __cplusplus_cli
  #error DllMain must be compiled to native code
#endif

BOOL APIENTRY DllMain( HMODULE hModule,
                       DWORD  ul_reason_for_call,
                       LPVOID lpReserved
                     )
{
    ...
}
```

The code you see here is a step in the right direction, but it is not the solution to all loader lock problems. You can still call a managed function from DllMain. In addition to that, there is another potential for executing managed code, which is discussed in the next section.

Initialization of Global and Static Variables

The Win32 SDK documentation for DllMain contains another important statement: "If your DLL is linked with the C runtime library (CRT), the entry point provided by the CRT calls the constructors and destructors for global and static C++ objects. Therefore, these restrictions for DllMain also apply to constructors and destructors and any code that is called from them."

This statement is especially important if you implement mixed-code DLLs. Constructors of native types can be executed by __DllMainCRTStartup to initialize global variables. These constructors can either be managed functions or call managed functions. In both cases, managed code would be executed under loader lock.

As an example, consider the following simple class:

```
// Lib5HelperClass.h

class HelperClass
{
public:
  HelperClass();

  // other members not relevant here
};
```

Even though this is a native class, the constructor can be implemented in managed code:

```
// Lib5HelperClass.cpp
// compile with "cl /c /clr Lib5HelperClass.cpp"

#include "Lib5HelperClass.h"

HelperClass::HelperClass()
{
  System::Console::WriteLine("HelperClass::HelperClass");
}

// other member implementations not relevant here
```

Let's further assume that this class is used to define a local variable in a source file compiled to native code:

```
// Lib5NativeParts.cpp
// compile with "CL /MD /LD /EHs Lib5NativeParts.cpp " (continued on next line)
//               "/link Lib5HelperClass.obj /out:Lib5.dll /implib:Lib5.lib"

#include <iostream>
using namespace std;

#include "Lib5HelperClass.h"

HelperClass g_helper;

extern "C" __declspec(dllexport) void f()
{
  cout << "f called" << endl;
}
```

The client that is using this code is very similar to the client of the previous sample:

```
// Lib5Client.cpp
// compile with "CL /MD Lib5Client.cpp"

#pragma comment (lib, "Lib5.lib")
extern "C" __declspec(dllimport) void f();

int main()
{
  f();
}
```

This application also fails to execute, because the managed code in the HelperClass constructor is called during the native initialization of the mixed-code DLL.

DLLs and Module Constructors

To allow the definition of global variables, even when their constructor executes managed code, mixed-code assemblies provide a module constructor. In the context of application initializations, I have already discussed that the module constructor is the first managed method of an assembly that is executed. For DLLs, the CRT provides a module constructor that can initialize global and static variables. This means there are two ways to initialize global variables: via __DllMainCRTStartup (native initialization) and via the module constructor (managed initialization).

Visual C++ allows the programmer to decide whether a global variable should be initialized during DLL startup or during module initialization. Global and static variables defined in a CPP file compiled without /clr are constructed at the native initialization of a DLL (via __DllMainCRTStartup). If a CPP file is compiled with /clr, all global and static variables it defines are constructed in managed initialization (via the module constructor).

In the preceding sample code, there is a file Lib5HelperClass.cpp that is compiled with /clr, and a file Lib5NativeParts.cpp that is compiled without /clr. Since the global variable g_helper is defined in Lib5NativeParts.cpp, it is initialized at DLL startup, which causes the problems. If g_helper had been defined in Lib5HelperClass.cpp (which is compiled with the /clr switch), Lib5.dll would have been successfully initialized.

Initialization Timing Problems

To avoid executing managed code during DLL startup, it would be helpful if all global variables were initialized in the module constructor, but this could result in a situation in which native code accesses uninitialized global or static variables. There are two major scenarios in which this can happen.

To explain the first one, I'll demonstrate how to fix the problem I had with Lib5. In this scenario, the definition of HelperClass contains an additional method DoSomething.

```
// Lib6HelperClass.h

class HelperClass
{
```

```
public:
  HelperClass();

  void DoSomething();

};
```

In contrast to Lib5, g_helper is now defined in Lib6HelperClass.cpp, which is compiled with /clr. This ensures that the variable will be initialized during module construction, when execution of managed code is allowed.

```
// Lib6HelperClass.cpp
// compile with "cl /c /clr Lib6HelperClass.cpp"

#include "Lib6HelperClass.h"

HelperClass g_helper;

HelperClass::HelperClass()
{
  System::Console::WriteLine("HelperClass::HelperClass");

}
```

Now the native exported function f calls g_helper.DoSomething. To use g_helper in Lib6NativeParts.cpp, it must be declared via an extern declaration:

```
// Lib6NativeParts.cpp
// compile with "CL /EHs /MD /LD /Zi Lib6NativeParts.cpp " (continued in next line)
//                 "/link Lib6HelperClass.obj /out:Lib6.dll /implib:Lib6.lib"

#include <iostream>
using namespace std;

#include "lib6HelperClass.h"

extern HelperClass g_helper;

extern "C" __declspec(dllexport) void f()
{
  cout << "f called" << endl;

  g_helper.DoSomething();
}

// HelperClass::DoSomething is compiled to native code here
void HelperClass::DoSomething()
{
  printf("HelperClass::DoSomething\n");
}
```

Also notice that the function `HelperClass::DoSomething` is compiled to native code here. When a native client calls `f`, and `f` calls `g_helper.DoSomething`, no managed code is executed. Therefore, the module constructor is not called. As a consequence, the `HelperClass` constructor will never be called to initialize `g_helper`, and `f` will use an uninitialized `g_helper`. The output of a native client that just calls `f` would therefore be the following:

```
f called
HelperClass::DoSomething
```

Notice that there is no output from the `HelperClass` constructor, because it has not been called.

If `HelperClass::DoSomething` had been implemented in a managed object file, the module constructor would have initialized `g_helper` before `DoSomething` was called. In this case, the output would be what you expect:

```
f called
HelperClass::HelperClass
HelperClass::DoSomething
```

The second pitfall that can cause access to uninitialized state is also related to an unprecise separation of the compilation models. It is shown in this source file:

```cpp
// Lib7.cpp
// compile with "cl /LD /clr Lib7.cpp"

#include <stdio.h>

class HelperClass
{
public:
  HelperClass();

  void DoSomething();
};

HelperClass::HelperClass()
{
  System::Console::WriteLine("HelperClass::HelperClass");
}

#pragma managed (push, off)

static HelperClass g_helper;

void HelperClass::DoSomething()
{
  printf("HelperClass::DoSomething\n");
}
```

```
extern "C" __declspec(dllexport) void f()
{
  printf("f called\n");
  g_helper.DoSomething();
}
#pragma managed (pop)
```

Compared to the previous source files, this one looks quite convenient. Instead of two CPP files and one header file, only one file is needed here. As in the previous sample, the HelperClass constructor is compiled to managed code, the method HelperClass::DoSomething and the exported function f are compiled to native code. This is achieved via the #pragma managed construct. Since Lib7.cpp is compiled with the /clr switch, g_helper is initialized in the module constructor, not at DLL startup. The fact that g_helper is defined inside a code section that is compiled to native code does not change how it is initialized. When a native client calls f, the native methods printf and HelperClass::DoSomething are called. Since no managed code needs to be executed, the module constructor would not be called, and like before, HelperClass::DoSomething would be called on an uninitialized object g_helper.

To avoid access to uninitialized data, follow these rules:

- If you define a global variable in a CPP file compiled with /clr, define it as a static global variable so that it can only be used in the file in which it is created.

    ```
    static HelperClass g_helper;
    ```

- If the variable is needed in other files, as well, make it available via a getter function.

    ```
    HelperClass& GetHelper()
    {
      return g_helper;
    }
    ```

Since GetHelper is a managed method, the module constructor will initialize g_helper before calling GetHelper. Therefore, a valid reference to an initialized g_helper can be returned.

Similar rules exist for static member variables of native classes as follows:

- If you define a static member variable of a native class in a CPP file compiled with /clr, make sure that the variable is private.

- If the variable is needed in other files as well, make it available via a public static getter function.

To reduce the chance of accessing uninitialized data, you should follow another hint, too:

• Compile all methods of a class to either managed code or native code. Do not mix compilation models in a class. Had all methods of HelperClass been compiled to managed code, the initialization problem would not have existed. Providing a clear separation between managed code and native code is an important general rule that you should follow.

CRT Initialization in /clr:pure DLLs

Most of the information I have discussed so far applies only to mixed-code DLLs. For DLLs compiled with /clr:pure, the situation is different, because there are two significant restrictions as follows:

• DLLs built with /clr:pure can contain only managed code.

• DLLs built with /clr:pure cannot have functions with native calling conventions.

The first restriction removes a significant pitfall. Since there is no native code that could be executed, there are no initialization timing problems. All the CRT initialization is done in the module constructor.

Due to the second restriction, a powerful option is missing. Since functions with native calling conventions cannot be defined, it is not possible to export functions from a pure-IL DLL. For clients, pure-IL DLLs are only accessible via managed APIs. Therefore, pure-IL DLLs can only be called from managed clients. Consequently, pure-IL DLLs cannot delay-load the CLR.

Summary

In this chapter, I have discussed several implementation details concerning the initialization of the CLR and the CRT in different assembly types. As you have seen, this knowledge is necessary to prevent a range of special problems, most of which are related to the initialization of global variables.

Programmatically Updating the .NET Security Policy

The following sample application expects a path to a signed assembly as the command-line argument. It modifies the .NET security policy so that the passed assembly as well as all other assemblies signed with the same strong name will be executed with full-trust permissions. Since this application does not use the Reflection API from the FCL, even mixed-code EXE files can be passed as command-line arguments. Furthermore, it implicitly avoids name collisions caused by other CAS configurations. You can download this sample from the Source Code/Download section of the Apress web site (www.apress.com/).

```
// TrustStrongNameFromAssembly.cpp
// build with "cl /clr TrustStrongNameFromAssembly.cpp"

#include <vcclr.h>
#include <strongname.h>

#using <System.dll>

using namespace System;
using namespace System::Collections;
using namespace System::Text;
using namespace System::Runtime::InteropServices;

using namespace System::Security;
using namespace System::Security::Policy;
using namespace System::Security::Permissions;

void DumpHelp()
{
  Console::WriteLine(
       "Usage: TrustStrongName <assembly signed with public key to trust>");
}

PolicyLevel^ FindPolicyLevel(String^ name)
{
  IEnumerator^ levels = SecurityManager::PolicyHierarchy();
```

```
  while (levels->MoveNext())
  {
    PolicyLevel^ level = safe_cast<PolicyLevel^>(levels->Current);
    if (level->Label == name)
      return level;
  }
  return nullptr;
}


NamedPermissionSet^ FindNamedPermissionSet(PolicyLevel^ policyLevel, String^ name)
{
  if (!policyLevel)
    throw gcnew ArgumentNullException("policyLevel");
  if (!name)
    throw gcnew ArgumentNullException("name");

  for each(NamedPermissionSet^ nps in policyLevel->NamedPermissionSets)
    if (nps->Name == name)
      return nps;

  return nullptr;
}


CodeGroup^ FindCodeGroup(CodeGroup^ parent, String^ name)
{
  if (!parent)
    throw gcnew ArgumentNullException("parent");
  if (!name)
    throw gcnew ArgumentNullException("name");

  for each (CodeGroup^ cg in parent->Children)
    if (cg->Name == name)
      return cg;

  return nullptr;
}


void GetPublicKeyAndPublicKeyToken(
        String^ assemblyFilename,
        [Out] array<Byte>^% publicKey,
        [Out] array<Byte>^% publicKeyToken)
{
  pin_ptr<wchar_t const> wszAssemblyFileName = ::PtrToStringChars(assemblyFilename);
  BYTE      *pbStrongNameToken = 0;
  ULONG     cbStrongNameToken = 0;
  BYTE      *pbPublicKeyBlob = 0;
  ULONG     cbPublicKeyBlob = 0;
```

```cpp
  if (!StrongNameTokenFromAssemblyEx(wszAssemblyFileName,
                                     &pbStrongNameToken,
                                     &cbStrongNameToken,
                                     &pbPublicKeyBlob,
                                     &cbPublicKeyBlob))
  {
    DWORD err = StrongNameErrorInfo();
    throw gcnew Exception(
        String::Format("StrongNameTokenFromAssemblyEx caused error {0}", err));
  }

  // this code copies
  publicKeyToken = gcnew array<Byte>(cbStrongNameToken);
  Marshal::Copy(IntPtr(pbStrongNameToken), publicKeyToken, 0, cbStrongNameToken);
  StrongNameFreeBuffer(pbStrongNameToken);

  publicKey = gcnew array<Byte>(cbPublicKeyBlob);
  Marshal::Copy(IntPtr(pbPublicKeyBlob), publicKey, 0, cbPublicKeyBlob);
  StrongNameFreeBuffer(pbPublicKeyBlob);
}

int main(array<System::String ^> ^args)
{
  array<Char>^ hexDigits =
        { '0', '1', '2', '3', '4', '5', '6', '7', '8',
          '9', 'A', 'B', 'C', 'D', 'E', 'F' };

  Console::WriteLine("TrustStrongName");
  Console::WriteLine("Written by Marcus Heege - no warranties whatsoever");
  Console::WriteLine();

  if (args->Length != 1)
  {
    DumpHelp();
    return 1;
  }
  if (args[0] == "/?" || args[0] == "-?")
  {
    DumpHelp();
    return 0;
  }

  try
  {
    array<Byte>^ publicKey = nullptr;
    array<Byte>^ publicKeyToken = nullptr;
    GetPublicKeyAndPublicKeyToken(args[0], publicKey, publicKeyToken);

    Console::WriteLine("Public key:");
```

```cpp
    for each(Byte b in publicKey)
      Console::Write("{0}{1}", hexDigits[b >> 4], hexDigits[b & 0xF]);
    Console::WriteLine();

    StringBuilder sb(publicKeyToken->Length * 2);
    for each(Byte b in publicKeyToken)
      sb.AppendFormat("{0}{1}", hexDigits[b >> 4], hexDigits[b & 0xF]);
    String^ strPublicKeyToken = sb.ToString();
    Console::WriteLine("Public key token: {0}", strPublicKeyToken);

    PolicyLevel^ machineLevel = FindPolicyLevel("machine");
    if (!machineLevel)
      throw gcnew Exception("Machine level not found.");

    NamedPermissionSet^ npsFullTrust =
            FindNamedPermissionSet(machineLevel, "FullTrust");
    if (!npsFullTrust)
      throw gcnew Exception("FullTrust permission set not found");
    PolicyStatement^ polStmtFullTrust = gcnew PolicyStatement(npsFullTrust);

    String^ codeGroupName = String::Format("PKT{0}FullTrust", strPublicKeyToken);
    CodeGroup^ cgPKTFullTrust = FindCodeGroup(machineLevel->RootCodeGroup,
                                              codeGroupName);
    if (cgPKTFullTrust)
    {
      Console::WriteLine("Deleting existing code group " + codeGroupName);
      machineLevel->RootCodeGroup->RemoveChild(cgPKTFullTrust);
    }

    Console::WriteLine("Adding new code group " + codeGroupName);

    StrongNamePublicKeyBlob^ snpkb = gcnew StrongNamePublicKeyBlob(publicKey);
    StrongNameMembershipCondition^ snmc =
            gcnew StrongNameMembershipCondition(snpkb, nullptr, nullptr);
    cgPKTFullTrust = gcnew UnionCodeGroup(snmc, polStmtFullTrust);
    cgPKTFullTrust->Name = codeGroupName;
    machineLevel->RootCodeGroup->AddChild(cgPKTFullTrust);

    Console::WriteLine("Saving machine policy level");
    SecurityManager::SavePolicyLevel(machineLevel);
  }
  catch (Exception^ ex)
  {
    Console::WriteLine("Error occured: " + ex->Message);
    return 1;
  }

  Console::WriteLine("Succeeded");
  return 0;
}
```

∎∎∎

Measuring the Performance of Thunks

This appendix contains the application used to measure the performance of thunks in Chapter 9. You can download this sample from the Source Code/Download section of the Apress web site (http://www.apress.com).

```cpp
//////////////////////////////////////
// TestLibManagedParts.cpp
// compile with "CL /c /clr TestLibPart2.cpp"

static long g_l = 0;

extern "C" __declspec(dllexport)
void __stdcall fManagedFromDLL()
{
  ++g_l;
}

class __declspec(dllexport) NativeClassFromDLLWithManagedCode
{
public:
  void f()
  {
    ++g_l;
  };
  virtual void vf()
  {
    ++g_l;
  }
};

//////////////////////////////////////
// TestLib.cpp
// build with "CL /MD /LD TestLib.cpp /link TestLibManagedParts.obj"
```

```cpp
static long g_l = 0;

extern "C" __declspec(dllexport)
void __stdcall fNativeFromDLL()
{
  ++g_l;
}

class __declspec(dllexport) NativeClassFromDLLWithNativeCode
{
public:
  void f()
  {
    ++g_l;
  };
  virtual void vf()
  {
    ++g_l;
  }
};

/////////////////////////////////////////
// ThunkPerformanceManagedParts.cpp
// build with "CL /c /clr ThunkPerformanceManagedParts.cpp"

#define _WIN32_WINNT 0x400
#include <windows.h>
#include <iostream>
using namespace std;

static long g_l = 0;

using namespace System::Runtime::CompilerServices;

////////////////////////
// target functions called in different measurements

[MethodImpl(MethodImplOptions::NoInlining)]
__declspec(noinline)
void __stdcall fManagedLocal()
{
  ++g_l;
}
extern void __stdcall fNativeLocal();
```

```cpp
class NativeClassWithNativeCode
{
public:
  void __thiscall f();
  virtual void __thiscall vf();
};
class NativeClassWithManagedCode
{
public:
  void f()
  {
    ++g_l;
  }
  virtual void vf()
  {
    ++g_l;
  }
};
class NativeClassWithVirtualClrCallFunction
{
public:
  virtual void __clrcall vf()
  {
    ++g_l;
  }
};

#pragma comment(lib, "TestLib.lib")
extern "C" __declspec(dllimport) void __stdcall fNativeFromDLL();
extern "C" __declspec(dllimport) void __stdcall fManagedFromDLL();

class __declspec(dllimport) NativeClassFromDLLWithNativeCode
{
public:
  void f();
  virtual void vf();
};

class __declspec(dllimport) NativeClassFromDLLWithManagedCode
{
public:
  void f();
  virtual void vf();
};

/////////////////////////
// helper class for performance measurements
```

```cpp
class MeasureHelper
{
  static long long perfFreq;
  int threadPriority;
  long long startCounter, finishCounter;

public:
  void StartMeasuring();
  void StopMeasuring();
  double GetMeasuredTime();
};

//////////////////////////
// functions that perform the actual measurements
extern int numberOfCalls;

typedef void (__stdcall* PFN)();

void __stdcall MeasureCallsFromManagedCaller
                    (PFN pfn, const char* szFunctionName, bool bIndirect)
{
  MeasureHelper mh;
  mh.StartMeasuring();
  pfn();
  mh.StopMeasuring();

  cout << mh.GetMeasuredTime()
       << "s\tfor 10e8 " << (bIndirect ? "indirect " : "") << "calls to "
       << szFunctionName << " from managed code" << endl;
}

#define IMPLEMENT_MANAGED_MEASURE_FUNCTION(targetfn) \
void __stdcall Call_from_managed_code_##targetfn() \
{ \
  for (int i = 0; i < numberOfCalls; ++i) \
    targetfn(); \
}

#define IMPLEMENT_MANAGED_MEASURE_FUNCTION_INDIRECT_CALL(targetfn) \
void __stdcall Call_indirectly_from_managed_code_##targetfn() \
{ \
  PFN pfn = &targetfn; \
  for (int i = 0; i < numberOfCalls; ++i) \
    pfn(); \
}

IMPLEMENT_MANAGED_MEASURE_FUNCTION(fManagedLocal)
IMPLEMENT_MANAGED_MEASURE_FUNCTION(fNativeLocal)
```

```
IMPLEMENT_MANAGED_MEASURE_FUNCTION_INDIRECT_CALL(fManagedLocal)
IMPLEMENT_MANAGED_MEASURE_FUNCTION_INDIRECT_CALL(fNativeLocal)
IMPLEMENT_MANAGED_MEASURE_FUNCTION(fManagedFromDLL)
IMPLEMENT_MANAGED_MEASURE_FUNCTION(fNativeFromDLL)
IMPLEMENT_MANAGED_MEASURE_FUNCTION_INDIRECT_CALL(fManagedFromDLL)
IMPLEMENT_MANAGED_MEASURE_FUNCTION_INDIRECT_CALL(fNativeFromDLL)

void __stdcall Call_via_clrcall_pointer_from_managed_code_fManagedLocal()
{
  void (__clrcall* pfn)() = &fManagedLocal;
  for (int i = 0; i < numberOfCalls; ++i)
    pfn();
}

#define IMPLEMENT_MANAGED_MEASURE_MEMBERFUNCTION(classname, targetfn) \
void __stdcall Call_member_from_managed_code_##classname##targetfn() \
{ \
  classname* p = new classname(); \
  for (int i = 0; i < numberOfCalls; ++i) \
    p->targetfn(); \
  delete p; \
}

IMPLEMENT_MANAGED_MEASURE_MEMBERFUNCTION(NativeClassWithManagedCode, f);
IMPLEMENT_MANAGED_MEASURE_MEMBERFUNCTION(NativeClassWithNativeCode, f);
IMPLEMENT_MANAGED_MEASURE_MEMBERFUNCTION(NativeClassWithManagedCode, vf);
IMPLEMENT_MANAGED_MEASURE_MEMBERFUNCTION(NativeClassWithVirtualClrCallFunction,vf);
IMPLEMENT_MANAGED_MEASURE_MEMBERFUNCTION(NativeClassWithNativeCode, vf);
IMPLEMENT_MANAGED_MEASURE_MEMBERFUNCTION(NativeClassFromDLLWithManagedCode, f);
IMPLEMENT_MANAGED_MEASURE_MEMBERFUNCTION(NativeClassFromDLLWithNativeCode, f);
IMPLEMENT_MANAGED_MEASURE_MEMBERFUNCTION(NativeClassFromDLLWithManagedCode, vf);
IMPLEMENT_MANAGED_MEASURE_MEMBERFUNCTION(NativeClassFromDLLWithNativeCode, vf);
};

//////////////////////////////////////////
// ThunkPerformance.cpp
// build with "CL /clr ThunkPerformance.cpp /link ThunkPerformanceManagedParts.obj"

#define _WIN32_WINNT 0x400
#include <windows.h>
#include <iostream>
using namespace std;

////////////////////////
// target functions called in different measurements

static long g_l = 0;
```

```
void __stdcall fManagedLocal();

__declspec(noinline)
void __stdcall fNativeLocal()
{
  ++g_l;
}

class NativeClassWithManagedCode
{
public:
  void f() ;
  virtual void vf();
};

class NativeClassWithNativeCode
{
public:
  void f()
  {
    ++g_l;
  };
  virtual void vf()
  {
    ++g_l;
  }
};

#pragma comment(lib, "TestLib.lib")
extern "C" __declspec(dllimport) void __stdcall fNativeFromDLL();
extern "C" __declspec(dllimport) void __stdcall fManagedFromDLL();

class __declspec(dllimport) NativeClassFromDLLWithNativeCode
{
public:
  void f();
  virtual void vf();
};

class __declspec(dllimport) NativeClassFromDLLWithManagedCode
{
public:
  void f();
  virtual void vf();
};
```

```
////////////////////
// declarations of functions that perform the actual measurements
int numberOfCalls = 100000000;

typedef void (__stdcall* PFN)();

void __stdcall MeasureCallsFromNativeCaller
                    (PFN pfn, const char* szFunctionName, bool bCallOnce);
void __stdcall MeasureCallsFromManagedCaller
                    (PFN pfn, const char* szFunctionName, bool bCallOnce);

#define IMPLEMENT_NATIVE_MEASURE_FUNCTION(targetfn) \
void __stdcall Call_from_native_code_##targetfn() \
{ \
  for (int i = 0; i < numberOfCalls; ++i) \
    targetfn(); \
}

#define IMPLEMENT_NATIVE_MEASURE_FUNCTION_INDIRECT_CALL(targetfn) \
void __stdcall Call_indirectly_from_native_code_##targetfn() \
{ \
  PFN pfn = &targetfn; \
  for (int i = 0; i < numberOfCalls; ++i) \
    pfn(); \
}

IMPLEMENT_NATIVE_MEASURE_FUNCTION(fManagedLocal)
IMPLEMENT_NATIVE_MEASURE_FUNCTION(fNativeLocal)
IMPLEMENT_NATIVE_MEASURE_FUNCTION_INDIRECT_CALL(fManagedLocal)
IMPLEMENT_NATIVE_MEASURE_FUNCTION_INDIRECT_CALL(fNativeLocal)
IMPLEMENT_NATIVE_MEASURE_FUNCTION(fManagedFromDLL)
IMPLEMENT_NATIVE_MEASURE_FUNCTION(fNativeFromDLL)
IMPLEMENT_NATIVE_MEASURE_FUNCTION_INDIRECT_CALL(fManagedFromDLL)
IMPLEMENT_NATIVE_MEASURE_FUNCTION_INDIRECT_CALL(fNativeFromDLL)

#define DECLARE_MANAGED_MEASURE_FUNCTION(targetfn) \
void __stdcall Call_from_managed_code_##targetfn();

#define DECLARE_MANAGED_MEASURE_FUNCTION_INDIRECT_CALL(targetfn) \
void __stdcall Call_indirectly_from_managed_code_##targetfn();

DECLARE_MANAGED_MEASURE_FUNCTION(fManagedLocal)
DECLARE_MANAGED_MEASURE_FUNCTION(fNativeLocal)
DECLARE_MANAGED_MEASURE_FUNCTION_INDIRECT_CALL(fManagedLocal)
void __stdcall Call_via_clrcall_pointer_from_managed_code_fManagedLocal();
DECLARE_MANAGED_MEASURE_FUNCTION_INDIRECT_CALL(fNativeLocal)
DECLARE_MANAGED_MEASURE_FUNCTION(fManagedFromDLL)
```

```
DECLARE_MANAGED_MEASURE_FUNCTION(fNativeFromDLL)
DECLARE_MANAGED_MEASURE_FUNCTION_INDIRECT_CALL(fManagedFromDLL)
DECLARE_MANAGED_MEASURE_FUNCTION_INDIRECT_CALL(fNativeFromDLL)

#define IMPLEMENT_NATIVE_MEASURE_MEMBERFUNCTION(classname, memberfn) \
void __stdcall Call_member_from_native_code_##classname##memberfn() \
{ \
  classname* p = new classname(); \
  for (int i = 0; i < numberOfCalls; ++i) \
    p->memberfn(); \
  delete p; \
}

IMPLEMENT_NATIVE_MEASURE_MEMBERFUNCTION(NativeClassWithManagedCode, f);
IMPLEMENT_NATIVE_MEASURE_MEMBERFUNCTION(NativeClassWithNativeCode, f);
IMPLEMENT_NATIVE_MEASURE_MEMBERFUNCTION(NativeClassWithManagedCode, vf);
IMPLEMENT_NATIVE_MEASURE_MEMBERFUNCTION(NativeClassWithNativeCode, vf);
IMPLEMENT_NATIVE_MEASURE_MEMBERFUNCTION(NativeClassFromDLLWithManagedCode, f);
IMPLEMENT_NATIVE_MEASURE_MEMBERFUNCTION(NativeClassFromDLLWithNativeCode, f);
IMPLEMENT_NATIVE_MEASURE_MEMBERFUNCTION(NativeClassFromDLLWithManagedCode, vf);
IMPLEMENT_NATIVE_MEASURE_MEMBERFUNCTION(NativeClassFromDLLWithNativeCode, vf);

#define DECLARE_MANAGED_MEASURE_MEMBERFUNCTION(classname, memberfn) \
          void __stdcall Call_member_from_managed_code_##classname##memberfn();

DECLARE_MANAGED_MEASURE_MEMBERFUNCTION(NativeClassWithManagedCode, f);
DECLARE_MANAGED_MEASURE_MEMBERFUNCTION(NativeClassWithNativeCode, f);
DECLARE_MANAGED_MEASURE_MEMBERFUNCTION(NativeClassWithManagedCode, vf);
DECLARE_MANAGED_MEASURE_MEMBERFUNCTION(NativeClassWithVirtualClrCallFunction, vf);
DECLARE_MANAGED_MEASURE_MEMBERFUNCTION(NativeClassWithNativeCode, vf);
DECLARE_MANAGED_MEASURE_MEMBERFUNCTION(NativeClassFromDLLWithManagedCode, f);
DECLARE_MANAGED_MEASURE_MEMBERFUNCTION(NativeClassFromDLLWithNativeCode, f);
DECLARE_MANAGED_MEASURE_MEMBERFUNCTION(NativeClassFromDLLWithManagedCode, vf);
DECLARE_MANAGED_MEASURE_MEMBERFUNCTION(NativeClassFromDLLWithNativeCode, vf);

struct MeasureData
{
  const char* funcName;
  PFN testFunc;
  bool managedCaller;
  bool indirectCall;
};

#define MANAGEDCALLER = 1
#define NATIVECALLER = 2
#define DIRECTCALL = 1
#define INDIRECTCALL = 2
```

```cpp
#define MEASURE_ENTRY_MANAGEDCALLER_DIRECTCALL(targetfn) \
  { #targetfn, Call_from_managed_code_##targetfn, true, false }
#define MEASURE_ENTRY_MANAGEDCALLER_INDIRECTCALL(targetfn) \
  { #targetfn, Call_indirectly_from_managed_code_##targetfn, true, true }
#define MEASURE_ENTRY_NATIVECALLER_DIRECTCALL(targetfn) \
  { #targetfn, Call_from_native_code_##targetfn, false, false }
#define MEASURE_ENTRY_NATIVECALLER_INDIRECTCALL(targetfn) \
  { #targetfn, Call_indirectly_from_native_code_##targetfn, false, true }
#define MEASURE_ENTRY_MANAGEDCALLER_MEMBER(classname, memberfn) \
  { #classname "::" #memberfn, \
    Call_member_from_managed_code_##classname##memberfn, true, false }
#define MEASURE_ENTRY_NATIVECALLER_MEMBER(classname, memberfn) \
  { #classname "::" #memberfn, \
    Call_member_from_native_code_##classname##memberfn, false, false }

void Measure(MeasureData* pMeasureData, int cMeasureData)
{
  for (int iEntry = 0; iEntry < cMeasureData; ++iEntry)
  {
    MeasureData& md = pMeasureData[iEntry];
    if (md.managedCaller)
      MeasureCallsFromManagedCaller(md.testFunc, md.funcName, md.indirectCall);
    else
      MeasureCallsFromNativeCaller(md.testFunc, md.funcName, md.indirectCall);
  }
}
/////////////////////////
// Entry point
int main()
{
  // execute once to ensure JIT compilation has been done
  fManagedLocal(); fManagedFromDLL();
  NativeClassWithManagedCode n1; n1.f(); n1.vf();
  NativeClassFromDLLWithManagedCode n2; n2.f(); n2.vf();

  MeasureData md1[] =
  {
    MEASURE_ENTRY_MANAGEDCALLER_DIRECTCALL  (fManagedLocal  ),
    MEASURE_ENTRY_NATIVECALLER_DIRECTCALL   (fManagedLocal  ),
    MEASURE_ENTRY_MANAGEDCALLER_INDIRECTCALL(fManagedLocal  ),
    {"fManagedLocal (via __clrcall pointer)",
        Call_via_clrcall_pointer_from_managed_code_fManagedLocal, true, false},
    MEASURE_ENTRY_NATIVECALLER_INDIRECTCALL (fManagedLocal  ),
    MEASURE_ENTRY_MANAGEDCALLER_DIRECTCALL  (fManagedFromDLL),
    MEASURE_ENTRY_NATIVECALLER_DIRECTCALL   (fManagedFromDLL),
    MEASURE_ENTRY_MANAGEDCALLER_INDIRECTCALL(fManagedFromDLL),
    MEASURE_ENTRY_NATIVECALLER_INDIRECTCALL (fManagedFromDLL),
```

```
      MEASURE_ENTRY_MANAGEDCALLER_DIRECTCALL  (fNativeLocal   ),
      MEASURE_ENTRY_NATIVECALLER_DIRECTCALL   (fNativeLocal   ),
      MEASURE_ENTRY_MANAGEDCALLER_INDIRECTCALL(fNativeLocal   ),
      MEASURE_ENTRY_NATIVECALLER_INDIRECTCALL (fNativeLocal   ),
      MEASURE_ENTRY_MANAGEDCALLER_DIRECTCALL  (fNativeFromDLL ),
      MEASURE_ENTRY_NATIVECALLER_DIRECTCALL   (fNativeFromDLL ),
      MEASURE_ENTRY_MANAGEDCALLER_INDIRECTCALL(fNativeFromDLL ),
      MEASURE_ENTRY_NATIVECALLER_INDIRECTCALL (fNativeFromDLL )
   };
   Measure(md1, sizeof(md1)/sizeof(*md1));

   MeasureData md2[] =
   {
     MEASURE_ENTRY_MANAGEDCALLER_MEMBER(NativeClassWithManagedCode          , f ),
     MEASURE_ENTRY_NATIVECALLER_MEMBER (NativeClassWithManagedCode          , f ),
     MEASURE_ENTRY_MANAGEDCALLER_MEMBER(NativeClassWithManagedCode          , vf),
     MEASURE_ENTRY_MANAGEDCALLER_MEMBER(NativeClassWithVirtualClrCallFunction, vf),
     MEASURE_ENTRY_NATIVECALLER_MEMBER (NativeClassWithManagedCode          , vf),
     MEASURE_ENTRY_MANAGEDCALLER_MEMBER(NativeClassFromDLLWithManagedCode, f ),
     MEASURE_ENTRY_NATIVECALLER_MEMBER (NativeClassFromDLLWithManagedCode, f ),
     MEASURE_ENTRY_MANAGEDCALLER_MEMBER(NativeClassFromDLLWithManagedCode, vf),
     MEASURE_ENTRY_NATIVECALLER_MEMBER (NativeClassFromDLLWithManagedCode, vf),
     MEASURE_ENTRY_MANAGEDCALLER_MEMBER(NativeClassWithNativeCode          , f ),
     MEASURE_ENTRY_NATIVECALLER_MEMBER (NativeClassWithNativeCode          , f ),
     MEASURE_ENTRY_MANAGEDCALLER_MEMBER(NativeClassWithNativeCode          , vf),
     MEASURE_ENTRY_NATIVECALLER_MEMBER (NativeClassWithNativeCode          , vf),
     MEASURE_ENTRY_MANAGEDCALLER_MEMBER(NativeClassFromDLLWithNativeCode , f ),
     MEASURE_ENTRY_NATIVECALLER_MEMBER (NativeClassFromDLLWithNativeCode , f ),
     MEASURE_ENTRY_MANAGEDCALLER_MEMBER(NativeClassFromDLLWithNativeCode , vf),
     MEASURE_ENTRY_NATIVECALLER_MEMBER (NativeClassFromDLLWithNativeCode , vf)
   };
   Measure(md2, sizeof(md2)/sizeof(*md2));
}


//////////////////////////
// helper class for performance measurements

class MeasureHelper
{
  static long long perfFreq;
  int threadPriority;
  long long startCounter, finishCounter;

public:
  void StartMeasuring()
  {
    if (perfFreq == 0)
```

```cpp
    ::QueryPerformanceFrequency((LARGE_INTEGER*)&perfFreq);

  // boost priority to avoid thread scheduling side effects
  threadPriority = ::GetThreadPriority(::GetCurrentThread());
  ::SetThreadPriority(::GetCurrentThread(), THREAD_PRIORITY_TIME_CRITICAL);

    ::QueryPerformanceCounter((LARGE_INTEGER*)&startCounter);
}

void StopMeasuring()
{
  ::QueryPerformanceCounter((LARGE_INTEGER*)&finishCounter);

  ::SetThreadPriority(::GetCurrentThread(), threadPriority);
}

double GetMeasuredTime()
{
  return (finishCounter - startCounter) / (double)perfFreq;
}
};

long long MeasureHelper::perfFreq = 0;

void __stdcall MeasureCallsFromNativeCaller
                  (PFN pfn, const char* szFunctionName, bool bIndirect)
{
  MeasureHelper mh;
  mh.StartMeasuring();
  pfn();
  mh.StopMeasuring();

  cout << mh.GetMeasuredTime()
       << "s\tfor 10e8 " << (bIndirect ? "indirect " : "") << "calls to "
       << szFunctionName << " from native code" << endl;
}
```

Index

You Need the Companion eBook